AMERICAN
FEAR

AMERICAN FEAR

THE CAUSES AND CONSEQUENCES OF HIGH ANXIETY

PETER N. STEARNS

Routledge
Taylor & Francis Group
New York   London

Routledge is an imprint of the
Taylor & Francis Group, an informa business

Routledge
Taylor & Francis Group
270 Madison Avenue
New York, NY 10016

Routledge
Taylor & Francis Group
2 Park Square
Milton Park, Abingdon
Oxon OX14 4RN

Printed in the United States of America on acid-free paper
10 9 8 7 6 5 4 3 2 1

International Standard Book Number-10: 0-415-95542-4 (Softcover) 0-415-95540-8 (Hardcover)
International Standard Book Number-13: 978-0-415-95542-3 (Softcover) 978-0-415-95540-9 (Hardcover)

Visit the Taylor & Francis Web site at
http://www.taylorandfrancis.com

and the Routledge Web site at
http://www.routledge-ny.com

CONTENTS

ACKNOWLEDGMENTS

Various people have provided stimulating suggestions for this book. I thank Roy Rosenzweig, Mary Francis Forcier, Mary Hildebeidel, Deborah Stearns, and Eryq Dorfman, among others. For research assistance, Earnie Porta, Veronica Fletcher, James Halabuk, Patricia Condon, and Bill Kendall have my real gratitude. Debbie Williams and Alicia Smallbrock provided great help in preparing the manuscript. I benefited greatly from comments by two anonymous readers. My sincere thanks also to the Routledge editor, Kimberly Guinta.

PREFACE

A 2005 newspaper article wondered, though a bit jocularly, whether the United States was suffering the social equivalent of a panic attack. A small town in Maryland (population 1,400) had installed surveillance cameras on the town hall, paid for by the Department of Homeland Security, with the police chief arguing that terrorists might pass through on their way to other targets. "You can't ever tell." The state of Kentucky received a similar grant to protect bingo parlors from attack, while the city of Grand Forks, North Dakota, had deployed a $145,000 bomb-dismantling robot against a backpack vagrants had left under a pine tree, which turned out to contain bricks.

Not surprisingly, a host of businesses and agencies increasingly try to profit by fanning the flames of fear. An arms manufacturer suggests that, without more investments in its direction, the nation risks losing control of the skies. University research centers routinely seek and win federal research dollars by highlighting fears of biological or critical infrastructure attack. A key former federal official, who once urged citizens to buy duct tape to seal their homes against terrorist poisons, gains a post on the board of Home Depot, a leading purveyor of duct tape.

Symbolism keeps pace. The Federal Emergency Management Agency Web site for kids uses as its mascot a hermit crab dubbed Herman, apparently because the species, when confronted by danger, immediately scurries to hide in a new shell—the model, it would seem, for national response to disaster.[1]

There seems little doubt that citizens of the United States are being made to fear in ways that make them uncomfortable and that leaders are making dubious decisions about policy and resource allocation.

Several recent studies, both before and after September 11, 2001, have highlighted the problem. This book amplifies the argument in several new ways.

The fact that the book joins a modest but impressive existing literature suggests that a genuine problem has been identified—though, of course, we must prove the case—but also raises the question: why another effort?

Part of the response rests in the seriousness of the issue, and the need for several voices to help us grapple with it, beyond telling good stories about oddly inflated responses to real or imagined threats. But there is more: this book attends to fear levels concerning domestic issues but deals particularly with the relationship between fear and foreign policy, adding a vital dimension to existing fear studies. It also provides a careful assessment of fear levels, beyond reference to undeniably fear-soaked messages from the media. Most important, it explores the causes of our current dilemma—an exploration essential to any discussion of remedies. Most of the recent analyses—and they have great strength—have emphasized manipulation by television stations or federal agencies desperate to capture public attention and willing to inflame fear in the process. The approach tells part of the story, but not all of it. And it tends to lead to pleas that the entities currently sponsoring fear simply stop—which is indeed desirable but, frankly, not very likely, since the authorities involved have obviously discovered a successful formula and may see little reason to mend their ways. (Indeed, many are not merely manipulative; they share in the fears themselves.)

What is needed—and what this book provides—is not only additional diagnosis of the problem, but a careful look at the several factors that have created it. Exploitation is part of the pattern, but so are wider changes in American culture. Only if we see contemporary fear as the result of these several forces can we hope to come to grips with it.

The public itself is directly engaged in the current climate of fear—not merely the subject of nefarious pressures from the outside. And the public must also be part of the solution. A deeper probe of this facet of contemporary American emotional experience is essential.

Americans need to work on controlling public fear. The challenge is real, but the response will not be easy—for it goes well beyond calling fearmongers to task. Yet, we can win against an excessive emotion—and indeed, we have won in the nation's past—if we gain a fuller sense of why fear has taken such a hold on us. We need to think about an emotion that too often, in recent decades, has defied thought.

A century ago, a number of optimistic American publicists proclaimed that a modern society should be able to eliminate fear:

Fear is the greatest source of human suffering. Until comparatively recent times nature has been something unknown and the
unknown has been a constant source of terror. It is believed to be
full of supernatural and possibly hostile agencies. Devils, demons,
and indignant deities, an angry and jealous God, possible future
and retributive punishments, earthquakes, and eclipses—all have
contributed to make the life of man miserable. This burden of woe
has now been lifted. Another view of nature now prevails. Man
cast off fear and finds himself master of nature and perhaps of
all her forces, while in religion the gospel of love is casting out
the dread monster of fear. But it is not only fear of supernatural
agencies that we have escaped, but also fear of political upheavals
connected with despotic governments and social instability. Few
of us appreciate the profound security that we now enjoy: security
of life, property, and reputation.[2]

Voices of this sort in one sense sound distant and strange today. But
we should not be misled. Contemporary Americans are still part of a
culture that very much wants to bypass fear. Our expectations remain
high; it's reality that has proved recalcitrant. Ironically, in seeking to
avoid fear we may have become more fearful than necessary. Our emotional vulnerability has increased. It's time to understand this complex
evolution better and to reassess the results.

I

Establishing the Cause for Fear Excess

1

INTRODUCING FEAR

This is a book about American experiences of fear, arguing that national reactions to the dread emotion, both in personal and in public life, have exhibited crucial distinctive features in recent decades. Americans collectively, in other words, show some different responses to broadly comparable fear situations than do counterparts elsewhere. It is also a book about changes in American approaches to fear that have made many Americans more vulnerable to anxieties about fear and have encouraged more agencies to play on these anxieties than was true in the national past. These are big claims, hard to prove fully, but important to consider as we examine one of the dominant emotions in contemporary American public life.

Fear is not, of course, an endlessly variable emotion. Virtually anyone can be made to experience fear. Many societies have demonstrated proclivities to fear—one need only think of the "great fear" that swept over the French countryside in 1789, when peasants believed reports that landlords were about to rob them of their livelihood and reacted violently in response. Or the British fear of invasion by Napoleon that prompted postings of guards to monitor the English Channel, not only at the time, but for decades thereafter in what was clearly an irrational extension of initial emotional response. Contemporary examples abound. In talking about American fear, then, and about the emergence of contemporary versions of American fear, we are not arguing that Americans or their society are entirely unique. At most, current national experience suggests some loading to one end of a normal continuum. The Japanese, with an inevitably low crime-rate, are inordinately afraid of crime and respond with exaggeration (and often, a mistrust of foreigners) when cases do come to light. Chinese citizens take precautions against SARS, for example, in covering light switches with plastic, even though the disease has lapsed.

One of the book's arguments, in fact, though we won't belabor these comparisons, is the broad similarity between the contemporary United States and recurrent situations in societies past where fear overcame reason. Many traditional societies, for example, experienced colonial rule as a loss of control—understandably enough—and responded with periodic great fears. In India, rumors of British use of beef or pork fat to grease bullets—though inaccurate—triggered a major panic in the mid-1850s. Rumors of British-caused animal disease spread fear again in the 1890s. The United States, though a modern, noncolonial society, has its own fears of loss of control—to foreign threats, but also to a national government many Americans have come to mistrust. Rumors operate in this context as well, though we'll see that contemporary media often serve a rumorlike role as well. The result is recognizable historically—one of several episodes of a society open to periodic deep fears—but surprising in terms of the American self-image of modern rationality and emotional cool.

Fear is a variable social emotion—often contagious, often affecting group behavior and social policy—but it is often an individual experience. Individuals also encounter fear differently, depending, of course, on the provocation but also on individual temperament. No social generalizations can omit the personal variable. Stephen Crane's great book on the Civil War, *The Red Badge of Courage*, dealt with individuals who had more trouble living up to certain ideals of fear containment than did some of their colleagues. In dealing with contemporary America, we must not discount the many people who handle fear fairly calmly, who display great courage either because of their stolidity or (in another definition of courage) who manage to override real fear when it comes to a crunch. There is no American fear experience that supersedes personality variables. And even people who display considerable fear when presented with remote threats, can rally with real bravery when an actual challenge emerges—another, situational complexity on top of sheer personality. Further, there are doubtless subgroup cultures regarding fear, in what is after all a very diverse society—and we will certainly have to consider some group reactions, including gender reactions, that have long played a role in promoting different formulations where fear is involved.

It's vital to be clear here. This book does not discount the many Americans who continue to display many forms of courage, including, of course, the military personnel and other frontline people most

commonly praised for bravery, but also many others who display cou.
age in other ways—including protesting military action at real threat
to their social respectability and personal freedom. We are not even
arguing that there are fewer courageous Americans than in the past—
though we will note some interesting changes in the ways certain agencies, like the military, handle fear. We do contend, however, that there
are also either more fearful Americans than there once were, or that
their voices are louder or more sought after and publicly authorized—
or both. The point about subcultures and great personality differences
remains, along with the insistence on continuing courage in American life; but there is still a collective set of standards and reactions that
deserves attention and that does reflect both a certain distinctiveness
and some real change from the past.

The book will develop three main strands of recent American fear,
showing how they increasingly coalesce from the cold war onward. The
first involves a serious reevaluation of personal fear and also the risk,
especially but not exclusively in childhood, under the aegis of watchful
psychologists and other new-style experts eager to protect innocents
from a potentially overwhelming emotion. The second deals with media
uses and promotions of fear. The third strand highlights collective reactions to danger, and particularly to foreign threat. Here we deal both
with a growing desire for assured safety, for protection against risk—
demonstrated among other ways in a distinctive panoply of warnings
and precautions—and with notable anxieties about menace from foreign people and foreign places. These strands all developed in a society
that was in many ways unprecedentedly secure, with declining rates
of disease, with growing assurance against premature mortality. They
developed, in other words, in ways that were not entirely rational, save
insofar as they reflected a lack of normal experience with fear-inducing situations, an inexperience that could help explain why fear, when
actually encountered, was both unfamiliar and deeply resented. The
reactions, whether rational or not, were deeply meaningful. Around the
three main strands—the approaches to the emotion itself, the media
components, and the new trends in collective response—we must also
deal with controlled fear in American entertainment—with the titillation of ever-more-daring amusement park rides, ever-more graphic—
movies and games, that allow people to display courage in essentially
controlled environments; and with health and death fears, and changing patterns of disease and degeneration, that may have promoted
anxiety despite the statistical gains in mortality and morbidity. This
is an expansive loom, but the threads do interweave and, in the process, explain both widespread American reactions and the temptation

to manipulate these reactions among various groups of experts and officials.

A MODEST APPETIZER: THE STRANGE
CAREER OF CURIOUS GEORGE

The main strands of this study involve synthesizing the strong American responses to real or imagined foreign threats, beginning with the Red Scare of the 1920s and extending obviously to the cold war and the war on terrorism when it became clear that an isolationist stance provided inadequate protection. We pick up the contemporary aspects of this theme in the following chapter, to begin the difficult task of determining whether any unusual features were involved or whether we're simply dealing with logical responses to growing global involvement in an obviously messy world. The other strands are less familiar, involving the concomitant reconsideration of fear and risk in other contexts and the role of media guidance in emotional life. Here too, ensuing chapters will provide further analysis. But we begin with a vignette that indicates the strong forces of change involved in this aspect of American emotional standards and that suggests, as well, the potential relationship between personal, even seemingly trivial, changes in the culture of fear and ultimate public response.

Curious George, a reasonably popular book series for young children that began in the late 1940s, was written by immigrants from Germany (H. A. Rey and his wife Margret). The initial stories involve George, an irrepressible monkey, getting into all sorts of terrifying situations: he's kidnapped, jailed in a dark prison infested with mice, trapped in a helium balloon, falls off a skyscraper and breaks a leg ("he got what he deserved," a callous bystander remarks) amid other mishaps, all of which he manages to endure with reasonably good spirits after initial fear. The Reys, Jewish refugees (H. A. Rey himself was a German army veteran from World War I), began their writing in Europe and reflected a European sense that children could be exposed to frightening images without damage to their psyches, indeed perhaps with some benefit in terms of thinking about how they would handle fear in real life. But while the initial books in the series sold well enough to maintain publisher interest, the tone was antithetical to the changing culture developing for young American children—where, according to adults at least, fear-producing situations should be eliminated to the greatest extent possible. This impulse had already been amply displayed from the 1930s onward, in the Disney-ed dilutions of traditional folk tales like Cinderella (where the evil stepsisters originally suffered brutal physical punishments), and now it applied to the curious monkey. By the fourth book in the series, issued in 1952, George no longer gets into scary adventures, and he's surrounded by loving, supportive human beings who carefully supervise his activities so that he won't encounter trouble. By the fifth book in the series, the Reys actually yielded to psychological and pediatric experts on the publisher's staff, which further reduced the opportunity for any emotionally challenging adventure. George himself becomes anxious, eager to stay around home for the sake of safety. (Also, the vocabulary was dumbed down, in response to findings that children were not capable of handling many words, but that's another story.) When anything untoward does occur, George becomes immediately frightened and vows never to court danger again. As his surrogate human father figure intones, "I was scared, and you must have been scared too. I know you will not want to fly a kite again for a long, long time." Fear still occurs, but obviously it is now irredeemably bad, and sensible people (and humanoid monkeys) will avoid its risk at all costs. And children, as personified by George, are themselves easily frightened, deserving all possible reassurance and protection instead of nonchalance (the dominant motif in the original books of the series) or injunctions toward courage. Fear will occur in childhood—the last George book was designed to reassure children facing hospitalization—but it should be minimized as much as possible, surrounded by maximum reassurance and support—a set of lessons that might teach some children that the emotion was not only unpleasant but undeserved, and that sources of fear should be removed or punished.[1]

This new attitude not only differed from traditional European norms but also, as we will see, from earlier American standards as well, where presenting fear situations to children, and particularly to boys, was regarded as normal, character-building fare. The change in approach— which did not, of course, eliminate actual fear in childhood, but rather affected reactions to it by children themselves and by surrounding adults—was based on every good intention, founded on a new idea that children were too fragile to handle fear or to be urged to do so.

OPTIONS FOR FEAR

As we will see in discussing this transition more fully, the new expertise did not exactly deal with long-term consequences of the new approach to fear in terms of adult reactions to the emotion. The proximate goal was protection of children's psyches. Reigning experts did believe that careful guidance of childhood emotions would produce well-balanced adults, free from the traumas and "festering" caused by poor socialization earlier on. In that vein, they might well believe that handling fear would improve with new-style childhood nurturance, and the argument might well make sense. Certainly, as again we'll discuss more fully later, stories of fear-soaked childhoods, in which children were not only not sheltered from fear, but exposed to direct uses of fear in discipline, easily induce horrified reactions according to contemporary standards; the resultant adults must have been basket cases.

But what if this calculation is wrong, that at least somewhat more open exposure to fear in childhood actually prepares less frenzied adult response; and that cushioning in the modern American manner—granted all sorts of deliberate and accidental deviations from the norms—makes people less able to cope, more resentful when confronted with fear-inducing situations? A key question, impossible to answer with absolute certainty, but essential to explore as part of the contemporary American fear equation. And not only children are involved; so are their parents, taught to be terribly anxious, fearful even, when thinking about threats not only to their children's security, but also to their presumed emotional fragility. Soccer moms, it turns out, at least if the 2004 election is any guide, can easily be converted to fearful moms, and the historical shifts in emotional signals may have a lot to do with the conversion. The argument here, on the burdens of overprotectiveness, applies both to the results of socialization and to new tensions on the part of the socializers themselves.

PROBING THE CAUSES OF DISTINCTIVENESS AND CHANGE: BEHAVIORAL HISTORY AND EMOTIONS RESEARCH

While the principal focus of this book is on fear, as an urgent American policy and personal issue, the treatment also serves as an example of behavioral history.[2] The book argues, in other words, that significant (and probably distinctive) national reactions can be fully understood only through historical analysis. They do not constitute perpetual, inevitable, or purely natural reactions, even given the magnitude of current threats such as terrorism. They emerge from changes, in this case beginning to develop early in the twentieth century when fear itself came up as a new topic and, simultaneously, the nation encountered novel and uncharted foreign entanglements. As the discipline that most explicitly assesses change, while trying to deal with causes and attendant continuities, history has to play a growing role in explaining

ourselves to ourselves. Contemporary fear, in my judgment, can illustrate the strengths of this new/old analytical approach superbly.

Not surprisingly, indeed very desirably, fear is beginning to attract
various kinds of analysis. Interestingly, a huge surge in emotions
research over the past two decades did not highlight fear—there was
more interest in anger, seen to be an American problem, or emotions
that directly affected family life, like gratitude or lack thereof.[3] While
fear drew a bit of attention from the budding field of emotions history,
here too it was not a major focus and the work that was done was not
directly applied to contemporary public life.[4] From this more public
vantage point, a prescient book argued, in 1999, that American fears
were heavily misdirected, an argument we will pick up (and credit) at
various points in the following pages.[5] More recently, post–September
11, the political manipulation of fear—or the political advantages of
fear, from those who almost welcomed this new emotional focus as an
antidote to the selfish materialism of the 1990s—has drawn comment.[6]
Much of this work is useful, in highlighting the Bush administration's
zeal to promote and capitalize on fear, but it generally lacks a wider perspective or any particular focus on more general perceptions and experiences of fear. One book, by political scientist Corey Robin, features
a discussion of the role of fear in selective Western political theory,
from Hobbes onward, as a springboard for analysis of the use of fear in
American race relations and labor disputes, with more sweeping comments on why fear or anxiety have come to figure so prominently in
American political messages from both left and right.[7] Here too, there
is much to value, including the basic idea that American leaders have
come to see fear as a foundation for national unity in the absence of
confidence in more positive programs. But Robin's work, though historical in a sense, lacks any attention to the role of fear in wider American behaviors, or to the evolution of fear as an emotion. The behavioral
history of fear, and from this a fuller understanding of fear's public
place, has yet to emerge, and it will add greatly both to our grasp of the
phenomenon, beyond the wiles of politicians, and to a more realistic
discussion of options and remedies. By the same token, fear history will
provide added credence for this approach to the analysis of contemporary behavioral patterns more generally.

This book's goals will be amply met if, through focused historical
inquiry rooted in current concerns, it persuades some Americans, and
some American leaders, to reconsider their reactions and roles in the
current fear equation. And if, by providing a particularly significant
case study, other analysts are encouraged to apply the behavioral history lens to a range of additional topics, creating a new juncture between

history and contemporary understanding, between history and vital facets of policy and social life.

PRELIMINARY CONSIDERATIONS

The book's intent, particularly where fear itself is concerned, raises some personal but particularly political issues that must also be addressed briefly by way of introduction.

The personal can be handled quickly enough, without becoming a distraction either now or on later reflection. Just as I have no desire to have this book discount manifold examples of ongoing American courage, so I do not want to imply some special emotional qualities for myself. I was very interested in fear, or at least in courage, as a boy, reading a good bit about torture—wondering how I'd stand it (badly, I assumed)—and about battle heroism, with some favorite early twentieth-century books that dramatized children's bravery. So there may be an older preoccupation, and concern about potential personal inadequacy, that informs this study. I certainly have no basis for setting myself up as someone who has demonstrated particular fearlessness and advises fellow citizens to follow suit. I have not, to be sure, been personally moved by great anxieties about encounters with terrorism, but this is not a matter of bravery so much as annoyance at excessive warnings and some corrective sense of probabilities. But I base none of the following analysis on personal qualities.

Indeed, I have actively shared in many of the behaviors I will discuss on the more personal side. As a parent, for example, I was quite concerned about protecting my children from unnecessary fright (trying to do better in this regard than I thought my father had done toward my sensitive self). Thus, in writing about parental standards, I in no sense claim some tough-minded personal exceptionalism, some superiority over the standard American middle-class pack. I do believe, however, that some norms that we have come to take for granted as clear advances in child protection, both psychological and physical, may need to be rethought at least to some extent, as they contribute to larger public attitudes that are (in my judgment) demonstrably undesirable. Overprotective parenting harbors its own fears, and this is another facet that needs to be reviewed.

There is a final personal angle. I am, I confess, motivated in part by a sense that, having lived through the cold war, I was more than a bit misled about the risks involved. I am eager not to fall into similar gullibility regarding terrorism, and even more eager to have the American public shielded from similar excesses and their policy results. With all the advantages of hindsight, it seems clear that Americans were over-cautioned about the dangers of Soviet attack during various passages of the cold war, just as they (we) were stimulated into a host of actions—Vietnam, most notably—on the basis of misleading anxieties about the domino effect of Communist conquests. The warnings, of course, may have helped prevent the development of a global aggressiveness that, with one or two exceptions, was not otherwise present in a fairly conservative Soviet leadership—it's impossible to prove the contrary. The warnings certainly may have emanated from sincere belief in threat, encouraged further by quite accurate estimations of the horrors that would result from full-scale nuclear conflict. While military-industrial budgets were promoted by cold war fears, and surely played some role in their stimulation, there is no reason to deny a mixture of genuine concern along with the self-interest of key national leadership groups. But the fact remains: the danger was rarely as great as the American public was often urged to accept. And while I was no bomb shelter builder—I did at one point consider putting some provisions in the trunk of my car, as was briefly recommended in the early 1960s, but dismissed the idea out of laziness and a realization that, given Boston traffic, I would never get out of town if a threat materialized in any event—but I certainly spent a lot of time wondering if the end was likely to come. And I do, now, regret my credulousness, and this historical reconstruction undoubtedly plays a role in the book's line of argument.

Which leads to my next main introductory concern—the issue of partisanship. The question of fear is undoubtedly part of the infamous red-blue cultural/political divide in the United States. A poll at the end of 2004, indicating that 53 percent of all Americans favored civil liberties restrictions on Muslims in the United States (including citizens) in the interests of better security, revealed the typical gap: most in favor of such restrictions were Republicans, conscientious church goers, and regular watchers of TV newscasts; least in favor were Democrats, more secular, and people who obtained news from other sources (or, conceivably, simply didn't follow the news much). Fear played an obvious role in the 2004 presidential elections, with Republicans explicitly urging voters to reject the Democratic ticket because it would protect the United States less well; Vice President Cheney at one point directly argued that electing the Kerry-Edwards ticket would increase the chance of terrorist attack. A 2005 gubernatorial race in Virginia saw the Republican candidate try to push fear buttons in calling attention to real or imagined threats of crime and illegal immigration.

And there is the still more amorphous problem of dissecting American reactions at all, in a climate in which some politicians—and they again are disproportionately Republican—try to paint any inquiry not simply directed as condemning terrorist evil as offering aid and comfort to the enemy. This is not a book about terrorism itself, but about responses to it. There is no attempt to see terrorism as anything but a serious problem that must be forcefully addressed. But American responses are not simply natural or inevitable; they have their own role to play in dealing with the menace. The ultimate argument is that better understanding of the emotions involved is fundamental to sound policy. Terrorism is, after all, an alternative to conventional warfare mainly in its effort to provoke fear instead of mustering proportionate force. Fighting terrorism involves, perforce, the best possible grasp of fear.

This book will contend, then, not that terrorism should be ignored and certainly not that it should be excused, but that fears have been overplayed, and in some cases blatantly manipulated (not just by politicians). But there is no reason to accuse those involved in fighting terrorism by invoking fear with bad faith or cynicism; there is a real problem here, and they undeniably feel a heavy weight of responsibility. I hope, in other words, that the following analysis will not be automatically rejected by "red" readers. We are all interested in sensible, constructive responses to current and foreseeable threats. An open discussion of what these responses should be, in light of a larger emotional context, will be beneficial, across partisan lines. The book is not designed to favor any conventional partisan purpose—after all, most Democrats have also argued that we should be afraid but that they would handle dangers better. And there have been times where liberals led in pushing fear messages. Indeed, some conservatives even today plausibly argue that certain "blue" advocates themselves exploit fear distinctively, for example exaggerating the consequences of global warming to the point of near-hysteria. It's time for a new look by most of those involved in current partisan struggles around fear reactions—ideally including those in various camps whose political fortunes have benefited from fear responses.

In sum, the book, though critical of some recent policies, including the interesting juxtaposition of color coding for terror warnings and notices of abducted children, is not intended as yet another academic indictment of the current administration, providing comfort to liberals but little persuasiveness beyond their ranks. It intends, instead, to invite a more general dialogue about constructive emotional responses to contemporary threats.

EMOTIONAL CHANGE

One additional preliminary, not as obvious as the issues of partisanship, will quickly occur to most readers as the argument progresses, and so must be identified at the outset. Is it realistic to talk about shifting or socially variable emotional responses? Aren't these responses hardwired into the human psyche, particularly in the case of such undeniably basic emotions as fear, the body's stimulus to flight back when human beings more clearly recognized their animal nature? How much does culture matter, where emotions are concerned, and how can the impact of change be traced?

This involves an old debate among emotions researchers, and it would be misleading to pretend it has been resolved.[8] Many psychologists and biologists prefer to study the invariant aspects of emotion—the extent, for example, to which peoples almost everywhere can recognize the same emotional facial signals (including those reflecting fear). Other disciplines—some social psychology, and certainly many practitioners in anthropology, sociology, and history—focus more on the ways emotions are culturally constructed, and hence vary among different societies and also, potentially, change over time. Yet, while preferences do diverge among various clusters of scholars, there is general agreement that emotions, even those as basic as fear, contain a mixture of ingrained impulse and a degree of cognition that evaluates and, to some degree regulates, the same impulse; and cognition, in turn, is shaped by cultural cues as well as the vagaries of individual personalities.

Fortunately, this study of fear does not need to engage this whole debate directly, though of course it depends on some notion of emotion as (partly) culturally constructed. For the main argument is not that actual fear has changed—we have already noted that we are not contending that the percentage of courageous Americans has declined—but rather that its public context has altered, and that policies based on this context have shifted dramatically as well. It has become more acceptable (particularly for men; women probably had more latitude in the past as well in American culture) to talk about fears, and therefore (to some extent) to acknowledge them to oneself. A quick illustration: sociologist Cas Wouters has noted the striking readiness of American pilots, preparing for action in the Gulf War in 1990, to acknowledge to journalists how frightened they were, obviously not feeling that this acknowledgement was either inappropriate or unmanly (or detrimental to military effectiveness).[9] The scene would have been inconceivable, in a military-journalist encounter, in either of the world wars. This does not mean that the pilots felt more fear than their counterparts earlier in the twentieth century, but simply that the public culture surrounding fear had shifted dramatically, allowing openness instead of considerable concealment.

Public cultures of fear do not flow from nature, though of course they revolve around an emotion that is partly innate. Some cultures enjoin stoicism, an insistence that fear not be expressed to others, even to oneself. Others, like the contemporary American, find fear more troubling, manageable only if somehow vented, and truly uncomfortable even then. The variance can be considerable, over time as well as across cultures at any one time.

Different cultural contexts, in turn, have obvious policy implications. Three generations ago, President Franklin Roosevelt offered one of his most memorable phrases on the subject of emotion: "The only thing we have to fear is fear itself." The plea might still resonate today, but it would surely seem at least somewhat anachronistic, and it certainly is not the line of argument urged on the public by policy makers in recent years.

But different contexts also have potential bearing on actual emotional experience as well. If a culture urges the appropriateness of a reaction, the reaction becomes more common—and vice versa. There are a number of recent examples. Jealousy became more firmly reproved by the 1920s than it had earlier in the United States, and it is not hard to demonstrate that the number of people claiming not to be jealous went up, that those who felt jealous worked harder to conceal—and that, probably at least, the actual incidence of jealousy declined.[10] The same applies to the growing dislike of grief during the same time period; grief-stricken people had more trouble finding a sympathetic audience and, again probably, more people worked on not acknowledging pronounced or long-lasting grief in the first place.[11] In the other direction: envy became more openly approved, as part of the adjustments to consumer capitalism in the United States. Children, once criticized for showing envy, were now encouraged, within limits, because the emotion would spur them to want nice things.[12] And without much question, more people began to acknowledge and act on the emotion in the process, and, again quite probably, more people began to feel envy in the first place.

Social rules for emotion count considerably: they shape public responses—no-fault divorce followed in part from strictures against jealousy and anger in marriage, while prohibitions against publicly posting student grades followed from new hostility to jealousy and shame.[13] Social rules condition personal responses and self-authorizations concerning natural emotional impulses. In late twentieth-century America, new cautions against intense emotion encouraged a distinctive level of concealment and anxious checking with others, according to several comparative studies.[14] Correspondingly, increased permission to express certain emotions promoted the emotion in turn, in part through direct imitation.

All this means that social expressions of emotion can change, often considerably, and this is vividly true for fear in recent American history. The change is important in itself; it shifts what people admit to themselves; it will often affect the actual incidence of the emotion as well. This study of fear relies on the first claim, about social expression, and easily slides over into the second, about self-acknowledgment. We cannot be as definite about the third—whether the number of fearful people goes up as well—but there are more than straws in the wind on this point as well. While the incidence of courage may not have diminished, the number of emotional fence-straddlers, once silent or cautious but now ready to admit or to act on fear, may well have increased. The overall package, involving some remarkable adjustments in the ways fear is felt and handled, with significant consequences at both public and personal levels, can be clearly established, without contesting the importance of some irreducibly natural components when it comes to individual encounters with fear.

SOCIAL FEARS

Americans are certainly not unique in fearful reactions to foreign threat. Europe offers some classic cases, as noted earlier. Various societies, historically, encouraged emotional responses to longstanding enemies. For probably several centuries, Turkish parents thus invoked fear of Russians as part of their disciplinary package for children—if you don't behave, the Russians will get you. Invasion threats often triggered fears.[15] Rumors of the Spanish Armada, in the England of 1588, spread wildly in advance of the fleet's defeat; the political theorist Thomas Hobbes claimed that his mother was frightened into premature delivery: "My mother was filled with such fear that she bore twins, me and together with me fear"—and he claimed that his own interest in the emotion in public life stemmed from this sequence.[16] Given new media, through which anxieties can spread more quickly, and probably also increased awareness of how fear can be used to spur mass loyalty and mass action, the role of emotional reactions to foreign threat may have increased still further in our own age. Use of contemporary propaganda to villainize opponents—as in the accusations about German brutality in World War I, to take one familiar example—could easily promote as well as reflect deep seated-fears.

Many Japanese were openly and understandably afraid when Americans and other Westerners pushed into their country after 1853. Here was a nation that had been substantially isolated from broader international contacts for two and a half centuries, suddenly forced into new levels of interaction by the muzzles of Western guns. (Perry's visit was followed by another American mission and a larger British fleet, all demanding open Japanese markets and other concessions.) Fear and uncertainty ran high among ordinary people as well as the leadership. Many believed, calling on older ideas from the folk religion, that this kind of disruption could only occur because Japanese society itself had fallen into imbalance, with corruption at the top, protest from below; even before the Western visit, religious pilgrimages had increased, a sign of unease. When a major earthquake struck in 1855, it was taken as a cosmic punishment both for social disarray and for foreign pressure (or rather, for the government weakness that made foreign pressure irresistible). At the same time, other commentators viewed Perry's arrival as a welcome corrective for a society that was ailing, a spur to new action. While a faction of samurai began to organize for resistance to the foreigners, arguing that Japan had no need for new contacts, on the whole the combination of Western arrival and the connections associated with natural disaster provided unifying symbols for a politically fragmented nation. Within fifteen years, Japan began to respond amazingly positively to the challenges of what was for the island nation an unprecedented global context. Understandable fear—following from the lack of recent experience in dealing with major external pressure—generated a kind of anxiety that was open to additional, logically unrelated threats. But the end result proved extremely constructive, as the apparent magnitude of danger, even if artificially exaggerated by folk beliefs about the causes of natural disasters, prompted a dramatic revision of attitudes and policies toward the wider world.[17]

This is, of course, just one example of fear responding to foreign menace. Yet it is instructive in two respects. First, again, it reminds us of the obvious: that current American fears can be usefully compared to reactions of other societies when the international framework shifts in challenging ways. Our recent emotional response is hardly unique. Without believing that our society was being punished for transgressions—efforts to blame American misdeeds for the terrorist attacks of September 11 were quickly reproved—the United States was also in the throes of new concerns about national purpose, complete with pronounced religious revival. Some Americans, while deploring the attacks, did believe that fear could revivify a larger, less selfish national commitment, as the Japanese reformers had argued a century and a half before.

But the differences are striking. Compared to the Japan of the 1850s, the United States is a supremely powerful nation, with a long history of international involvement—yet our fears about the outside world may be surprisingly similar to those of a relatively weak Japan with very little international experience of any sort. Does the similarity rationally attach to the threat of terrorism, or are we overdoing (or being encouraged to overdo) the emotional response? It's extremely difficult to calculate reasonable fear potential, but the Japanese example provides some spur to reflection. Will our fear, like that of the Japanese a century and a half ago, lead to constructive response and a new sense of purpose, or will it encourage a more primitive kind of lashing out, facilitated by the very reality of American power? The returns on this second question are not yet in, but initial indications are hardly encouraging. Fear has neither united Americans nor encouraged particularly thoughtful response; we simply want to be rid of the emotion and punish its sources, real or imagined.

So while fear of foreign threat crops up in many situations, always bringing some irrational overtones, there is reason to explore the magnitude of American reactions and, possibly, some of the particular kinds of irrationality involved. The analytical challenge here must not be denied: it would be far simpler if American fears had no comparative or historical precedent, but obviously this is not the case. Proving that the public climate became more fearful than the threat warranted is no easy task, though fortunately (at least for analytical purposes) showing how this fit a wider pattern of personal and public fear is less difficult. Some fears are less well grounded than others, some responses less constructive than others. This book seeks to work this fuzzy but vital boundary, beginning with the following chapter.

ANALYTICAL HURDLES

The idea of a special problem with fear in contemporary America may come hard, for at least two reasons. We are accustomed to thinking of political fear as something that occurs in blatantly despotic societies, not in our own. We know something, at least, of how fear was used in Nazi Germany, particularly of course against Jews and other minorities but as a means of preserving loyalty among ordinary Germans as well. We know a bit about fear in Stalin's Russia, with arbitrary arrests, terror-induced self-accusations, executions, and exiles. And we hear of the use of fear in more contemporary political regimes, with accounts of torture, unexplained disappearances, and assassinations. The growing human rights outcry against torture, one of the major additions to world opinion in the past twenty-five years, reminds us of how other societies promote fear and of how much right-thinking people now disapprove of these routines.[18] But it is harder to think of political uses of fear in our own open, democratic society—yet these uses truly exist, even aside from the accounts of American uses of illegal torture on certain kinds of foreign prisoners. Manipulated fear is something that happens to others, not to ordinary, law-abiding Americans. Yet, as scholars like Corey Robin have pointed out, and as the less scholarly can see around them, fear is a reality in the United States.[19] It has motivated policies in the past—from Red scares to McCarthyism and beyond—and it motivates policies today. Fear sells goods, in contemporary America, and it sells public responses as well. We cannot evade its role by pointing to more familiar, conveniently foreign examples.

But this leads to the second hesitation about discussing contemporary, public American fears: an understandable belief that, if we have fears, they are quite rational, not a topic requiring pointy-headed intellectual analysis. After all, the terrorist threat is genuine, just as the cold war threat was genuine, and that's really all that need be known. An argument that seeks to acknowledge the problem of terrorism, and the reasonable amount of fear terrorism induces, but that goes further to talk about unnecessary or counterproductive levels of fear, risks seeming needlessly complicated, even disloyal. Surely one of the reasons that few major political figures have tackled fear head-on involves the difficulty of distinguishing between essential and damaging ranges of the emotion, and the real risk that, in urging a reduction of fear, one will be vulnerable to accusations of liability should some new attack occur in future. (The issue of the timidity that stems from concerns about liability for risk helps explain many aspects of the climate of fear in the United States, including the responses to terrorism since September 11, 2001.)

This book argues that fear is a very real factor in American public life—not just a problem in foreign despotisms past or present, that it impinges on a wide variety of Americans and not just mistreated political prisoners, that it is by no means entirely a rational response to threat—and that it must be hauled out for analysis because it reduces our capacity for clearheaded policy. The problem is not entirely new, but it has emerged historically—Americans were not always so collectively open to fear. It looms large in political life but it is not political alone, calling on a larger emotional repertoire established over several decades. It even contributes to the gap between American and international opinion—many publics, not intrinsically anti-American but accustomed to a higher level of risk, simply do not understand how afraid we have become, how much of our lashing out results from emotional vulnerability.

Wider discussion of fear will be difficult. No society likes to confront its distinctive emotional sores. Fearfulness is hardly part of our preferred national image. The partisan overtones add to the complications—while both political camps play on fears, the conservative use has become more blatant and troubling, if only because conservatives have gained national ascendancy. The indisputable fact that the nation faces real risks is perhaps the central complexity: the line between fear, and fearing too much, is not easy to draw. But we have come, as a nation, to fear excessively. Many Americans, if they step back a bit from the daily barrage of news, can see how the employment of fear has increased. Behavioral history, that explains the current pattern through its emergence over time and relates political manipulations to a broader shift in the outlook toward fear, will help sort through the puzzle. Fear must be seen in a new light if we are to loosen its hold.

For we have come not only to fear too much, but also to react with undue resentment when we realize we have to fear at all. Our emotional responses contrast with our own past and with the experiences of other contemporary societies not faced with outright invasion or the deliberate incitements of an outright police state. We may fear because, as Corey Robin argues, our political leaders serve us no more inspiring alternatives. We may fear because, in our heart of hearts, we realize that our recurrent international arrogance almost invites response—or at least because we're involved with a range of international engagements with which, despite patriotic bombast, we're far from comfortable. We certainly fear because of nearly a century of well-intentioned but misguided attempts to sanitize an unavoidable emotion. And we certainly fear because we have, as a nation, operated in a state of warlike readiness for over sixty years—arguably a duration that no society, particularly one not previously accustomed to militarism, can easily manage without emotional dislocation. And we certainly fear because, ironically, we do not discuss fear enough.

2

THE DISTINCTIVENESS OF AMERICAN FEAR

The terrorist attack on September 11, 2001, was unprecedented, in its technology, its range of destruction, its ability to reach well beyond its own regional sources. This means, by definition, that reactions to the attack are hard to compare to responses to foreign threats in other times or other places. But the comparison is essential despite its difficulty. We are contending that the emotions roused by the September 11 attacks, directly and in subsequent policy, went beyond logical necessity, and if this claim, however cautious, is to go beyond mere assertion, it needs some juxtaposition with roughly similar (never exactly similar) experiences elsewhere.

The focus is on placing the contemporary in relevant comparative context—with comparisons ranging in past time and across recent space. The goal—and it is challenging—is to demonstrate real distinctiveness for current emotional reactions, using this contemporary standard as the trigger for subsequent historical explanation—the standard sequence in behavioral, as opposed to conventional, historical analysis. For the ultimate purpose is not only to show how many Americans have departed from other norms in reaction to severe threat, but also to demonstrate why; turning then back to further consequences and possible remediation.

Take a look, just for a first impression, at the structural reactions to vulnerability and fear, with some sense of comparison and history in mind. Consider the concrete barriers surrounding monuments and public buildings in Washington, D.C.—some of them conceived even before September 11, but with rapid escalation thereafter. The Washington Monument was surrounded by large and exceptionally ugly slabs: there was no question that fear trumped aesthetics in the contemporary American vocabulary, though by 2005 (the slabs were initially placed in the mid-1990s, after the Oklahoma City bombing) they had at last been superseded. Compare this to the British reaction to the more frequent incidents of IRA violence a decade ago. Downing Street, where the prime minister resides, was closed to pedestrians, and a chain crossed the entry to the road; but there was no huge apparatus, and some sense of tastefulness remained. Compare also to earlier threats to the United States itself, including attacks on the White House by Puerto Rican nationalists: following these earlier incidents, security was beefed up, but public visibility and freedom of movement were largely maintained.

American embassies have become virtual bunkers. In Abu Dhabi, admittedly in a tense part of the world but not a country itself in turmoil, a visitor cannot park within three blocks of the American compound, despite available lots. The whole edifice is surrounded by fortress-like bunkers, and two ranks of military security must be passed before there is any sense of welcome or even normalcy. The American nation parades its anxiety for all to see. The contrast with contemporary British measures, at its embassies, is again striking. In Abu Dhabi, for example, the British did ban parking directly in front of the embassy and constructed a higher wall—but one that remained attractive and in keeping with local custom; concrete slabs were not involved. And in this respect, not surprisingly, American fear proves contagious: the number of Arabs interested in visiting these grim outposts of fortress America, toward possible tourism or business, has dropped precipitously.

Comparison provides one vantage point on American fear. Purely domestic logic, or illogic, provides another. In 2005 the *Washington Post* reported on a California surveillance firm, employed to electronically trace school buses in the nation's capital. One monitor caught a bus that was traveling through the city well after the school day had begun. The operator immediately wondered if the bus had been hijacked, if this was a terrorist attack. It turned out that there was no problem at all; the bus was simply taking kids on a field trip.[1]

Why, as first thought, assume a terrorist hijacking? Possibly this was a reasonable reaction from a firm paid to prevent the worst, particularly in the still-vivid aftermath of September 11 and given the location. But possibly—why not think of a field trip first, hardly an uncommon event, or even some maintenance issue?—a sign of modest hysteria, or at least the kind of reaction that promotes hysteria. Why does fear emerge so quickly, in a nation still, by any comparative measurement, fairly secure?

The interpretation of these examples is admittedly complex. The threat to American public buildings and embassies is real. (The bloody attacks on two compounds in Africa, causing the greatest damage to local residents, must not be forgotten.) Britain, after all, though a terrorist target, was lower on the priority scale, and while it suffered bomb attacks at facilities in Istanbul it had no recent experience, at least prior to 2005, to match the destruction of American embassies in East Africa. It is quite possible to justify the measures that have been taken—ugliness, after all, may be a small price to pay—or even to urge still more. But there is arguably something unusual about the extent and blatancy of fortified America, just as there is something unusual about immediately jumping to worst-case imaginings when a school bus gets lost. And there is always the question of whether bunkers and other vivid reminders reassure a nervous populace, or simply remind them to be ever more afraid.

A final early impression to bring back the comparative element: The brutal attacks on the London public transportation system, in July 2005, were obviously far smaller in scale than those of September 11, and observers were quick to point out that, though devastating, the bombings did not introduce the kind of new methodology that might be disproportionately scary—like flying airplanes into buildings. Deaths reached at most 7 percent of levels that had occurred on September 11, and there was none of the symbolic fright of planes ramming into bastions of world capitalism and national defense. So it was, objectively, easier for people not directly associated with the attacks to keep their cool. Nevertheless, the calm in the city, within hours of the attacks, was striking. American reports emphasized "remarkable calm" and the "absence of panic." Almost directly reversing the post–September 11 American lament that "everything has changed," people in the street pointedly noted that "I don't think (the attack) will change anything at all." Few events were disrupted—there were a couple of cancellations in sports, and West End theaters were dark for one night. Busses (one had been blown up) resumed operation within hours, to full complements of passengers—one of whom noted wryly, "If you get blown up, you get blown up." No flights were canceled. Many Britons deliberately planned to go to work the next day, simply to prove a point—and while subway traffic was somewhat below par, it was considerable. (Indeed, subway traffic in the United States also fell the next day, though not as much.) Some people interviewed admitted fear, usually adding "a bit" and quickly noting "but you have to carry on." One man, too injured to stay at work, nevertheless boarded the same-numbered bus that had been bombed the previous day, just to show his mettle. Newspapers encouraged no fear, but rather took a tone of anger and defiance: one headline screamed, "Bastards." Police officials, responsible for safety, were admittedly edgier, issuing concerned warnings about possible further danger and shooting an innocent foreigner. But a contrast remained.

Media covered the attacks on the Underground with zeal, though of course subterranean explosions permitted little dramatic footage of the September 11 sort. But given the prominence of media hyperbole on September 11, and its role in shaping emotion, the saturation approach to the terrorism in London is worth note. It did not generate panic, for the most part—which means either that media themselves are partly shaped by dominant public emotional reactions, or that an insistently courageous public reaction can trump media manipulation, or both. A point to remember as the analysis digs deeper.

It was even interesting that, a week after the event, it was President Bush who used the attacks for remarks that were interpreted as a claim that the goal was to scare Americans, though he added that there would be no loss of nerve under his administration. And that, in the wake of the attack, in what one columnist called the only real panic reaction in the whole affair: two American military bases in southeastern England forbade personnel from going to London because of security risks. The ban was attacked by British officials, who viewed it as a concession to terrorists, and American authorities rescinded it when they realized that there was a "public communications issue."

Again, the comparatively modest magnitude of the London attack encouraged greater tranquility on the spot. But it was also true that respondents took deliberate delight to evoking a national image of stolidity and rationality. And they had the benefit of knowing what earlier American reactions to terrorism had been; it had already been clear, as government spokesmen indicated in explaining why Britain would not move toward fear-evoking nationwide color-coding, that the British fancied themselves as rather different (and, implicitly, emotionally superior). Now there was a chance to illustrate the claims directly, in the process strongly suggesting that a different kind of national culture toward fear was in play.

We must, of course, go beyond impressions, to more systematic comparisons. The point of this chapter is to demonstrate the proposition already advanced hypothetically: that American reactions to fear are different from those in other places and from those in the American past, granting all the incomparabilities of the case studies that can be adduced. The further points will be, then, to explore why this distinctiveness has emerged and whether it serves any useful purpose beyond employment for well-meaning therapists and grist for the mills of political manipulators. But first, the demonstration itself is essential.

SEPTEMBER 11 EMOTIONS

Polling data soon after the September 11 attacks demonstrated that a near-majority of Americans had experienced active fear. Fifty-two percent were strongly (18%) or somewhat shaken—with 33 percent reporting being frightened often or sometimes. This meant of course that 47 percent professed no particular emotional response, an important division, but the dominant emotional reactions were impressive nevertheless. Over 60 percent of the population cried on September 11—which suggests grief more than fear. Half of all adults reported worries about the safety of loved ones in the weeks after the attacks. Large majorities professed willingness to sacrifice in order to promote safety—including acceptance of higher taxes or restrictions on energy. Between 61 and 71 percent of all adults believed that civil liberties should be curtailed. A full 68 percent felt very or somewhat concerned about being personally affected by a subsequent attack.[2]

Reactions varied by group, of course. Those nearest the attacks were more emotional than people in other regions, and knowing a victim mattered as well. Women and young people were more emotional than others; Hispanics varied from other ethnic groups slightly. Higher levels of education reduced emotionality as well. Interestingly, in light of later developments, Democrats felt more fear than Republicans, the latter presumably comforted by greater faith in President Bush.

A Carnegie Mellon study explored divisions in emotional responses from a slightly different angle. Americans who reacted to the events of September 11 with anger were more optimistic, certainly less fearful, than those who emphasized fear—and this was part of the division between men and women. All groups were profoundly influenced by media coverage, however, in their emotional responses, and this tended to privilege fear. Furthermore, while most individuals claimed to feel that they were personally less vulnerable to terrorism than average, they still saw a high personal risk of harm or death by terrorism—another prod toward fear and an interesting capacity to personalize responses—a point to which we will return.

The dominant responses, as well as the divisions, persisted. A later report suggested that most people continued to say that while the attacks had "shaken their own personal sense of safety and security," only a third still actively worried about their safety in public places. Related divisions—about fifty-fifty—involved predictions about future attacks or whether it is possible to prevent all or most future terrorism in the United States. It remained tragically easy to scare groups of Americans: in 2004, for example, a stray plane in protected Washington airspace led to hundreds of civil servants running from their buildings and phoning relatives to render their last goodbyes. Flight, rather than more prudent realism, showed what vivid emotional memories remained.[3]

The dispersion of fear was intriguing, particularly when the terrorist attacks were soon amplified by incidents in which anthrax was sent through the mails. Some Americans not only stopped using airplanes, they also refused to ride busses or take trains—or did so only feeling "scared, so scared." One mother, worried about anthrax, forbade her children, all in their late teens or early twenties, to open letters. Parents everywhere were afraid to send kids trick or treating (exaggerating a longstanding set of anxieties about Halloween that had origins independent of September 11). "Nobody wants to do anything anymore," a waiter noted six weeks after the attacks, who heard talk of fear while he served tables in a Midwestern town. "Good rational people are frightened in a way they've never been," added a business traveler. And a psychological consultant noted what became increasingly obvious: "The fear has generalized to other situations that are probably safe."[4]

Emotional responses also mattered. Not only did emotions lead to support for particular policies, such as the USA Patriot Act restrictions on normal wiretapping and immigration procedures, they also correlated with mental health symptoms of anxiety or depression. Particularly interesting was a link with levels of information about ongoing current events, such as the retaliatory attack on Afghanistan. Though fearful Americans kept up with the news as well as others, they had far less accurate knowledge about actual national policy or findings about terrorism. Emotionality, it seemed clear, was affecting rational capacity—just as it could in more personal aspects of life. What the polling data could not convey, though what was also true and significant, was that the level of emotionality itself was a new phenomenon, the product of historical change.

EMOTIONAL CHANGE FROM PEARL HARBOR TO SEPTEMBER 11: 1941

The Japanese attack on Pearl Harbor was a massive surprise to the Americans targeted. Though the bombing lasted only a few hours, it left more than 2,400 dead, including 68 civilians. Confusion reigned at the naval base, while civilians rushed to blacken windows and avoid nighttime lights in case a follow-up occurred. Dozens of ships were sent to sea to disperse any subsequent target. And while the attack focused on an island outpost, not anything like a national heartland, it did seem legitimate to fear the possibility of submarine bombardment on the Pacific coast and, once Germany was involved, on the Atlantic as well. There were several sightings in ensuing months. Preparations for air raids, with the London blitz experience in mind, extended even to small towns in the Midwest that duly appointed wardens who patrolled the streets looking for chinks in blackout curtains. Air raid sirens were widely installed, with monthly practice drills. The nation was literally at war, and some sense of vulnerability to what would six decades later be called the homeland persisted for several months. Many people on both coasts expected attacks.

The initial bombardment inspired some individual panic, though not in public expressions outside of Honolulu (and even there to a limited extent). Few people saw much purpose in outward emotion, at a time when open expressions of fear were not in vogue. A few children later recalled anxious mothers, though interestingly they themselves often professed to find the moment "exhilarating," which means that parental upset was kept in sufficient bounds that children did not absorb the signals they would six decades later. Some men, in fuller contrast, immediately rushed to sign up for military service (a phenomenon that recurred to a lesser extent in the days after September 11). Variety of response and its privacy were accompanied by a swift change in tone, often within a few hours. Bewilderment quickly yielded to a sense of anger and resolve, along with confidence in national strength. A Michigan man later described this reaction as he and his wife learned of the attack while on a Sunday drive: "There was an immediate concern, uncertainty, panic, a feeling that you needed somehow to seek a place where you'd be protected .... [But as we drove home] I remember our feelings. First it was indignation, then it turned to anger, and by the time one went to work the following morning it was determination. 'They can't do that to us.'"[5]

More broadly, none of the accounts of the early stages of the war dwells on fear, whether the focus is on personal recollections or a wider historical canvas. Tabloids like the Hearst papers screamed of Japanese espionage and sabotage, and that undoubtedly promoted some emotion—particularly among Japanese Americans. Generally, however, reactions quickly turned to the duty or excitement of military service, or to war industry jobs (a relief after the doldrums of the Depression), and, for many young women, the lure of new work opportunities and some new social outlets as well.[6]

In this context, one set of sources is both representative and revealing, and provides particularly useful comparative fodder for the oral recollections after the September 11 attacks.

Within a few days of the Japanese attack, a government agency interviewed Americans on the street, essentially at random, to determine reactions. Some of this interviewing stretched on into the following month. Ten field workers from the Archive of American Folk Song, established in the Library of Congress in 1928, fanned out to do "man-on-the-street" conversations, to collect the reactions of ordinary Americans. Over two hundred of these interviews, some framed in terms of "Dear Mr. President" letters, sit on the Library of Congress Web site, and they constitute an invaluable resource. Of the 210 on file, only eight, less than 4 percent, mention fear.

Several topics predominated. There was immense faith in the American military. Respondents disagreed about how long it would take to push back the Japanese (and, soon, the Germans). Some expected victory in a year; others urged greater realism, it would take a while. But there was no doubt about ultimate outcome. Interestingly, and possibly reflecting no small amount of racism as well as some recollections concerning World War I, there was more concern about the task against the Germans than about the Japanese threat.

Discussion also focused on the Japanese themselves. Was the attack unfair—it was agreed it was awful—or was this a legitimate act of war? Should the United States retaliate in kind against Japan when circumstances permitted?

Timothy Sullivan, a machinist in Buffalo, responded to the specific question: "Did you experience any fear or excitement?" The reply: "No, I didn't because after all I had pretty good faith in our navy." Mr. Sullivan disclaimed any hatred against the Japanese—he didn't think he hated anybody, but he "didn't like any of this stab in the back business." He realized that American cities might be bombed, but he presumed he could bomb back in retaliation. As to his personal future, "now this thing is upon us," he would "just fall in line with whatever is offered." "You feel that you'll have to make some sacrifices?" "I suppose. The same as we all did in the last war."

Sullivan was also asked about the nation's obvious lack of preparation for war. He freely admitted Americans weren't ready. But there was no need for anxiety. "We've never been ready for anything, but we've always been able to meet it." He was absolutely confident in the justice—he called it honesty—of the American cause. He knew it would be a long war. He admitted anxiety on only one point, what would happen to his children if we should lose the war. But he moved quickly from this topic, ending by professing his absolute faith in President Roosevelt, even though he had always otherwise voted the Republican ticket.

An intriguing interview. There is the one small link with September 11 responses, when the interviewer compelled attention to family reactions, but otherwise the contrasts are remarkable. Sullivan knew the American leadership and military were unready, caught by surprise, he knew modern war was tough, prolonged, and even unpredictable, but his confidence and sense of the task at hand were calm, unruffled. Why were his responses so different from those of a later generation, also caught by surprise, but in a society with a far vaster military and a far longer military track record? [7]

Matt Mansfield, in Tucson, Arizona, had jumped into the war effort by January 1942. He was supremely confident about Roosevelt's leadership—"the best job of any man that could possibly be handling this very critical situation." He was selling war bonds and raising money for the Red Cross. He was working harder than before—he managed a JC Penny store—and giving up some leisure expenses, and he was "mighty happy" to sacrifice whatever the army needs. "And of course we're giving up some of our best young men and we're happy to do that." "The war will be a big job, but we will win." [8]

An interviewer in Nashville noted, somewhat vaguely, that a certain amount of confusion and "hysteria" greeted the war news among African Americans. But he affirmed that while "Negroes" were concerned about their place in the war effort they were eager to defend democracy. Local pastors used the occasion to attack previous lack of preparedness, selfishness, and divisiveness—shown particularly in racial discrimination. But now Americans were awake to the real threats and would work to make a better world.

Miss Fadie France, an (African American) YWCA secretary in Nashville, acknowledged that the attack was expected, given what the Japanese had been doing to China for the past four years. She noted that she had perhaps not fully internalized the serious business of war: "just a mild excitement that naturally comes with mass action, the usual response of an individual to group psychology." No animus against the Japanese, just its leaders. They would lose. "My faith and belief in the superiority of the United States is childlike in its entirety." This despite the nation's continued unfairness to minority groups.

A teacher in New York, focused on "the safety of the children," noted ruefully that her school had the latest safety equipment but that when it was built, "nobody thought of bombs." By January she was helping to run air raid drills. "The children think it's great fun. They have absolutely no fear and the morale is excellent." It's the teachers' job to ready the children to defend democracy. We can all do without cars and washers if necessary, but the schools must go forward.

Max Weissberg, also of New York, had served in World War I. He'd promised his mother he'd be back soon when she started to cry. In fact, it took quite a while to get back. "Confidence is ninety-nine percent of your battle, and if everybody would feel that way they'd all come back. I think it's a great way to feel."

Mrs. Hannah Watkins was a housewife in Nashville. She'd been in Paris and "saw fear" when the Nazi aggression began. "But the resentment that we feel from the Japanese aggression makes us determined to fight until victory belongs to the democracies." W.C. Curry added that "this is the gravest period in our country's history …. Courage, vigilance, and dogged determination to win should be our slogan."

A teacher in Indiana did mention being afraid, but only that his income would go down so much that his professional career would be jeopardized. But he was glad to be a teacher because of the "real opportunity and challenge" to help explain that the people now our enemies would someday have to be respected as citizens of the better world for which the war is being fought.

Sam Coffee of Austin admitted worry—about "the prices." But he marveled at national unity. "I never saw such cooperation on earth." If prices could be kept near normal, there was no way the war would be lost. But even if the prices rose, everyone would back the war. Everybody admired President Roosevelt, who had done more for farmers in the South than any predecessor.

Howard Belker, a cab driver in Denver, was asked what his reactions were "when this news came along." "Well, I don't know that I could say that I had any definite reaction … except to say that, well I just felt 'well, here it is and what's the use of worrying about it.'" And added: "Well, I feel this way: I had a good sleep last night and I ate well today and I'm going to continue to do so." He planned to enlist.

A bellboy added that it all seemed "kind of sudden," and the resulting war was going to take a long time. He too planned to enlist.

Several other Denverites, all planning to sign up or expecting to be drafted, commented on the surprise aspect, some saying also that it had been obvious it was "coming," dividing as to whether this suggested Japanese duplicity more than unacceptable unawareness on the part of the government. But there was absolute confidence that Japan would be beaten, and then Italy and Germany too. "Let's get into it and get it over with." "If they just give us a chance we'll show them what we can do."[9]

This was simply not the United States of sixty years later. A single sidebar on fear that was closely linked to family, though only when an interviewer suggested the link in the first place; a professed eagerness to sign up with the military (even this, far more extensive in 1941 than in 2001); the element of surprise and unreadiness; some sense that it was time for action, time to strike out—these constituted a few limited bonds between reactions to the two catastrophes. And we must not forget wider parallels. The course of World War II would lead to internment of Japanese Americans, a more drastic response than that administered to Muslim Americans after September 11, though fueled by very similar emotional anxieties and resentments. But in the immediate aftermath of surprise attack, the confidence level was dramatically different—in ultimate victory, in the existing government and president: it has to seem nostalgic or naïve or both, to a contemporary observer. And the emotional tone was a distinctive animal entirely, with the distinction continuing even as the war proceeded. Where fear is concerned, and if Pearl Harbor is a sufficiently comparable case, our contention about change over time is proved.

Furthermore, the tone of the post–Pearl Harbor interviews was largely confirmed by wider public behaviors as World War II progressed. The communities that appointed wardens to check on blackouts, against the possibility of London-like bombing attacks, were more resolute than fearful. Public commitment to campaigns such as savings bonds or even accumulating waste tinfoil for the war effort provided a sense of participation that neither expressed nor encouraged substantial panic, even in the initial months before it became clearer than an outright attack was unlikely. The fears undoubtedly felt when sending a husband or son off to war were not publicly expressed. This was not a highly emotional war.[10]

EMOTIONAL CHANGE: SEPTEMBER 11

Quite obviously, fear hit New York City. A woman jogging in Battery Park, near the World Trade Center, became frantic, then "truly terrified," as events multiplied. Crowds gathered, seeking comfort in community. As the buildings collapsed, "the terror was palpable." The woman raced to her boyfriend's apartment, convinced the whole city might be under siege. A group of friends camped out together for the ensuing night, "all too scared to be separate." In later days, as the worst crisis passed and people were able to return to homes in lower Manhattan, a woman scoffed at the leaders who were urging a return to normalcy. "My neighborhood never will go back to normal, and neither, I fear, will I. I am depressed and anxious for a very real reason." Stories of this sort, from people in direct proximity to the attacks, multiplied, and they were understandable and painfully credible.[11]

What was interesting was that reactions from places distant from the attacks were almost as vivid, the sense of immediacy and sudden insecurity almost as great.

Linkages might involve family members directly involved. A teacher in Springfield, Virginia, learned about the attack on the Pentagon. "In my mind something as fantastic as that could never have happened in my lifetime." She and many others in the school were afraid for parents or other loved ones who worked in the Pentagon or nearby. In this case, her relatives did manage to come home safely, and gradually the fears quieted somewhat. But—and this was three years later—"every time I see images from it I get a little emotional." Her fears by this point had turned personal, knowing that she could be killed in some similar attack. Interestingly, the teacher herself made the comparison with Pearl Harbor—"on both of these days America was caught off guard and thus suffered a lot." And, perhaps aided by the perspective, she admits that the fears—first for relatives, then for herself—have stilled somewhat. "For the most part my life has not really changed because I did not know anyone killed in the attacks and daily life has gone on much as before"—some heightened airport security aside.[12]

This sense of balance gradually regained was not always the case, and high emotions did not necessarily have anything to do with possible familial involvement.

Nancy Sanders wrote her reactions down a month to the day after the attacks. She was visiting her parents, planning a day of shopping, when the news began to unfold. The attack on the Pentagon seemed particularly unsettling, because it showed someone was "seriously attacking our country." As the television accounts continued, Sanders could not stop thinking about those who had died: she began crying and could not stop, "I was crying for our nation's safety." She could not leave the house, partly because of the riveting repetitions on screen, partly because "we were so afraid for our safety and didn't know what was coming next." Worry and sorrow continued in the days and weeks after the events.[13]

Still more striking was the rawness of many emotions even in accounts written much later, where the recollection of first reactions, many months after the attacks, built into an apparently durable emotional wound.

A worker in Rochester, New York, describes how he reacted to news about the attacks on the World Trade Center, as he listened to his radio soon after arriving on the job. He heard the announcement about the first tower hit, initially not believing the news, assuming it was some kind of joke. His coworkers "took it with mild shock," assuming it was some horrible accident. Then the announcer, his own voice reflecting the sickening sight on television, came back with the word of a plane hitting the second tower.

At this point someone in the office rolled out a TV set, and everyone became glued to it. "No emotion. I couldn't feel anything." And the worker even managed to take some routine calls about invoices and charges. Then came the news that the Pentagon was hit as well. "The pit in my stomach dropped even further. What the hell is going on here? This is America! We don't have these problems. We don't have terrorists! That's something you hear about in Israel, not in the USA! I was scared. I was worried. What if we're next? What if the bridge I cross is next? What if I'm personally next?"

Then the towers collapsed. "I knew at that point the world changed." "I wish I didn't have to remember that day. I wish we had our innocence again. I wish that none of this ever happened. But now, three years later, it has happened. A memory which will never be forgotten."[14]

Brandie Washington was in New Orleans, planning her child's first birthday party. She wrote also her recollections about three years after the event. A friend called with the news, which immediately made her nervous because she thought the reference was to the Center in New Orleans, which her mother visited periodically. She soon got the site clarified, but scarcely felt relieved. "I couldn't believe that something like this would happen in our country.... I cried in disbelief and fright," grabbing her daughter to hold her close. Soon, calls were essential to establish that some relatives in the New York area were not involved (they weren't, save in terms of inconvenience and their own fears). She kept newspaper clippings and wrote about her terror and anger in a journal she planned to save for her daughter, so she could answer later history questions about what September 11 was all about. "Even though it didn't affect me directly it has definitely taken a toll on me and the way I live my life." Ms. Washington felt rage at the Pakistanis who were shown rejoicing in the attacks; she detailed her heartfelt grief for the families who suffered loss; and she had her own fears.[15]

Stephanie Boaz, in Texas, had just given birth to a new son. She saw both towers attacked, as she lay in her hospital bed. "I remember feeling this horrible, deep pain inside. All I knew is that I wanted my son with me, because I was so afraid. What next, the hospitals? I remember thinking that I could be next." If terrorists could hit these buildings, they must be able to strike anywhere. She held her son all day, and later filled six pages of his scrapbook with materials on the day. "I think it is very important that he understands the relevance of that day, when he's old enough to understand about the lives lost and the feelings of insecurity that swept across the nation."[16]

The nature of fear varied. Some expressed deep emotion but with vague targets. Many quickly became afraid for themselves and/or for their families. Large numbers felt deeply that the fabric of national life had been torn. The sense of personal involvement in momentous tragedy and fundamental change ran strong, propelling but also reflecting the strong emotional stirrings.

A woman in Fort Campbell, Kentucky, put the point fairly clearly. She saw the attacks on television and immediately screamed for her husband. But he was in the military and had to leave for work, as his facilities needed to be locked down against terrorism. "That day I didn't stop crying it hurt so bad." The personal element was obvious in this case—the woman's husband returned two days later to say that he would soon be deployed to Afghanistan. But it was a more diffuse personal involvement that mattered more. "Terrorists didn't just take thousands of lives but they actually took part of our freedoms. One of the freedoms they took from us is not to be afraid, but we are now—[she was writing in December 2003]—are more afraid than ever. I know I did not lose anyone at September 11 but I and everyone in America had lost the chance to relax and not worry as much."[17]

A woman in western Pennsylvania described her horror as the attacks unfolded on television. Her shock and fear virtually "short-circuited" her brain. Finally managing to head for work, she saw the streets of her small town almost deserted because "people were afraid to go out." Rumors flew, including the reports that one plane was headed to attack Pittsburgh or "coming our way. "We were petrified." People left work to pull their children from school. When the crash of the final plane was registered, forty-five miles away, "it was a reaction of utter terror. It could have just as easily hit us. "I ended up having post-traumatic stress disorder and many long sleepless nights." Only when she was able to visit the crash site as a memorial service a year later did she gain any peace. She vowed an annual pilgrimage to express her grief and keep the emotional demons at bay.[18]

Jessica, in Canton, Ohio, heard about the attacks on a car radio. Her feeling at first was that someone was playing a terrible joke. Then she saw people crying in their cars, as traffic virtually halted. She'd visited the trade towers just a few months before and had marveled at the sight, so different from the sights of her small hometown. This was a "fortress," it couldn't fall. Jessica drove home, "getting more and more terrified along the way." This was again a palpable fear—she could barely get her house key out because her hands were shaking so. She then called her mother—"I think we all wanted our mothers on that morning"—and felt, even though her mother projected calm in response to her screaming, that both of them agreed that "the world was ending." She managed to make a ten-minute trip to her mother's house despite her "terror," gaining comfort from a motorist who stopped at a red light who honked his horn, seeing her in tears, and mouthed "it's going to be okay." She felt, in retrospect, that this saved her sanity. Writing not quite two years later Jessica concluded: "I'm still not over what happened that day. I moved to Chicago, and I get nervous when I see low-flying planes or when too many sirens are blaring at once. I wait for the news that it's happened again. I used to be so naïve, so innocent. I felt so safe and I didn't even know it. Now I'm afraid."[19]

A teacher in Illinois talks of the torture she felt as she tried to work with her students even as the news unfolded. "I have never felt such fear as an American. I was afraid. I wanted to be home with my husband and with my children." She was instructed not to talk with her students until right before dismissal, and then to tell them not to worry. "That was the most difficult task I have ever been given. I was afraid, very afraid, and I could hardly hold back tears when trying to assure my students .... I do not know anyone that died in September 11, however the people that did are the people of us all .... I feel the loss of them everyday, I remember, and I will never forget."[20]

Stories of this sort are hardly the only evidence about reactions to the events of September 11, but they provide particularly interesting comparative opportunities the Pearl Harbor data. Here, in both instances though in somewhat distinctive formats, we have accounts of individual reactions. Their contrasts, obviously, are striking—and the other findings, like the polling data discussed above, largely extend the conclusions that result. Americans had changed in response to major disaster and outside threat. Many individuals, in the wake of September 11, would mention Pearl Harbor as precedent of a sort, as a similarly "defining event"—though many also ignored the linkage in their insistence that the nation had never before been violated. Whatever the relationship, the public emotions that ensued were quite different.

Funded by the Alfred Sloan Foundation, the City University of New York and George Mason University began in 2003 to collect stories about September 11 and its aftermath, urging ordinary people to send in their accounts. By August, 2005, 11,708 Americans had contributed in some fashion. Their memories produced the striking impressions of fear and emotional turbulence suggested in the individual vignettes.[21]

They also yield a statistical breakdown. When coded for words like "afraid," "fear," "nervous," "anxious," "worried," and "scared" the data show a substantial minority willing, even eager, to admit their emotional reaction. Over 18 percent of all respondents stated, for the most part without apology, their involvement in fears or anxieties, and often of course adding the ongoing emotional impact. This figure doubtless undershoots the actual percentage, because using code words can miss additional synonyms or other surrogates, but there is no point belaboring statistical niceties. A substantial number of Americans felt, admitted, and retained fear as a response to the events of September 11, and, as we have seen, this included people close to the events but also ones quite distant from them. The stories they were willing to write for an archive largely confirmed the clearer statistical findings from tireless pollsters: many Americans, probably a majority, had felt active fear as the attacks echoed and reechoed (see Table 2.1).

Statistics also echo other characteristics that shine through individual accounts. Not surprisingly, targets of emotion were sometimes rather vague. But when fears could be pinned down they far more often involved self and family than the country as a whole. (Again, this confirmed polling data taken in the more immediate wake of the attacks.) As others have noted, a striking aspect of the September 11 accounts involves the narrow focus, the use of individual and small group as primary frame of reference, the personal investment in emotional response. Even general political concepts like patriotism crop up amazingly infrequently in the stories—at a 6 percent rate (political leaders get only 5%), compared to the 21 percent of the stories that deal with family; the personalization is truly striking.[22]

PEARL HARBOR AND SEPTEMBER 11

American responses to September 11 departed markedly from the reactions to Pearl Harbor. Judging by available evidence—which needs to be assessed further below—Americans were over three times as likely to be afraid, and the level of their fear, when expressed, ran much deeper as well. They were also—and this seems an obviously related point—much quicker to connect attack with personal and familial situations. They were, further, much less likely, when discussing emotional response, to turn immediately to statements of confidence in American government. These changes had occurred despite major advances in educational levels, which the post–September 11 polls suggested might have muted emotionality.

Table 2.1

Afraid.

451 stories/610 uses of the word	Percent	n
1. Not afraid	4.68	29
2. Irrelevant	39.1	242
3. Afraid for self	7.7	48
4. Afraid for family	7.2	45
5. Afraid for Country	8.4	52
6. Unclear/vaguely afraid	32.7	203
Total	99.78	619
Afraid at all	56	348

Fear.

1,038 stories/1,097 uses of the word	Percent	n
1. No fear	5.7	63
2. Irrelevant	42.3	464
3. Fear for self	8.6	94
4. Fear for family	7.1	78
5. Fear for country	6.3	69
6. Unclear/vague fear	29.9	329
Total	99.9	1,097
Report fear at all	51.9	570

Nervous.

160 stories/172 uses of the word	Percent	n
1. Not nervous	5.2	9
2. Irrelevant	2.3	4
3. Nervous for self	46.5	80
4. Nervous for family	13.4	23
5. Nervous for country	9.8	17
6. Unclear/vaguely nervous	22.6	39
Total	99.8	172
Nervous at all	92.4	159

Anxious.

100 stories/103 uses of the word	Percent	n
1. Not anxious	3.8	4
2. Irrelevant	1.9	2
3. Anxious for self	37.8	39
4. Anxious for family	29.1	30
5. Anxious for country	6.8	7
6. Unclear/vaguely anxious	20.3	21
Total	99.7	103
Anxious at all	94.1	97

(continued)

Table 2.1 (continued)

Worried.

786 stories/790 uses of the word	Percent	n
1. Not worried	11.3	89
2. Irrelevant	39.5	312
3. Worried for self	8.9	71
4. Worried for family	14.0	111
5. Worried for country	9.8	78
6. Unclear/vaguely worried	16.3	129
Total	99.8	790
Worried at all	49.2	389

Scared.

914 stories/981 uses of the word	Percent	n
1. Not scared	9.2	90
2. Irrelevant	28.7	282
3. Scared for self	12.9	127
4. Scared for family	16.5	162
5. Scared for country	7.8	77
6. Unclear/vaguely scared	24.7	243
Total	99.8	981
Scared at all	62.1	609

Note: Of all 3,762 respondents who mentioned *afraid, fear, nervous, anxious, worried,* or *scared,* 2,172 or 57.7 percent reported positively feeling that emotion. Of all 11,708 responders (as of August 13, 2005), 2,172 or 18.5 percent reported feeling either *afraid, fear, nervous, anxious, worried,* or *scared.*

To be sure, 18 percent is not the whole story. Most obviously, the September 11 accounts were under no obligation to refer to emotions at all, since these were free and spontaneous responses; many simply involved stories of what the authors saw from their vantage points and other descriptive accounts. In contrast, the Pearl Harbor interviews directly raised emotional issues. In this sense, the statistical contrast—18 vs. 4 percent—masks even greater differences in actual anxiety levels—a point corroborated by the polling data that suggest a near-majority experienced considerable or acute fear in the days and weeks after the attacks. The September 11 stories themselves contain further clues: a somewhat smaller but interesting percentage of the spontaneous stories referred to fear or related emotions only to claim that the emotion had not been experienced. One can, admittedly, wonder why then the emotion was raised at all, and surely some of the deniers were protesting too much. In contrast, the Pearl Harbor interviewees were often directly asked about emotion, so their high confidence levels, though not necessarily entirely truthful, involved less need for elaborate denial. It is also true that many of the September 11 stories, whether focused on fear or not, went on to refer to other reactions, like the quick public outpouring of grief and anger, the urgent references to national unity, the blossoming of flags and bumper stickers bent on conveying strength of purpose and defiance. Nancy Sanders, after recounting her horror and fright, quickly turned to the claim that the terrorist act "will make our nation stronger," expressing her pride and confidence in being an American. The outpouring of flag waving itself raised some questions: it expressed assertiveness, but also perhaps a need to cover up unacknowledged fears in symbolic bombast. But even taken at face value, the September 11 stories, juxtaposed with the Pearl Harbor interviews, suggest some important contrasts in public mood and internal emotional diversity.[23]

Five other contrasts at least partly explain the divergence in response. First, and this is no trivial matter, there is the question of nature of evidence. The post–Pearl Harbor accounts resulted from random interviews—not too many, to be sure, but sufficiently congruent to be fairly persuasive. We have compared these data to materials spontaneously submitted (whose emotional tenor, however, was further confirmed by other data). Both sets involve a rather wide array of ordinary Americans, spread over many regions. But it is obviously possible that people whose emotional reactions were unusually vivid were most likely to take the trouble to write in about their feelings, compared to a possibly more placid majority. Clearly, comparing 4 percent to 18 percent may imply a very misleading statistical precision—though all indications suggest that 18 percent is, in fact, well on the low side of emotional reality.

But there is another difference, which pulls us back to the need for further explanation. While a certain number of the September 11 stories reflected notes jotted down at the time, a surprising percentage of the emotional scars were still vivid two years after the event. And this despite the (to date) absence of subsequent tragedies on American soil. Post–Pearl Harbor confidence and calm were not the results of passage of time and the distraction of intervening developments; they emerged right away. Even four years later, admittedly under provocation of some overt manipulation by national politicians, a significant number of Americans were willing to turn away from conventional support of Democrats to the anti-terror banners of the Bush administration on grounds of ongoing fears—the famous conversion of pro-Clinton/Gore soccer moms to pro-Bush terror moms, eager to support the party that seemed most clearly to respond to their leading current concerns for their children. For a significant number of Americans, the events of

September 11 created fairly durable fear, again in contrast to Pearl Harbor, and this fact alone is impressive, requiring additional analysis.

Evidence and durability aside, there is a second comparative issue to contend with: Pearl Harbor and September 11 were themselves different. About the same number of Americans died, which is not a trivial similarity. But the vast majority of the Pearl Harbor dead were military. While this was shocking, it may be argued that Americans will get less upset about military than about civilian deaths, because military life imposes some acknowledged risks and because it is harder to transpose military losses into a sense of personal and familial vulnerability than in cases of attacks on ordinary folk. (But it is also true that we have come to resent military deaths much more than we once did, which is an argument for change rather than a chance to explain it away.)

The attack on Pearl Harbor was a surprise attack on the United States, but on a remote part of the nation, where tragedy was harder to internalize than when the national core was directly hit. Hawaii was not only distant, but it was not even a state in 1941. Though Pearl Harbor was followed not only by grim and bloody warfare but also by the concerns about coastal attack, it is possible that September 11 reactions expressed a sense of personal threat, a there-but-for-the-grace-of-God-go-I response that the onset of World War II and a Hawaiian tragedy simply could not generate. As several of the stories indicated, it was easy, after September 11, to wonder about whether the next attack would involve one's own office or one's own commute; Pearl Harbor in this sense too may have seemed more remote. Finally, while the Japanese attack intended to create American fear it was less focused on the goal than is terrorism, where emotional exploitation is the primary aim.

Part of the difference in emotional response involved real differences in events and contexts. It is impossible to prove that, had September 11–like events occurred in 1941, Americans would have responded differently. But, admitting this complexity, it remains likely that more is involved. After all, shock was great in both cases. Tensions had been building with the Japanese, to be sure, but the same had certainly been true concerning Islamic terrorists. Surprise but partial preparation existed in both cases. Not only was the death rate rather similar, but the symbolic component was not totally different. The Japanese were hitting an American fleet for specific military purposes; the act was not terrorism in a literal sense, but, in the process, they attacked a key expression of American power. Possibly, to be sure, the idea of facing a conventional if fearsome military opponent was easier to handle than the amorphousness of terrorism, but this particular proposition could be stood on its head as well: more fear might be called up for a conventional war, where there was clearer knowledge about future sacrifice and loss and direct, fairly recent experience in what world war was all about. And befuddlement at hatred of the United States, a prominent part of the September 11 response, surely could be duplicated in 1941, with awareness of how vividly Japanese leaders were inculcating bloodlust among their citizenry. In both cases, American naiveté, the surprise that people we didn't know could want to hurt us, could be brought into play.

Furthermore, the contrast in objective setting should not be pressed too far, lest we confuse our recent memory of September 11 with the long-forgotten historical reality sixty-five years ago. Many people in 1941–42 did believe that invasion was likely. Many did believe that foreign agents might be operating in their midst. Many saw the grim course of the first months of the war, with a steady diet of Japanese advance, far worse than the comparable aftermath of September 11. There was much to be concerned about, and there was concern—but not widespread avowed fear; as motivation for the war effort, policy impulses ran in the opposite direction, seeking to promote calm resolve. Nor, finally, was there any significant partisan use of fear. The emotional contrast between World War II and September 11 is far greater than any difference in the levels of perceived threat.[24]

Grant, then, that part of the increase in fearfulness, between the two attacks, has to do with objective differences in specifics, there is still a problem to be explained. Even if differences in situation do enter in, they arguably do not adequately explain the huge discrepancy in emotional response. At risk of pretending undue precision: distinctions in the nature and location of the attack might account, say, for a 40 percent variance in emotionalism; they do not predict the almost total contrast between assurance and widespread fear. There are, to be sure, other differences, but they begin to be part of the contrast in response, not just a reason to downplay the comparison.

Take for example the obvious change in media potency. Americans *heard* about the Pearl Harbor attacks. They did experience tabloid journalism, bent on depicting spies and foreign agents at every turn. They might soon see pictures of carnage in newspapers and magazines and, if they chose, could add detail in the newsreels at movie houses. But they had the news *before* the visuals; the visuals were far less graphic (and were in black and white, not color) and, above all, were far less ubiquitous. Even if one were prone to the mesmerization of disaster, it was simply harder to engage sixty years ago. Add to this important distinction the genuine shock and horror of the newscasters themselves as the events of September 11 unfolded. Pearl Harbor was big news, but few of the radio reporters who conveyed it were directly involved; they had time to digest before they sought to express emotional cues. Even the difference in time zone, compared to the immediacy of events in the Eastern Daylight orbit, played a role.[25]

The huge changes in media unquestionably explain a lot. But, it can be argued, they simply form part of a genuine and larger shift in emotional response, rather than preempting this shift. It is impossible to prove that Americans in 1941, faced not only with a September 11 but with the media immediacy of 2001, would have responded differently from their descendants six decades later. Yet change in media, and the far greater importance of media not only in stimulating but also in guiding public emotional response, was part of the shift of emotions themselves. Revealingly, as already noted, Britons of 2005, with the same media intensity as their American counterparts, responded to terrorism more in the Pearl Harbor manner—highlighting once more the extent to which, in dealing with American reactions over time, more than media are involved. The vast difference in representation between 1941 and 2001 here becomes part of a larger pattern of change—though part of the explanation as well.

There is a fourth set of factors—beyond differences in events, in media, and in the nature of evidence—that is surely in play. American culture itself had changed. Confidence in government had dwindled—hence the striking reduction in emotional stolidity based on a belief that the authorities could take the problem in hand. After September 11, Americans were proud of their military, eager to appeal at least briefly to national unity, but they could not avoid fears through wide-ranging confidence in leadership. Partisanship also more clearly affected responses in 2001—with people alienated from the president initially more fearful, but later Republicans more eager to take advantage of enduring fearfulness. The 2001 data and collected stories reveal a marked increase in attention to self and family, a quick association of fear with personal attachments in notable contrast to the almost complete—one partial exception—of familial linkages in the Pearl Harbor interviews. This personalization was surely related to the retreat from confidence in political institutions and leadership, with each trend reinforcing the other. American worries about children had also escalated— parents were referred to as helicopters, hovering anxiously over their progeny and accordingly quick to link any general disaster to a familial frame of reference. With political confidence lower, despite some comfort in postdisaster displays of unity, it was easier to believe that threats had to be faced as individuals and as families, not in terms of society at large. Revealingly, in the September 11 stories, only a minority of fear and anxiety references applied to the nation; far more were directed at self or relatives. Here, too, American culture had changed, with a larger number of people "bowling alone" and accordingly more vulnerable.[26]

And finally, fear, too, had altered, becoming easier to feel and to admit. Here again, the contrast between Pearl Harbor and September 11 reactions, though partly explainable through other factors, is quite real. Whatever they "actually" felt, Americans in 1941 were at pains to wish to seem ready to get on with the job, to avoid the distraction of personal emotion. This was simply not the case sixty years later, where fear bobbed to the surface more readily. The shifts in responses involved major alterations in cultural norms—good, bad, and indifferent—involving state, individual, and emotion itself. Fear had become harder to handle but easier to admit. Loss of wide confidence in the government encouraged a tendency to view danger in personal terms, with stronger resultant emotional overtones. Anxieties about children reflected a greater belief in the vulnerability of the young, a greater sense of parental responsibility, but this, too, was part of the new equation of fear. Key changes in relevant American culture were connected, and they revolved around emotionality as the centerpiece.

A fifth set of historical contrasts also applies, related to fear factors and also helping to explain their durability. Following Pearl Harbor, in 1942, the American government did indulge one clear panic reaction, the internment of 100,000 Japanese residents, most of them citizens. Policies after September 11 avoided this extreme, partly because of the shame of the prior incident; but considerable public support for measures against Muslim Americans, and actual profiling and harassment in fact, suggested some similar impulses. But with internment as a huge exception, engagement in World War II led the government otherwise to emphasize positive activities for the public—not only support for the war effort in general terms, but also savings plans, collection of materials, and other activities that created a sense of involved commitment and surely helped reduce or prevent any fears that Pearl Harbor itself, and ensuing threats of coastal attack, might have generated.

In contrast, post–September 11 reactions emphasized the importance of normalcy combined with deliberate invocations of recurrent fear. Ordinarily people had no special tasks. Other than watchfulness, there was nothing much for ordinary Americans to do. There was no need to sacrifice—despite a willingness to do so: the government would cover the costs of a war on terror with growing deficits, while the public was urged to return to consumer indulgence just as quickly as possible, to keep the economy afloat. Wars resulted, but they were fairly distant and, for the first two years, involved few troops, so the sense of widespread citizen engagement was limited. These different policies may have been fully justified by the nature of the threat and the intervening increases in economic dependence on consumerism: but they did nothing to help people feel that they were participating in any special effort in ways that could help refocus emotional concern.

Then there was the decision, as part of what quickly became known as homeland security, to highlight color codings of threat levels. Here was a deliberate effort to link to other approaches to risk—to weather dangers but particularly to codings adopted to identify missing children. Revealingly, of the levels selected the top three—dangerous, high, and elevated—were all ominous; it was particularly unclear why the third level, at yellow or elevated, was less dire than number two's orange. And officials and the public alike could be fairly sure that threats would not drop below these fearsome levels in the foreseeable future. As the Washington, D.C., police chief noted, reflecting September 11 emotionality more generally: "We will never be at green again. Normal was redefined on 9/11. Normal is yellow."

It will be some time before federal documents will be sufficiently available to allow scholars to explore more fully the reactions behind decisions like color coding: how much this was an essential response to the special qualities of the terrorist threat—again, in contrast to massive but more conventional warfare; how much it was intended to set up opportunities for political manipulation; how much it reflected fears on the part of officials themselves, eager to share their anxieties and pass on to a wider public the responsibility for any second disaster—the balance among these overlapping factors cannot be fully known at present. We do know that other governments, also concerned about vulnerabilities after September 11, made different decisions. The British explicitly rejected color coding and quickly moved to minimize public fears. The American response was both more varied and more open-ended. Its capacity for prolonging fear was enhanced when, within three years, government officials began contradicting each other about threat levels, one agency sometimes minimizing current danger while another proclaimed that al-Qaeda was "90 percent" ready to attack the nation again (as in May 2004). Fears did in fact wane with time and no further assault, but emotional vibrations lasted longer than might have been true with a different set of official guidelines.

EMOTIONAL CONTRASTS: THE U.S. AND OTHERS

What is clearly distinctive historically, as Pearl Harbor responses are juxtaposed with those of September 11, is also distinctive as the United States is aligned with contemporary counterparts. The basic chronological contrasts that distinguish recent responses from those of six decades before, in emotional valuations and emotionally implicated policy consequences, in turn emerge strongly in a second set of comparisons. Pearl Harbor and September 11 have the merit of occurring within a single national context, around surprise attacks of considerable magnitude, for a common national framework limits certain variables. Comparing September 11 with recent reactions to terrorism elsewhere reduces the importance of variables such as media, where contemporary exposures are widely shared across national lines, while admittedly introducing a different set of complexities. This second swath will also suggest a current American approach toward fear, enhancing the need to seek larger explanation. Americans have not only come to fear more than they did in the past; many of them also fear more, or at least more openly, than their counterparts elsewhere.

Proving that American reactions to September 11 were comparatively unusual is at least as challenging as showing that they represented national historical change. Terrorist activities elsewhere lend themselves more neatly to comparisons with terrorism against the United States than Pearl Harbor does, but they are never tidily precise, with regard to victim tally or symbolic significance. There is nevertheless something of an accumulation of cases that is suggestive if not absolutely definitive, and that combines with the comparison over time.

We have already suggested an alternative British model developed in response to World War II, maintained on the whole in fact of terrorist activities associated with Northern Ireland and applied again (despite some strongly sympathetic reactions in principle to September 11 itself) to terrorist bombings on the London subway in 2005. The British incidents, particularly in 2005, were all smaller than those of September 11 and doubtless easier therefore to withstand. But they did accumulate, particularly during the struggles in Northern Ireland, which makes the reluctance to show fear somewhat more interesting.

Israeli patterns are even more interesting. Again, no single terrorist incident compares to those of September 11, but the early twenty-first century revival of the Intifada certainly created a recurrent series of civilian bombings whose cumulative effect was or could have been arguably greater than that of September 11.* And the result has triggered fear, but not the outpouring of free-floating public anxiety that September 11 occasioned in the United States.

One comparison is revealingly precise. Suicide bombings on Israeli busses, one of the main forms of attack in the early twenty-first century, generate definite but on the whole modest disruptions in patterns of ridership. Passenger levels on the affected routes normally drop about 20 percent, mainly among occasional rather than regular users. There is little impact on ridership in other cities, little impact as well on patronage of neighboring venues such as coffee shops. And bus drivers themselves stay on the job. Finally, even on the affected routes ridership tends to rebound within a few months. In other words, arguably, most Israelis react to terror as a low-probability event, something to think about, and doubtless to fear, but not productive of widespread panic.

The contrast with September 11 is striking. Passenger use on domestic airlines overall, throughout the continental United States, plunged by 60 percent for two months after September 11, then stabilized awhile at a 25 percent reduction, then dipped even further (fueled in part by an economic downturn) into early 2003, by which point the drop reached well over 30 percent. The reaction was larger than after an Israeli suicide bomb—even when the bomb was the latest in a series of several attacks per month. It lasted far longer than in the Israeli case. And it was distributed over a far wider geographic area—nationwide rather than regional. American fear spread farther. It deeply touched people themselves distant from the attack—as the qualitative reactions to September 11 themselves suggest. It clearly spilled over into other activities and sites not dependent on air travel, such as attendance at public events or car-based tourism—a contrast to the Israelis' continued patronage of neighboring shops. And the fear was very hard to shake off despite the absence—in contrast to the Israeli case—of ensuing events.

The same Israeli commitment to normalcy showed in the policy of gradually reopening shops and cafes after suicide bombings. Mike's Place in Tel Aviv, for example, near the U.S. Embassy, was up and running two weeks after a deadly attack. A nearby nightclub was repainted within two days after another incident. It is hard to imagine comparable

---

* If this was a thorough discussion of terrorism, rather than emotional reactions, we would need to probe state-sponsored terrorism as well as the nongovernmental variety. In focusing on Israeli reactions, there is no intention of ignoring the extent to which Israeli and other governmental actions sometimes, in their random damage among civilians, also have strong terrorist qualities. Certain patterns of American bombing might arguably be put in the same category. The issue is extremely important but not directly germane to this argument.

American reactions, granted the complexity of comparison in the absence of direct experience with suicide bombings on American soil. Americans would hesitate longer to frequent a scene of violence; they would have a greater impulse to memorialize the sites; they would be more preoccupied with grief and fear.

Somewhat ironically, one study suggests that Israelis in New York, after September 11, showed more fear than their counterparts back home in part at least because of sheer emotional contagion from American colleagues and media.

As always, comparative objections must be noted as well. Israelis doubtless have more sheer need to use busses than Americans to use planes—they may be just as scared, or even more so, but simply lack the range of options to indulge their fear. An economist's study, oddly uninterested in national comparisons, emphasizes the importance of routine-mindedness compared to the more occasional habits of many plane passengers, and there may be some truth in this. But terror in Israel, though less spectacular, is arguably objectively scarier, because of its recurrence, its focus on daily activities, its frequent victimization of children (almost entirely absent from September 11). Yet the cultural repertoire seems to emphasize grief and anger more than fear—not an entirely different mixture from its contemporary American counterpart but distinctive in the balance among components. American fear again stands out.[27]

Other comparisons can, of course, be adduced. France's experience with extensive terrorism during the Algerian war, with plastic bombs planted in pedestrian thoroughfares, elicited heavily armed police but no sign of public panic. Jordanian reaction to bombs that devastated three hotels, in 2005, featured defiant marches (and some quiet sympathy for gestures of protest against the American invasion of Iraq—a separate component) more than widespread fear, and interestingly there were no significant repercussions, even among the newly increasing band of tourists, in nearby Israel/Palestine.

The most interesting comparative analysis, however, derives from the bombings of commuter trains in Madrid in March 2004. The attacks, it must first be noted, differed greatly from those of September 11 in terms of fatalities: about two hundred people died, with an additional fifteen hundred injured. Score one for the inevitable problems of comparative precision. In other respects, however, the comparative potential improves. The attacks, it quickly became known, were impressively well coordinated. Ten bombs had been set to explode essentially simultaneously, and seven indeed did go off. The devastation and scope of planning combined with the obvious assault on daily commuter lifelines to provide dramatic challenge to the people of Madrid and, to a degree, of Spain more generally.

Fear and confusion prevailed at first, amid widespread television reportage and the open scenes of wreckage and bloodshed. Observers cited "chaos" and "paralysis" in Madrid. "This is so savage you can't even describe it," one lawyer exclaimed. Additional anxiety resulted from initial uncertainty about responsibility for the attacks—it might have been the Basque separatist group, ETA, long involved with lesser acts of violence, or it might have been (and indeed was) an arm of al-Qaeda that was simply a bit slow in claiming authorship. Not surprisingly, many Spaniards rushed home or remained reluctant to go out in public.

But the striking contrast with the United States and September 11 was the brevity of the dominant fear response. Within hours, literally on the same day, hundreds of Spaniards went out to seek outlets for blood donations for the victims. Even more widely, street protesters took to the roads. Joined by members of the royal family, nearly two million people in Madrid alone participated in a march against terrorism, the day after the attacks. "We must show the world we are not afraid," an elder-care worker noted. Nationally, demonstrations embraced at least eleven million people. Anger, in other words, and a defiant sense of unity and determination quickly predominated over other emotions in the Spanish response—much like the reactions in Britain over a year later, and despite the greater scale of the Spanish attacks. Radio Free Europe quickly reported the focus in public opinion: "not to let terrorists win." While some parents held their children back from public transportation, or warned them how to escape from trains, the majority of Spaniards returned quickly to normal travel patterns, with only a few reporting lingering fears or anxieties about future attacks. And despite grief and memorial services, there has been no impulse to turn the bombings into an occasion for some sort of massive public monument, in the fashion of Oklahoma City.[28]

Contrast was compounded by the equally quick hostility to initial government measures to limit civil liberties in response to the attacks. New border controls and personal data collection, not dissimilar to the USA Patriot Act approach, won wide condemnation. It was also interesting—though specific circumstances applied here—that whereas American reaction tended to favor the incumbent government, then and later, Spanish reaction included voting out the established party several days after the bombings, in favor of a socialist roster that previously had been given little chance. Some government bumbling and misinformation, plus a belief that Spanish involvement in the coalition in Iraq (long condemned by the socialists) was wrong and a factor in drawing terrorist attack, led to this outcome.[29]

The main point, however, is the quick emphasis on defiance over fear, not just in principle but in open public action—despite the invitations to further urban attacks that this action might have facilitated. This was simply different from the United States.

For the evidence unquestionably accumulates: France, Israel, Spain, Britain, and Jordan suggest a dominant pattern of reaction and leadership, examples that emphasize the distinctiveness of recent contemporary public emotion in the United States. And this, like the comparison over time, suggests the need to find explanations that go beyond inevitability, and suggests as well the need to evaluate distinctive consequences in ensuing policy as well as in both private and public mood.

Comparison is always disputable. The complexities of the Pearl Harbor/September 11 juxtaposition—a comparison over time rather than space—demonstrate this abundantly. The attacks of September 11 had unique qualities, in size and symbolic impact—particularly in contrast to terrorism in other contemporary cases—and these must not be downplayed. There is no way definitively to prove that Spaniards or Britons or Israelis would not have replicated American emotions had the attacks of September 11 happened to them, just because they proved markedly more stolid in dealing with smaller catastrophes.

Alternatively, comparative differences may be granted but dismissed simply on grounds of greater experience with public violence. Spain had dealt previously with Basque attacks, Britons with the IRA, Israelis with repeated episodes. American distinctiveness, in the second line of argument, does exist but does not require much analysis beyond citing national virginity (and this is, of course, what many Americans implicitly claimed at the time).

And yet Americans did have relevant experience, as with Oklahoma City or attacks on nationals abroad, quite apart from the earlier example of Pearl Harbor; they simply chose, in the main, not to cite it. Their suffering was greater in September 11 than that of foreign counterparts, at least in terms of single incidents, but not enough greater to wipe away the more abundant emotionality and its greater durability.

There is, then, an emotional issue to be explained, over time—in contrast to prior national experience—and comparatively across geographic space.

There is one final component of reactions, like those in Spain 2004 or Britain 2005, that may have contributed to the quick defiance and its contrast with American patterns: knowledge of the American response itself. Without directly criticizing American September 11 reactions, many people in Europe and elsewhere had been able to decide that the American response was not what they wanted for themselves—a reaction of fear and public retreat. They made their own comparisons, in other words, and this combined with other factors—such as British memory of Churchillian precedent—to generate the prompt insistence on acts of public solidarity combined with quick return to normalcy.

PERSISTENCE

American fear, post–September 11, contrasted with the national past; it contrasted with reactions elsewhere. A final measure of distinctiveness focuses on emotional persistence. As time passed, American emotions cooled a bit. Uses of air travel returned to normal levels with the average traveler professing little or no anxiety. Young people tossed aside fear more quickly than other groups. A 2005 student poll saw terrorism a distant third among fears, behind indebtedness and unemployment. (Even so, students were likely to know more about terrorism than about foreign or even domestic political issues, suggesting perhaps that nonchalance was somewhat skin deep.)

Deep fear, however, lasted a surprisingly long time. An October 2002 poll showed professed fear levels little changed from a year before, even though many habits had seemingly normalized. Most people continued to assume another attack was coming. American students in Madrid, in 2004, were more upset by the subway bombings there than most natives were, often crying, often assuming other attacks were imminent—again, a sign of the rawness of emotions. Americans in Israel also reacted far more vigorously than did Israelis. Obviously, persistence was encouraged by many politicians and media figures, eager to draw attention to news stories, hoping to curry voter favor. Frequent color-coded warnings and even the possibility of arbitrary arrest under the USA Patriot Act served, according to many observers, to keep emotional levels high. Programs designed to cope with fear, like those by the Red Cross, showed awareness of the depths of American feeling, but they might have unintentionally sustained it through ongoing warnings about psychological damage.[30]

The presidential elections of 2004 revealed the depth and impact of fear persistence. A number of surveys showed how many women, former soccer moms of the 1990s, were turning into "security moms," ready to vote on the basis of whatever candidates talked most elaborately about terrorism and the need for countermeasures. The result was that the voter gender gap, which had long saw women favoring Democratic candidates because of their willingness to spend on education and family welfare, steadily disappeared. As President Bush increasingly emphasized security themes, maternal preference for Democrat John Kerry virtually evaporated. In 2000, Al Gore had beaten Bush by 10 percentage points among female voters, but by September 2004 Bush actually had an 11 point advantage over Kerry in this same group. Within months, a Kerry lead, typical for Democrats, of about 50–36 points among women had vanished or even reversed. Women previously concerned about abortion rights, guns, and the environment now put fear first.

Individual women made the transition clear. As one noted, "I have recently become a soccer mom—and I'm a security mom too. I take the job seriously and I expect my president to take it serious. When I tuck my daughter in at night, I want to know that my president is watching my back and keeping me safe." Here, obviously, the personalization of September 11 reactions continued, entering the political arena directly. As a Planned Parenthood organizer noted, ruefully considering the erosion of her normal constituency: "There is no question the Bush administration is playing the fear card as much as they possibly can...to keep attention off his dismal record on the many policies that women (normally) care about." The summer seizure of a Russian school by Chechyan terrorists contributed as well, however remote the connection: "If your kid can't be safe in his own school—there's nothing more horrific." [31]

Feelings of vulnerability, in other words, showed little sign of recession. As in the initial reactions, women maintained the feelings more than men, and women with children most of all.

Special features of September 11 doubtless help explain this final persistence measure, just as they help explain change and comparison. But it remains fair to insist, with persistence as with comparison and change, that more is involved. Emotional wounds should have healed more quickly. Some combination of media zeal, political manipulation, and an unusually fertile emotional climate prepared a set of American emotional reactions that went well beyond the inevitable.

CONCLUSION

The memories continue, and so does the emotional resonance. Little incidents, hardly significant in themselves, show how pervasive and commonplace an exaggerated rhetoric about fear has become. A 2005 book review, commenting on a new work by Salman Rushdie, notes how, sixteen years ago, it seemed so strange that a man should have to live under the threat of Islamic terrorists on the other side of the world:

"but now we all live that way." Rushdie, of course, had seen a death sentence passed against him by an Iranian ayatollah in 1989, and a $5 million bounty placed on his head. Whether "we all" have to live as he has, since September 11, might be open to some discussion; but the fact that the similarity could even be claimed was intriguing. The fear remains, and hyperbole ensues.

Again in 2005 an exhibition of paintings from the centuries of plague in Italy, between 1500 and 1800, opened at the Worcester Art Museum in Massachusetts. The curator was a professor of Italian studies at Boston College. He had begun organizing the exhibit before September 11, but then was immediately impressed with the similarities between the threat of devastating disease and the contemporary threat of terror: "We were living in this state of utter helplessness …. The specter of terrorist-disseminated plagues … has kept us in a state of collective anxiety, if not of panic. We have come to realize, as they did, that fear is our new reality. For a brief time we had confidence that science would overcome anything. Now we return to something older."

The comparison is fascinating. Plague hit Italy frequently in the early modern centuries, following the devastating "black death" of the fourteenth century in which up to 25 percent of the European population was wiped out. Major epidemics occurred several times, and individual cities suffered almost every year. Does this provide a relevant standard for contemporary terrorism? The helplessness theme may certainly strike a chord. The possibility of devastating, terrorist-induced disease may haunt us as well, though of course it has not happened yet. But, uncertain futures aside, and with due respect for the admirable goal of promoting art exhibits, is the linkage really plausible, given the vast disparity in the (at least thus far) levels of threat to human life? The comparison says more about a public emotional state, about the subjective aspects of the American reaction to terrorism, than about objective grounds for fear. Clearly, many Americans continue to have some difficulty in mapping their fear reactions—a sign of the novelty of the threat, perhaps, but unquestionably also a symptom of some unusual features of contemporary emotional standards as well.

II
Causes and Contexts

3

SEARCHING FOR CAUSES

The conclusion that contemporary Americans have become unusually fearful compared to other people in roughly comparable situations, at least in collective public reactions, and also that their reactions have changed compared to the national past, cries out for explanation. This brief chapter posits some key directions, while also suggesting that other possibilities can be dismissed. The goal is to set the parameters for the next stage of inquiry.

Faced with the data in the previous chapter, several reactions are possible, and indeed several might be combined:

- Deny that there is anything distinctive about American patterns and simply argue that chapter 2 is wrong. Obviously, those who insist on this response will have been generous indeed if they have read to this point, not to mention if they continue reading. An alternative, but it's really the same response: disasters like those of September 11 are so dreadful that they justify any combinations of fear, grief, and anger that people may choose to develop. There's nothing to explain. In the same vein, some may feel that the horror of the attacks should focus all attention on the evils of the perpetrators: any study of American reactions might seem to dilute guilt or distract from the necessary response.

The attacks on the World Trade Center and the Pentagon were horrible and disorienting. People directly involved, because they were there or had close relatives in the buildings, might indeed be allowed any of the responses people generate when something awful happens, with no need to explore more elaborate causation. But wider reactions, including fearful policy response, can't be dismissed so readily, particularly when they differ so markedly from responses to similar threats elsewhere or previously. There is something to explain.

And as to distracting from guilt: the attacks were awful, the perpetrators were foul, and we must work for ways to prevent terrorism. But American responses enter into this equation as well. We're not accountable for the attacks themselves, but we must be in charge of what we do thereafter. Intelligent reactions require self-knowledge, and mere ranting against terror or evil will not get the job done.

A final variant—and this one can't be fully disproved one way or another—would be to argue further against comparability. IRA threats in Britain were nothing compared to the events of September 11. Pearl Harbor is interesting but, after all, it was far away, not nearly as relevant to personal safety.. The death toll was comparable but not only was it more distant but also mostly military, another buffer against personal relevance. The Spanish train explosions didn't kill nearly as many people and the targets didn't have the same national iconic quality. And so on. The issue of comparability is indeed tricky, as the previous chapter discussed; no disaster is ever quite like another, indeed no set of evidence about emotional response is ever quite like another. The fact that many Americans believed that they faced an unparalleled danger after September 11 is interesting, but the reaction goes deeper, and there is need to establish an explanation rather than to dismiss the issue of causation. The attack was terrible, and it unquestionably had distinctive features: no one else, ever, has had two skyscrapers blown up by civilian aircraft. But the whole affair was not so definably worse than attacks in other places and other times that the differences in reaction are wiped clean. While the loss of life was tragically great, the violence was time-specific compared to repeated terrorist acts in other societies that have generated less frenzied response. Granting the difficulty of comparing disasters, there remains something to explain.

Some weeks after September 11, the *Washington Post* ran a set of opinions by foreign observers. Among the most interesting was the view of a Mexican journalist, who noted that the events of September 11, dreadful as they were, killed only half the people that the Mexico City earthquake had done. His judgment: get over it already. Possibly unfair, since natural disasters may warrant less emotionality than disasters caused by human hand—but interesting.

- Americans have insufficient experience with tragedy, so their otherwise seemingly exaggerated response is understandable on grounds of naiveté. There is something to explain, in other words, in American fear responses but the explanation is simple. There's no reason for complicated analysis. People who favor this approach need not regret having read this far, but they may wonder about whether they should keep reading.

This dismissal is really challenging, and it may be partly correct. People who display more sangfroid than the American public in the face of terrorist acts—the Israelis, for example, or Parisians who experienced the long series of bomb attacks in the 1960s, or the Spanish with the commuter train explosion—have had long and also recent experience with war and misfortune, either directly or through what their parents handed down. Americans have a more modest track record, and have long been accused of over-optimism and misplaced innocence because wars have touched them so slightly in the past, at least since the 1860s.

A striking quick reaction to September 11, on the very day and repeatedly since, was "nothing will ever be the same." The line was understandable in the heat of the moment, though a historian may be pardoned for immediately dismissing the thought as silly and historically uninformed. But the currency and durability of the sentiment were more important than its inaccuracy. Surely it partly represented a belief that American soil had never been violated in serious fashion before (though—obviously enough by this point—I would argue that it had more to do with dismay at the emotional turmoil the attacks generated than with a real belief that some national virginity had been violated by a level of aggression previously kept at bay).

One of the first American reactions to the terrorist attacks on London in July 2005 was to note British familiarity. After all, London had been bombed far more terribly decades earlier, and there was the more recent experience with IRA activities. While the relevance of events sixty years ago might be questioned, it is true that many Britons, returning to normal the day after the bombing, directly referred to Winston Churchill's slogans and the gritty evacuation of Dunkirk, drawing directly on historical memories (not, given the ages involved, personal experience) from 1940. The British, in other words, did seem to react far more nonchalantly than we did (to an admittedly much less significant incursion), but while this is interesting—and perhaps, though no one said so directly, a bit embarrassing as we look back on our own alarums five years ago—it requires no intricate analysis.

Yet, if American soil has been relatively sacrosanct, the argument should not be overdone. Pearl Harbor hit American territory, and if distant Hawaii did not feel exactly like home to other Americans, the subsequent sightings of German or Japanese submarines off American coasts and the precautions against bombing even in Midwestern towns hardly induced a feeling of full security. And more recently Americans have been so often victims of mass terrorist attacks elsewhere that the unsullied innocence argument seems over-simple. We're not so unbloodied that the unprecedented qualities of September 11 alone warranted the pervasive sense of personal fear. We, too, could have devoted more attention to our basic familiarity with out-of-the-blue disasters, instead of treating each one—Oklahoma City, the embassies, and so on—as an unanticipated affront. Score a few points for the lack of experience argument, but we surely need more.

For the comparative memory angle is not, in fact, self-evident. Why did more Americans, in 2001, not hark back to the courageous response to Pearl Harbor, as the British did to their World War II precedents? Why no invocation of FDR to compare with the British ability still to take some inspiration from Churchill? Several factors may contribute: the British may well have superior historical memories—though Americans do seize on battle history as one of the aspects of the past they most cherish. Greater American partisanship may have pushed FDR to the sidelines, compared to a political climate in Britain that is less judgmental about the past. It's hard not to conclude that Americans fail to take full advantage of potentially inspirational past examples because more urgent emotions crowd out the field. This returns us, of course, to the need for further explanation.

Indeed, the argument that follows will seek to turn the inexperience argument partly on its head. Unfamiliarity with massive foreign violence on our soil cannot be contested. But it may be that excessive exposure to outside threat and the resultant deep fatigue, not emotional virginity, partly explains our current reactions. We have abundant experience with deep worrying about attack—we raised at least one generation of children who did not really expect to live to full adulthood, because of the apparent certainty of nuclear war. And we have extensive exposure to acts of mass terrorism against Americans though in other parts of the world. But this claim—of overexposure and nervous fatigue—must be part of a larger argument involving emotional reevaluations that are domestic as well.

- It all boils down to media manipulation. The ubiquity of television unquestionably provides both immediacy and incessant repetition for moments of great tragedy like September 11. Grainy newsreels and black and white pictures of Pearl Harbor provide no competition. Without question, media presentations and guidance help generate contemporary public emotions. Grief and disgust at the graphic violence in Vietnam greatly contributed to the turn of public opinion. While the American military has since learned how to ration images of violence, at least against American troops, there are no limits on the coverage of disasters like Oklahoma City or September 11. Virtually every waking citizen saw the twin towers collapse scores of times during the initial hours after the attack. The faces of raw fear, on the people fleeing the buildings, and then deep grief, became household experiences thousands of miles away. The contagion was inescapable, and shocked news anchors were ready to tell us what to feel in case there was any doubt. While the media argument weakens the inexperience gambit—after all, the same immediacy has brought us to other atrocities, like the embassy bombings in Africa—it may seem to excuse us from further explanation.

Terrorism of the September 11 sort has another peculiarity that reinforces the media role. Major attacks outside the specific war zones of the Middle East are infrequent. This encourages media to replay the singular events themselves, rather than getting caught up in the next disaster story as would be the case in a more orthodox war. Repetition pours salt on emotional wounds, even as we inevitably wonder when the next infrequent, unpredictable horror will occur.

Granting an important media role, that helps differentiate contemporary reactions from those of a pre-satellite-television era, it would be a mistake not to probe further. In the first place, comparative issues cannot be disposed of through the media argument. Media coverage was just as extensive in London or Madrid as it was in New York, yet while it revealed carnage and fear it also quickly reported spontaneous reactions of calm. The media help shape, in other words, but they also respond to a distinctive emotional climate—which means again that there is more to explain. Changes in the media must also be handled: broader shifts in popular culture, including an unprecedented wave of disaster fiction, may color news reporting, and certainly a new public openness to fear helps prompt media tone as well.

For there's the further question of public emotional hot buttons, available to the media but not created by them. American media delight in portraying both fear and grief, because a wide public responds with such grim fascination to emotions that are normally detested in contemporary culture. Most American hate to feel grief, save in some highly structured settings like a funeral home; yet precisely because of this revulsion, we seem endlessly attracted to the microphone shoved in the face of a parent who has just learned her child died in a house fire. The same applies to fear. An emotion that causes so much distress by contemporary standards draws viewers like flies. The media play up and play on our emotional vulnerabilities. They are unquestionably involved in explaining fear reactions. But they are conditioned by these reactions as well—the newscasters know the attractive power of conflicted emotions. Again, there is more to explain.

Several intriguing existing studies of fear rely almost exclusively on media manipulation by way of explanation. In point of fact, as we will show, the media role is complicated, even aside from the perennial question of how much the media can dictate without prior public readiness. In the chapters that follow we will show how media roles have changed as a result of wider shifts of public expectations.[1]

- There must be something in the national psyche that makes Americans easily turn to fear. National psyche arguments are difficult to assess, but they are usually too sweeping to be very satisfactory. In this case, the historical evaluation of recent American fear—the possibility of demonstrating that it is worse than it used to be (Pearl Harbor vs. 9/11)—knocks any over simple national character argument down fairly easily. Long-term components of American culture—there's no need to claim a clear-cut psyche—do help explain fear reactions, particularly where racial "others" are involved, as we will discuss in the following chapter; but they are supporting elements, not primary factors. There are some distinctive American fear traditions, or at least some distinctive elements, that cannot be ignored. But these apply mainly in combination with more novel factors, developing during the middle decades of the twentieth century; they cannot stand alone.
- American reactions do result from causation newer and more proximate than the enduring national character argument would allow. Some sort of recent, cosmic anxiety lies at their core, an anxiety then open to media manipulation and encouragement.

The most interesting candidate in this category, which we'll explore in chapter 5 along with another sweeping change, involves a sense of anxiety that has developed as the nation's world power has grown and possibly attains a point of overreaching. The majority of Americans do not explicitly acknowledge that national power has overextended or that some retaliation is inevitable. In fact, as September 11 demonstrated, they bristle at critics who try to find any justifiability in terrorists' motivations. But, so the argument runs, they are unconsciously anxious in any event.

The story goes that at the height of Napoleon's power, his mother used to wander around Fontainebleau Palace murmuring, "If only it lasts." There is a line of analysis, with some evidentiary claims behind it, that this is the mood that has emerged in the United States. The nation lacks long traditions of militarism or of widespread overseas imperialism, yet it has become a militaristic society and, though always with claims that "we'll get out soon," an empire-building one as well. Small wonder that subconscious fears about retaliation and reversal have built up, explaining fear reactions more generally.

This is an impressively imaginative argument. It may even be true, or partly true. The obvious problem with it, however, is the inability to substantiate it in any direct way. The evidence is interesting but at most suggestive, for what is unconscious—given the difficulty of placing the national majority on any relevant couch—yields speculative analysis at best. So, hoping perhaps to have our interpretive cake while eating it as well, we'll evoke this kind of argument but, admitting its reach, suggest that at most it helps establish a relevant new context, rather than providing a full explanation.

This then leaves the heart of the argument, where connections are much closer to the surface: new American approaches to fear began to develop, initially in personal and familial settings, some decades back. Increasingly widely established, they connected with related reconsiderations of risk and security. Together, these innovations began to shape public responses to threat, affecting both general reactions and policy determinations. The result generated two separate phases in the media approaches to fear, the first gingerly, then the second eagerly exploitative. Close parallels between what was being suggested about fear and security in personal socialization, and the wider response, are no accident—the one helped create the other. Add a growing national experience with foreign threat, developing during the same decades and at least initially conditioned in part by inexperience with such threat, and distinctive fear reactions became increasingly predictable. A culture of personal fear was revisited, in other words, even as experience with war and threat ultimately stretched nerves on another basis as well. New aversions to fear and risk intertwined with the perceived experience of foreign menace. In the combined result, reactions like those to Pearl Harbor became impossible. And if all this developed in a broader context also shaped by Napoleon's mother's reactions writ large, the explanation, strong enough already, becomes even stronger.

It is possible, of course, that a final causal factor should be involved: a still broader contemporary or at least Western-wide anxiety based on a sense that too many factors in life were escaping normal human control. Several recent studies have targeted fear as the dominant current emotion, without much reference to place; and one study identifies France, not the United States, as the "Fearful Society."[2] It is certainly possible that many countries, including the United States, participate in fears based on a sense that the privileged Western world position is eroding, that science and technology have spun out of balance, and that globalization unduly challenges more familiar centers of authority. "Fear," in this reading, may refer to a more purely cognitive approach, rather than outright emotion, but this distinction may be hard to draw. Americans have gained some special terrors, that require explanation, but the possibility that the emotion has a wider basis deserves consideration as well.

Substantial debate has emerged in recent years, among historians and also cultural studies scholars, about whether causation should be a primary target for analysis. Some contend that "meaning," rather than explanation, is what we should strive for. Meaning is good; when we turn in chapter 5 to the evidence about unconscious fears of imperial collapse we'll really be exploring this angle, more than precise causation per se. But ultimately, where both change and comparative distinctiveness are involved, there's no reason not to seek assignable causes as well. We can admit that, in history, causes are always debatable: the past does not allow laboratory verifiability. But it is often possible to build a plausible case, which is what we'll be arguing for American fear. The result is far more satisfactory than simply describing the phenomenon and urging a quest for meaning. And only with some sense of causation can we hope to come to grips with remedying any of the more pernicious aspects of the pervasive national reactions to fear.

4

THE ROOTS OF AMERICAN FEAR
Traditions

American culture launched a really distinctive approach to fear only in the twentieth century: there was no long legacy of public fearfulness. Indeed, current standards are particularly striking in their contrast with nineteenth-century norms, which quite explicitly called on Americans, or at least American men, to face fear directly and stare it down. There is no enduring national character in play here—indeed, reactions to Pearl Harbor already demonstrate an earlier willingness to confront threat without open emotional overtones.

One huge fear, of course, punctuated the colonial experience in New England: the witchcraft fears of the seventeenth century. These were not unique to North America in this period, and while they related to larger religious ideas discussed below, they had no carryover once the hysteria passed. To be sure, more recent episodes of collective emotion, most notably the McCarthy trials of the 1950s, would be dubbed witch hunts, with some accuracy; but their content and participants had nothing really to do with the classic colonial outburst. No relevant precedent was set.[1]

Two features of the nation's formative cultural experience, however, have remained relevant. The first involves a tendency to link fear to concerns about racial others, an important if hardly surprising component of the American cultural arsenal. The second, not necessarily more significant but more tantalizing, involves the persistence, or at least periodic recurrence, of an apocalyptic strain, ready to think in terms of catastrophe and mixing fearful prospect with rapturous hopes for the future and with a belief that some aspects of American society might justly be damned. This strand was not particularly unusual when it was transported from Europe to the New World. But its durability has been striking, in contrast to Europe's more thorough-going secularization, and its relationship to mainstream American culture remains both real and complex.

COLONIAL HERITAGE: ELEMENTS
OF NATIONAL CHARACTER

Coming to the New World was scary, back in the seventeenth and eighteenth centuries. African slaves, subject to the perils of capture and a hideous ocean passage, were often terrified. Olaudah Equiano, snared as a boy in West Africa, later left an eloquent account of his fears as he was separated from family, then from a sister, manhandled by strangers and the terrifying white sailors, prevented from the suicide that would have ended his fright. What the legacy of this fear was, in later African-American culture, is not easy to determine, but it warrants attention.[2]

Many African Americans, considering September 11 and majority reactions, noted their different perspectives. For them, and their historical experience, fear was not new. There was no sense that some fundamental innocence had been violated, because they had often encountered terror and undeserved violence.

White colonists could be afraid as well. Some early accounts talk of the intimidating, thick forests that spread down to the ocean floor, frightening people accustomed to a more tamed nature. More relevant to later American fears was the context this set for dealing with an obvious component of life in the New World, the need to interact with, or at least to contemplate, Native Americans. Here were peoples with dramatically different cultures and even economic systems, by no means always hostile but recurrently menacing in fact and even more often in perception. Not only their strangeness, but also their mistreatment at the hands of whites, could create a pervasive mixture of condescension and anxiety. Fear of Indians, and by extension the possibility of fears of other strangers, became part of the American cultural arsenal.[3]

The component was amplified and solidified by fears that developed concerning African slaves. A rich historical literature, applying to many slave societies besides the United States, documents the combination of hierarchical thinking and outright terror that applies to people who have been enslaved, particularly if they are marked, culturally or racially, as clearly different from the ownership group. Guilt and fears of rebellion or resistance merge to exaggerate the anxieties involved. Actual slave uprisings and the even more frequent incidence of individual violence fuel the fires. Nat Turner's Rebellion in Virginia in 1831, a slave insurrection in which fifty-one white people were killed, triggered huge reactions—many would argue overreactions—involving wild rumors of further attacks, the slaughter of many individual slaves, new laws punishing anyone teaching slaves to read or write (Turner had been notoriously literate), and massively increased surveillance. Obviously, many of these fears easily outlasted slavery itself, compounded by continued degradation of the now-free African-American minority.[4]

Part one of American fear, then, involves a persistent strand of deep-seated racial fears. Of course, these did not apply to all whites or to all interactions with racial minorities. There is no question that real resentments and imagined potential for retaliation built a picture of antagonism that easily survived into the twentieth century and beyond. A similar climate of fear, along with more prosaic economic rivalries, produced the mixture of anxiety and hostility that applied to Asian immigrants in the nineteenth century, leading to laws excluding further entry first to the Chinese, then to all East Asians by new legislation in 1917. Internment of the Japanese in World War II (in obvious contrast to the definite but less systematic reactions to German Americans even in World War I) was another extension of racial fear. Hispanics could also provoke fright, though it was long more regionally limited. Beliefs about violence and disease created much different immigration screening on the nation's southern border, around 1900, than where European immigrants were concerned; it also fed a significant pattern of lynchings of Mexican Americans—that horrendous expression of arrogance and fear—that rivaled the violence directed at African Americans. To add to the mix, unconscious guilt about the worst of ethnic treatments—the violence, the dispossession—could fuel a climate of unfocused fear that went beyond worries about retaliation while confirming anxieties about "others."[5]

Antipathy toward white ethnic immigrants, though frequently involving exaggerated beliefs about criminality, sexual degeneration, and disease, was less clearly marked, and less durable, than the fears associated with what seemed to be objective racial difference. European societies, like France, that received immigrants from Italy or Poland around 1900 had very similar beliefs about ethnic violence and inferiority. Overall, the United States developed a fairly commendable record, in comparative terms, of receptivity to white immigrants, with some fear but not an incapacitating emotional level.

But the same cannot be said about the racial minorities, though the strain of dealing with immigrants more generally may have exacerbated tensions for native-born whites. Many Americans retain strong traces of racial fears and a tendency to define more free-floating fears in racial terms. White immigrants themselves, such as Slavic, Italian, and, to a lesser degree, Jewish groups, quickly picked up the language and experience of prejudice and fear, another mixture of real encounters with African Americans in the cities amid job rivalries and housing tensions and the kind of emotional distancing that helped these groups blend with the dominant culture. Here was another element in the perpetuation of racially based fear. Despite some effort at self-discipline, this historic strand emerged fairly obviously in reactions to Arabs and Muslims in the wake of September 11. Quick attention to the issue of illegal immigrants was, for example, an obvious response to the attacks, but it also built on a longer tradition of fear-based nervousness about illegal entry, always focused disproportionately on "other" racial groups.*

Even aside from racial takes on terror, lingering fears of racial minorities provide an important and ongoing element in American public and emotional life. Fears, and the struggle to master or conceal them, feed direct racial tensions, contributing to very real animosities and retaliations from the minorities that in turn confirm the fears. They also feed a wider tension surrounding key racial minorities, beginning obviously with black men, that leads many whites grossly to exaggerate rates of outright and rhetorical violence, affecting not only the treatment of minorities themselves—as in the disproportionate imprisonments and executions of minority prisoners, a long tradition in the United States— but also the larger emotional stability of the white majority itself.[6]

The first tradition, then, carried from initial encounters with Native Americans and imported slaves, was a tendency to associate racial status with fear and to experience the racial mixing that proved inescapable in American life as a source of fear more generally. Here was a readily available component of the national emotional culture.

The second tradition was simply religious, and initially was not distinctively American. Christianity had long encouraged a certain degree of fear—which is not to say that other religions were entirely different. Jean Delumeau and others have traced the element of fear in popular Christianity during the medieval and early modern periods in Europe.[7] Castigations of original sin, invocations of the fear of death amid the obvious possibility of damnation, affected both public and private life, including the raising of children. Many Christian holidays were tinged

---

* And like so many extrusions of American fear, this one is underdiscussed. Many Americans, for example, know that the nation received a massive stream of immigrants in the 1990s—over nine million, in fact. Far fewer know that over 14.5 million illegals were expelled during the same decade. And while far more than fear was involved in this striking policy execution, an emotional component would be hard to deny.

with fear, sometimes adding older pagan elements to the emotionally relevant aspects of Christian theology. Halloween was an obvious case in point, with its linkage of magic and witchcraft to the celebration of the souls of the dead. Traditional Christmas also had fear components, as punishments could be visited upon children who had not behaved well; many regional customs had specific figures associated with this monitoring and retribution, alongside the gift-giving icons. At another level, popular belief often mixed fear and religion when children were born, associating certain kinds of children, such as those born with a caul, with bad luck and misbehavior inspired by the devil.

Christianity's association with fear must, of course, be very carefully stated. The religion also provided antidotes to fear, and those with faith could rejoice that God would protect them against undeserved torment and that there was a final reward that would erase any transient earthly suffering, whether physical or emotional. Many Christians, certainly including American Christians, have seen in their religion a vital alternative to facing the world afraid. This was true in the past, and it remains true today. God's order and beneficence, in the Christian view, argue against fear.

Yet Christian fear was there as well. Arguably, Protestantism further increased the emotional stakes for some Christians.[8] Key Catholic alternatives to fear, as in the ability to curry God's grace through special rituals, sacraments, priestly intervention, or even special faith in such intermediaries as the Virgin Mary, were stripped away, leaving many ardent Protestants more directly confronted with a judgmental God than had been true in more traditional iterations. Many Protestant preachers stressed divine anger against wayward behaviors, including pronounced emphasis on original sin. They urged the importance of salvation but also, amid the predestinarian strands, the limitations of human agency in achieving salvation; death could become more fearsome within this formulation.

Most obviously from the American standpoint, whereas Christian fear was beginning to tone down in Europe by the eighteenth century, thanks in part to more secular, Enlightenment-related modifications of doctrines like original sin, the process in the United States was more halting. A stronger remnant of fear-soaked religion remained current, even as many Christians modified their emotional signals, providing the second fear-related tradition that strongly colored the ongoing culture. A recurrent dose of millenarianism and apocalyptic anticipation both reflected and enhanced the Christian contribution to American fear.

The mere fact that religious commitments remained stronger in the United States than in Europe, through the nineteenth century and beyond, furthered traditionalist references. Catholic schools into the 1950s, for example, featured individual teachers who blithely warned their grade-school charges that the end of the world was near, and larger programs that invoked the fear of hell and eternal damnation as punishments for fairly common sins; and the messages could well be internalized, even on the part of children who sinned anyway. Only with Catholic reforms in the 1960s was this climate of fear more systematically rethought. Until then, Catholic emphasis remained surprisingly traditionalist, reflecting some of the peculiar features of Irish Catholicism (a distinct exception within European Catholicism more generally) and a sense of embattlement as an American minority. Sermons routinely invoked "all the threatenings of an angry God" and the "torments of the lost": "Ah! But when the sinner hears of a fire which is never going to be quenched, of a gnawing worm which shall never die, it strikes terror to his soul, you will see his face turn pale, you will see the tears start unbidden to his eyes." Fear, in other words, was central to discipline in a dangerous modern world. And while Catholic reform ultimately did seek to replace fear with more positive appeals toward love and intellectual assent, the fear rhetoric could return in fulminations against various forms of deviance, and it lingered of course amid older Catholics who had been raised in the earlier regime.[9]

An even more persistent traditionalist strand survived in Protestantism, and here there were few signs of softening even as the twenty-first century dawned. Historian Philip Greven has described three different Protestant cultures current in eighteenth-century America, one of which played on fear with a vengeance. Evangelical culture took firm root in American society during the seventeenth and eighteenth centuries, with outposts in many different Protestant denominations, from Puritanism through Methodism and even to segments of Quakerism, though it never won universal acceptance. For Evangelicals, fear began with religion, and informed both familial and social relationships. God was to be loved, but also feared, and children were "early taught to love, fear and serve the Lord." Angry judgments loomed; children were also urged to "fly from the Wrath to come." Fear of God easily translated into fears within the family; children were meant to fear their parents, and particularly fathers, though expressions of tender affection coexisted with this anxiety. As John Abott noted in the 1830s, writing to Evangelical mothers: "Fear is a useful and necessary principle in family governance," though it should be combined with positive measures. Children themselves were objects of fear as innate sinners. As the Puritan divine John Robinson put it, "they are a blessing great, but dangerous." The intense love for children directly translated into anxieties for their souls, depraved by original sin, and fear must be used to break their wills and instill obedience, amid open threats of hell and eternal damnation. Cotton Mather summed up the combination succinctly: "I will so use them [my children] that they will fear to offend me, and yet mightily love to see me...." Not only the rod, but also isolated confinement and other disciplinary devices brought fear home to children. Fear entered once more when Evangelicals were born again to the Lord: "See the Wrath of God was out against me, and I was in Immediate Danger of Stepping into the Flames of Hell." Fear, finally, translated for many Evangelicals into a sense of an outside world that was menacing and dangerous, requiring aggressive response in the name of God.[10]

Evangelicals, in sum, had a pervasive sense of fear, and they often transmitted this sense from one generation to the next. They sought to avoid fear, but they accepted its presence as normal and perversely essential in a sinful society. They found it entirely natural to use fear against others and to expect threat in return. In no sense did Evangelicals like fear, indeed they were schooled to cringe from it, but their upbringing and experience led them to incorporate it into their emotional arsenal as well as to assume its appropriateness for sinners.

The Evangelical component of American fear poses obvious complexities. It was not a purely American culture. Methodist emotional standards, after all, were born in England; it was John Wesley's mother, for example, who wrote about "teaching to fear the rod" as a necessary prod to obedience. It remains true, however, that this particular emotional strain was solidifying in colonial America at a time when it was receding in much of Christian Europe (the same deviation that would later apply to American/Irish Catholicism vis-à-vis larger European currents). And Evangelicalism persisted with impressive strength, providing an even sharper contrast with European patterns. Evangelicalism might sometimes lie dormant, as a public movement, but it never disappeared entirely, and it easily roused to renewed openness to expectations and uses of fear. Revival movements in the nineteenth century, new surges in the 1920s and again in the final decades of the twentieth century kept this emotional strand alive.[11]

Philip Greven, again, has charted the continuity of the Evangelical minority through assessment of contemporary childrearing. Books in the 1970s, by authors like Roy Lessin and Larry Christenson, were as committed to physical discipline and the centrality of obedience as the early Puritans had been. "Spanking is God's idea. He is the one who has commanded parents to spank their children as an expression of love. God holds you accountable for the discipline of your children.... If you fail to do so (properly), you will incur His wrath." Any more indulgent approach would doom children to depravity, "damn his body and soul forever." In the best Evangelical tradition, and in books that often sold over a million copies, parents were urged to tell their children they were acting as God's surrogates when they inflicted pain. "Explain to him…that if you refuse to obey God in the execution of His judgment upon his children, God will pour out His wrath upon you." These late-twentieth sentiments had their counterparts in earlier decades as well; complaints about excessive modern leniency and the need to "apply the rod…according to divine appointment" dot the Evangelical literature of the nineteenth century. The goal was unconditional surrender of the child's will, and complete obedience to parental command. Fear, specifically, receded in the more recent commentary, a partial bow perhaps to more modern emotional recommendations, but its acceptability remained. The injunctions that physical punishment should inflict enough pain, and last long enough, to draw tears and humiliation clearly presumed the impact of fear and its normalcy in the relationship between parent and God, and child and parent. The tradition continued.[12]

Further, of course, Evangelical promptings affected majority culture as well, sometimes as we will see provoking direct opposition, but sometimes with more sympathetic resonance. How else account, for example, for the currency of threats of death and punishment in the most popular reading books for children in the mid-nineteenth century? Thus McGuffey's *Fourth Eclectic Reader*, in 1866, where sixteen of twenty-nine poetry lessons concerned death: "Mother, how still the baby lies. I cannot hear his breath; I cannot see his laughing eyes; they tell me this is death." Now, this was not Evangelicalism pure and simple, for the poem went on to talk about the baby happy in a heaven where other family members could ultimately join him; but the remnant is clear, and a child might easily highlight the frightening transience of life which the verse so vividly brought home. It was hard for majority Protestants entirely to ignore the persistence of the deep sense of fear in one segment of their community. Evangelicals contributed to a more general if reluctant awareness of fear, and this fed American culture quite widely.

All of this was compounded, finally, by periodic invocations of the apocalypse—the millenarian strand in American life. Many Evangelicals themselves, expecting divine judgment and retribution, could easily be persuaded of the imminence of the world's end. The great revivalist churchman, Jonathan Edwards, was convinced that the "glorious work of God" would begin in America, with the end of the world close at hand. Apocalyptic sentiments was also fed by the importation of many millenarian sects from Europe to the United States, where religious freedom and cultural receptivity provided a more welcome home for prophecies of doom. It was in the 1790s, for example, that the founder of the Shakers, Ann Lee, came over from England, convinced that God had chosen Americans as a special people and that the Second Coming was imminent. The pattern would be repeated by religious and other utopians in the nineteenth century. Thus John Darby wrote in the 1860s of a Tribulation that would usher in seven years of misery under the Antichrist, followed by a Rapture in which believers would ascend to heaven. James Brooks in the 1880s, in New York, noted the unprecedented wickedness of the world around him, which would be answered by divine punishment in anticipation of Christ's return.[13]

The actual number of apocalyptic groups in the United States has usually been small, though at key points—and particularly in anticipation of the year 2000—a large number of small organizations, most with vigorous propaganda efforts, have been involved. Millions of Americans, not necessarily attached to any specific sect, have been and are aware of elements of apocalyptic thinking, ready to be pulled in if something goes wrong. Here, clearly, is a key reason for the public fascination with tales of cosmic doom, whatever the impact of the larger anxieties about world role sketched in the following chapter.

A classic example of the ready availability of apocalyptic fears occurred with Orson Welles' 1938 *War of the Worlds* broadcast in which he plausibly announced an invasion from outer space. Admittedly, the atmosphere was conditioned by growing anxieties about actual world war, but still the amount of fear the broadcast generated was startling. Some listeners added details to the broadcast, referring, for example, to giant sheets of flame that would engulf the entire nation, that clearly reflected apocalyptic data from the book of Revelations in the Bible, for they had not occurred in Welles' account itself. According to contemporary surveys, about one-sixth of the six million people who heard the broadcast believed it was true, a striking testimony to the strong current of American anxiety that predated full ascendancy into a global role or the dominant position of American science and nuclear weaponry in stretching human powers over the domain of nature.

The fact is that Americans had been recurrently bombarded by prophecies of the end of time. Again, the specific incidence involves impassioned minorities, often small ones at that; but the mood, particularly with repetition, could condition a wider public. Millerites in upstate New York expected the world to end in 1837, and amazingly the sect survived despite the ensuing disappointment. Other announcements, from individual preachers and larger sects, surfaced periodically thereafter; the zealot with an "end is near" sign became a staple in American cartoons, signaling obviously a majority rejection of the prophecies but also widespread awareness. The forecasts might draw ridicule, but, as with Evangelicalism more generally, an impressive number of Americans did share some belief, whether from Christian apocalyptic traditions or from other sources like the New Age partisans of different but equally terminal calendars.

We will later deal with the role of the apocalyptic minority, and its capacity periodically to reach into majority discourse, in discussing science fiction and UFOs, plus the larger reactions to the atomic bomb and the stresses of the cold war. There is little question that the existence of apocalyptic groups and traditions intensified hopes and anxieties about the nuclear threat and possible alien incursions, and ultimately about presumed government conspiracies to keep dangers under wraps. Periodically, mainstream films and television productions, like the *X-Files* movie and series, carried some of the apocalyptic visions over into standard pop culture.

By the same token, the climate created by Soviet rivalry and the bomb boosted apocalyptic sentiment, creating what one observer dubbed an "unrivaled period" of millenarianism in American life. Millenarian thinking, again as with Evangelicalism as a whole, surged forward in the final decades of the twentieth century. Fears triggered not only by nuclear competition and the cold war, but also by other developments such as recurrent tensions in the Holy Land could be intensified by the apocalyptic strain, and they intensified this strain in turn. In the 1970s prophets like Hal Lindsey even broke through to best-seller status, while radio broadcasts, from people such as David Welles of the Southwest Radio Church, drew huge audiences with statements like: "Our world is in a death-dive. We have peaked and now we're plunging rapidly to the end. Although Armageddon will be an awesome and terrifying experience for the world, it should be welcomed by the child of God as the day of vindication of our holy and sovereign Creator....What then should be the believer's attitude to the destruction of the world by fire? First of all, he should welcome it and pray for its nearness."[14]

Religion fed another form of millenarian thinking as the year 2000 neared. A bevy of engineers, fascinated with numbers, began to speculate on the precise timing of doom. In 1988 a former aerospace engineer, Edgar Whisenant, sold four million copies of a book explaining why this might be the year. (He later put out a revised edition pointing to 1989, though this sold less well.) Harold Camping, another retired engineer, later made the case for 1994, using numerical calculations working from the presumed time of Adam (11,013 B.C.). By this point bumper stickers were circulating with such slogans as, "If you hear the trumpet, grab the wheel," and monitoring organizations identified literally thousands of apocalyptic groups. Evangelical sects and larger religions like the Church of Latter-Day Saints embraced a fair share of millennial believers.[15]

The huge crest of millenarian sentiments in anticipation of the year 2000 revealed the strength of this stand of American culture—again, in contrast to the more purely celebratory anticipations throughout most of the rest of Christendom—while also explicitly creating a sense of dread that would spill over into reactions to September 11. To be sure, scattered apocalyptic prophecies surfaced in England (a staple around Hyde Park Corner), Switzerland, and even South Korea, but the trappings of a mass movement developed only in the United States. The volume of publications, paraphernalia, punditry group formation and networks, and above all radio broadcasts was extraordinary. For several years, for example, Jack Van Impe and his wife Rexella held forth on television almost every Sunday, forecasting the end of the world (anticipated between 1999 and 2003) and noting the markers available from the book of Revelations: ten members of the Common Market were precursors to the ten horns of the Beast of the Apocalypse; the number 666, used on many bar codes, became a numerological sign of the end of time; changes in the Holy Land betokened the destruction of the Jewish state, another apocalyptic marker, as the seven years of Satan's tribulation become imminent.

Like Evangelicalism, American millenarianism defies easy interpretation. In the first place, while apocalyptic expectations were unusually strong in the United States, they were not entirely unparalleled. It was a Swiss-led assemblage, though with American affiliations, that provided the most spectacular end-of-the-world group suicide in advance of 2000. The American peculiarity is real, but should not be pressed too far. More important is the complex millenarian relationship to fear. A true believer, after all, expected salvation amid the world's ruins. The Van Impes, for example, trumpeted the one-thousand-year reign of Christ that would succeed Satan's torments. For those with absolute faith, the millennial strand dramatically intensified a sense of vulnerability, but dissociated this sense from fear. Indeed, the greater the catastrophe, the greater the glee, for it hastened the final union with God. For other millenarians, however, it was difficult to be so sure: real fear, or at least anticipatory dread, escalated along with expectations of the Rapture. The apocalyptic strand was not homogeneous, even around themes such as government conspiracy, and tensions between hopes and fears were one of the key variables in the overall mix. Still, the connection with fear was strong. Just as Evangelicals increased familiarity with fear despite the promise of rewards for obedience to divine will, so millenarianism heightened an atmosphere of anxiety for many.

Finally, again as with Evangelicalism more generally, there is the question of impact on the nonmillenarian American majority. Mainstream Christianity, including Catholicism, carefully avoided predictions of the end of time; earlier experience had shown the risks of any effort at precision. And there were other American minorities not open to Christian apocalyptic doctrines of any sort. But the millenarian mood was hard to discount entirely. After all, enough reporting of the fervent beliefs in imminent catastrophe hit the general media that other Americans could hardly avoid an occasional twinge, and there was no comforting assurance of personal salvation to cushion the doubt in all cases. A sense of irrational worry might even impact purely secular calculations, as in the frenzied, and in the end largely unnecessary, concerns about a Y2K cyber catastrophe. Few Americans could totally banish a small but nagging question: what if the millenarians were right? And few could be sure, even as they concealed a sigh of relief that nothing unusual happened as 2000 and then 2001 rolled in, that the remembered anxiety did not play some small role in the emotional reactions to September 11.

American cultural tradition, in sum, provided two special sources of fear, along with the remnants of more general Christian uses of fear in religious and family discipline. Neither source was entirely unprecedented, but their vigor and combination had distinctive implications. Fears attached to race and Evangelical fears associated with God's wrath informed American culture at various points, a durable legacy of the two centuries in which the culture had first formed. The principal architecture of American fear came from different, even contradictory sources, but recurrent racial fears and the durability of some expectation of divine punishment were never entirely shaken off. Here was one of the fear elements, in a complex combination that would generate and distinguish key aspects of contemporary American emotional life.

The two early fear traditions may also help explain, in combination, aspects of the targeting of American emotion even today. It proves particularly easy to attach apocalyptic fervor to racial or foreign threats, real or imagined, converting certain kinds of international issues into battles against evil, legitimate foreign concerns into Satanic menace. We will note in later chapters how much scarier problems are when they have a foreign dimension, and while much of this focus relates to more recent history, it can connect with the older anxieties as well.

5

FROM SCIENCE FICTION TO REAL DEATH
New Contexts for Fear

From the middle decades of the twentieth century onward, Americans encountered two demonstrable changes directly relevant to the experience and evaluation of fear. They were exposed—or rather I should say, many of them willingly exposed themselves—to an increasing number of stories about cosmic destruction and they dramatically altered their approach to death.

Disaster stories have surely helped condition Americans to real, if far more limited, tragedies, and so directly feed into an account of contemporary national fear. But it is also possible, as chapter 3 suggested, that the stories reveal a deeper, if unconscious, insecurity about the nation's position in the world, a beneath-the-surface anxiety about collapse and retaliation. If this larger connection is true, then the stories not only directly prepare reactions to real tragedies, possibly making them seem larger than they are, but suggest a more profound psychic deficit that even more directly heightens the ominous quality of the same misadventures.

Changes in death were in one sense quite straightforward: a real revolution occurred that has protected modern Americans (and others in industrial societies) from unexpected death in ways literally unprecedented in the whole historical experience of the species. But while potentially reducing fear, it is not implausible to argue that unfamiliarity with death has actually heightened personal, and possibly also wider social anxieties.

Both of the changes briefly sketched in this chapter—the fascination with alien invasions and similar disasters and the new worries about death—build measurable developments into more speculative analysis. They set a context for the more specific changes that reshaped American fear, particularly since both have operated in chronological concert. Did they also reflect some deeper, almost pathological anxieties that help explain the distinctive contemporary American aversion to real-life fear? There is no desire to claim more certainty than the evidence allows: these are intriguing possibilities, though in both cases with some direct links to reactions to threat. There is no means of being too precise about how much the possibilities demonstrate. Both changes however, may help explain why many Americans seem to have become more fearful despite, arguably, having less to fear than they once had.

THE COSMIC THREAT GAMBIT

For several decades—and occasionally even earlier—Americans have displayed a real fascination with stories of global destruction and extraterrestrial invasion. This strand of popular culture links to fear in several ways: it has served to express the emotion, in a context of the nuclear arms race and the cold war. It may well have exacerbated fears, at least for some people, particularly when it connected to a larger apocalyptic vision. But it may also—and this is the point of sketching the strand at this stage in the argument—have unconsciously articulated an even greater insecurity, about a deeply risky underbelly of American power and American science, thus conveying far more massive anxieties than even atomic warfare and cold war competition generated. It has been suggested that H. G. Wells' *War of the Worlds* (1924)—an early entrant in the cosmic destruction genre—was not just a gripping story, not even merely a symbolic if early warning about passivity amid the growing threat of fascism, but a larger expression of expectations of retaliation for Britain's imperial overreach in world affairs—all written into the device of alien incursion.[1] The book's quick popularity in the United States suggests a resonant chord—possibly for this final anxiety as well as for the more obvious themes. The main point is that while the surge of books, films, and television shows about cosmic attacks and alien invasions has various explanations—including a delight in production values in a technologically minded society—it is not simply a logical result of international developments like the cold war, but may embody deeper-seated fears and guilt.

Exploring this theme requires a brief survey of the destruction genre itself—happily, well prepared by a number of splendid scholarly studies. We can then turn to the trickier issue of meanings.

One final preliminary: The idea of a cultural fascination with fear is hardly a contemporary invention. The nineteenth century had a wide-ranging agenda for popular terror, involving ghost stories, Poe-like mysteries, monsters à la Frankenstein, and an intriguing interest in burials alive. It was at least as possible to scare oneself silly one hundred fifty years ago as it has become today, if one put a mind to it in terms of available cultural fare—though we will later (chapter 8) discuss some escalations in this area as well. But the difference is also obvious: Victorian materials (and their contemporary descendants) focused on threats to individuals, at most to families or villages, not to whole societies. Grappling with monsters or the supernatural was a personal matter, not a question of social survival. Some definable set of factors has pushed what may be seen as a standard (at least Western) interest in fright to the more cosmic level. And while some of the factors are fairly obvious—the need to translate the stark new facts about the potential for nuclear annihilation, for example—there may, again, be some even deeper concerns involved.

The surge of American fascination with stories of global destruction and creatures from outer space began in the late 1940s, with the ensuing decade rated the golden age of science fiction. There were a few interesting forerunners, including, of course, the fact that science fiction efforts easily predated the popular explosion, some of them explicitly anticipating developments such as the atomic bomb. The first wide sightings of unidentified flying objects, though not yet so-called, occurred in the mid-1890s—suggesting (aside from the possibility that the objects were real) early concerns about repercussions that might result from the terrifying power and ambition of modern science and the impact of an older apocalyptic tradition that could make visitations or threats of this sort seem plausible. Receptions of the Wells book in the 1920s, then the massive fear associated with the Orson Welles 1938 radio broadcast about a Martian invasion, show wide if sporadic anxiety about the fragility of normalcy.[2]

The advent of the atomic age, in 1945, brought mixed American reactions, with some people delighted in the power of science and the possibility of curtailing national losses in World War II, others quickly noting the dawn of a new and terrible age. Popular references to potential species suicide were common for at least three years (see chapter 9). Unquestionably, the bomb also stirred apocalyptic groups, who saw the hand of God in the possible global destruction and who sometimes rejoiced in the opportunity soon to identify the truly saved. Officially, however—though we must return to this subject in chapter 9, when we deal more extensively with the buildup of reactions to military and foreign threats—most Americans accommodated fairly quickly, relying on careful government assurances, believing that the bomb provided vital defense against the Soviet Union, and immersing themselves in the more obvious joys of consumerism. Even the Soviet announcement of nuclear capacity, in 1949, did not trigger huge panic, partly because American authorities quickly promised an even greater shield through the hydrogen bomb.[3]

This is—many scholars have argued—precisely where science fiction came in, not only in books but in a growing array of films. Some of the material dealt with the possible results of nuclear war directly, like the powerful movie, *On the Beach*; David Bradley's 1948 book, *No Place to Hide*, sold widely. Others turned to space invasions as somehow a more acceptable, possibly because more allegorical, subject matter than the Soviet threat. Worries about both science and the cold war could find outlet in the growing spate of books and films dealing with mutant creatures, including ordinary insects suddenly becoming rampaging marauders. By the later 1950s, various television series began exploring the genre as well. Several scholars have tracked spikes in these media representations corresponding to specific crises, like the Berlin airlift, the Cuban missile crisis, and then in the early 1980s the bellicose cold war rhetoric emanating from the Reagan administration. Themes of destruction and attack could be variously handled: some were simply dire, others suggested human capacity to fight back, still others even depicted a more peaceful, post-attack world; political vantage points could be liberal, conservative, or purely neutral. The unifying point was that this material allowed many Americans to indulge fears in a symbolic setting, possibly to emerge more frightened than before, possibly to be cheered or distracted, but regardless to be able to express concerns about science, cold war rivalries, and a more general sense of menace that were too diffuse or embarrassing to be articulated directly or publicly.[4]

During this same period, Americans experienced an impressive set of encounters, or claimed encounters, with UFOs—unidentified flying objects. These encounters have been much studied and widely debated, and they still rouse so much emotion that any claim of objectivity is dubious. For our purposes, in one sense, it does not matter greatly whether some of the UFOs were real or not. There is no question that lots of people, from various walks of life, and often with obvious claims to ordinary good sense, thought the UFOs were real; many saw them directly. There is no question also, however, that the flying objects quickly related to cold war and nuclear concerns—many worried about saucers as Soviet weapons or, equally frightening, as American military ventures spun out of control. Media began playing up the UFO addition to the general interest in alien invasions very quickly. The first essentially contemporary UFO was sighted in 1947; the first widely popular resultant movie, *The Day the Earth Stood Still*, came out in 1951. Some of the interest was hopeful, at least in principle: aliens might be coming to try to save humanity from nuclear folly. But the whole idea of mysterious flying ships was unsettling, and popular representations turned increasingly ominous by the 1970s. The theme of alien masters sending creatures to mingle with ordinary people, possibly converting some of them into aliens themselves, lent an overtly conspiratorial and menacing tone to the whole phenomenon.

By the 1980s the aliens among us theme was becoming another cinematic staple. At this point part of the anxiety fed the political far right, with many convinced that the United States government was concealing information about the space invasions and was possibly conspiring with foreign or United Nations agencies to use alien attacks as a pretext to install some sort of comprehensive, elitist world government. But here too, the connections between minority passion and majority belief continued, partly because of the wide disseminations of stories, TV shows, and films. In the mid-1990s—even though direct sightings had dropped off—71 percent of all Americans believed the government knew more about UFOs than it had admitted and 50 percent claimed an outright official cover-up; 29 percent contended that the government had even made direct contact with the extraterrestrials. UFOs, like some other expressions of nuclear anxiety, became partly wrapped up in the special, apocalyptic culture distinctively vigorous and potent in the United States; but like other features of this culture the outcroppings were hardly sealed off from wider attention.[5]

In a powerful 1950s essay, Susan Sontag railed against the frenzy of cosmic destruction films as "the imagination of disaster," providing fantasy, not infrequently sugar-coated with attractive (if rarely effective) female lab assistants and happy endings, that diverted from the growing terror that really surrounded contemporary humanity. But the overall fantasy involved more than distraction. Some presentations were themselves terrifying, often barely glossed anti-Soviet hysteria, frequently reflecting ambivalence if not profound distrust about the powers of modern science. The impact of the genre, and the accompanying UFO frenzies, was surely diverse: some people were distracted or even amused; some were further frightened; some were polarized into extremist politics.[6]

It was revealing, of course, that Americans and American media played a disproportionate role in the whole culture of invasion and destruction. Whatever one's views of the full range of factors involved in the genre, including UFO debates, there seems little question that Americans were among other things expressing their special involvement in the nuclear arms race and the cold war. The genre had dimensions well beyond normal entertainment. A few UFO sightings occurred elsewhere; there were powerful science fiction writers in Europe, and excellent Japanese filmmaking around monster invasions; but the United States, and the American popular cultural market, were central to the whole phenomenon.

And this is where one returns to the provocative, if ultimately unanswerable question that goes beyond even unarticulated nuclear fears. Did the cosmic threat genre emanate not just from cold war and nuclear stresses, but also from a larger sense of vulnerability and guilt—among other things, because the United States itself had let the nuclear genie out of the bottle? Were the various films that showed that even the superpower United States might be brought down by outside attack suggestive of a largely unexpressed fear that this might be about to happen, or perhaps deserved to happen, that American strength and American science had reached into domains that risked incalculable consequences?

It was certainly revealing that, even with the cold war's end and well before September 11, 2001, the devastation and alien invasion fires continued to burn almost as brightly as ever. Apocalyptic presentations continued to answer some need, even as anxiety about the bomb and the Soviets receded (and before terrorism rekindled more obvious vulnerability). Literature declined somewhat during the 1990s; the most vigorous period of science fiction writing had passed. But, fueled by the huge expansion of cable television, series fare about attacks from outer space or alien penetrations actually increased, with the Fox channel and several cable outlets the most vigorous proponents. And major disaster motion pictures if anything received more play than ever. *Independence Day*, in 1996, was about alien invasion directly, and won wide attention; a number of films like *Armageddon* took up the theme of collisions with asteroids; *Deep Impact*, in 1998, with another all-star cast, focused on a comet due to impact earth. Various movies, including some remakes of earlier staples, dealt with alien takeovers of human bodies. A somewhat less cosmic series of films highlighted massive storms, or other natural disasters, that threatened whole cities if not human society more generally. A few movies picked up on new fears about global warming and resultant flooding.

Why, now that the cold war was over and the worst danger of nuclear confrontation diminished as well, did all this material keep on coming? Some people, possibly lots of people, had come to enjoy the genre. The leading films were normally issued in summer, hoping to draw teen-age audiences, part of an increasingly exploitative Hollywood effort to make sure that cinematic intelligence was put on hold between May and September. Increasing technological capacity and delight in gener-ating massively destructive special effects had their own role, helping to promote more visually powerful presentations that did not necessarily have much additional meaning. Cold war fears may have receded only slowly—we'll have to deal later with the not-implausible 1990s claim that some Americans "missed" the conflict—and there were the new environmental threats. Yet again, the question: was another factor still the unacknowledged uncertainty about American role in the world, a need to express anxious vulnerability, all the greater now that the nation had become the "only" superpower?[7] Did some Americans wonder if national pride, even arrogance, was simply asking for a comeuppance, for which cosmic disaster fare could serve as an acceptable anticipa-tion? Many Americans still liked to scare themselves; that much was clear. Did they also harbor larger forebodings?

THE CONTEMPORARY SPECTER OF DEATH

In this section we move away from what lies behind cultural representa-tions of invasion and destruction and focus on death itself, in a context in which the actual facts of death have been changing very rapidly.

Along with an intensifying emotional caution for children, dis-cussed in the following chapter, indeed closely related to it, were crucial changes in the reality and perception of death. Here was a further stim-ulus to uses of fear in marketing, and a direct contributor to reactions to perceived threats to security more generally. People have always feared death, with due regard for variations in personality and condition and with appropriate acknowledgment of the role of religious assur-ance for some. People certainly fear death still, and Americans hardly stand alone. Indeed, unusually great American religiosity, compared to contemporary Western Europe or Japan, may cushion the prospect of death for some, just as more traditional funeral practices, particularly in contrast to the more rapid spread of cremation in Europe, may pro-vide a greater degree of comfort.

Unquestionably, however, American death has changed dramati-cally in recent times, and unquestionably there have been some difficult adjustments. As with the socialization of fear itself, the chronological launching pad involved the initial decades of the twentieth century.[8]

By the middle of the twentieth century, the ordinary American adult had to think about death far less regularly than his or her counterpart in any past time. A relief in one sense, from any historical perspective, but also a challenge: would death become more difficult to face when its prospect did intrude, given its unfamiliarity? And there were two more regular encounters. First, anxiety about premature death actually increased precisely because it became less common; fear could easily concentrate on this issue. Second, certain kinds of death, encountered in public settings, including the military, became less palatable than ever before—not only premature, they also seemed particularly inappropriate, demanding explicit response and, in some cases, symbolic penance. Here too was a context for a cluster of emotions that could include fear.[9]

The death revolution—and the term is not too strong—had two major facets. First, young children stopped dying in large numbers, for the first time in human history. Between 1880 and 1920, in the Western world, infant mortality dropped from about 30 percent to under 10 percent, and the drop continued thereafter. Correspondingly, again for the first time in the human experience, the average family no longer had to expect any child to die. Maternal mortality virtually disappeared as well. By the 1930s, inoculations and new medicines, beginning with penicillin, beat back most deaths from communicable diseases. Attention shifted to less tractable degenerative diseases. All of this, in turn, had several major implications. The elderly became the only major death group, instead of one of two; death became unusual, statistically, and truly hard to handle for the other age categories. Also, worries about disease, though not necessarily greater than before, shifted from outside contagions to interior processes—like blood pressure—whose unseen and normally undetectable qualities could cause real concern.

The second major shift involved the movement of death's location from home to hospital, with the attendant reprioritization between clergymen and medical personnel as the leading experts in dealing with death. Most people no longer saw death or handled dead bodies, making the whole process more removed, possibly more frightening. At the same time, growing reliance on doctors meant an orientation toward fighting death rather than accommodating to it. For those confronting death, experience moved from familiar domestic settings to strange and intimidating acute care environments, from surrounding family to surrounding mechanical contrivances and bustling professionals for whom death was a defeat, the dying (once irretrievably hopeless) an unwanted burden.[10]

A third change followed from the two big transformations, probably inevitably, and it had its own impact on the emotional response to death. The previous apparatus available for dealing with death diminished rapidly; indeed, it was often explicitly attacked. Mourning declined from the 1920s onward; it became unusual to see draped doorways or black armbands. Grief itself was criticized, as a nuisance, an imposition on others, in a culture that wanted to emphasize the positive. Etiquette manuals, once full of rituals advising others how to deal with the recently bereaved, turned the tables by the 1950s: now, good manners required lessons to the bereaved themselves, so they would not bother other people. Extended grief was now a matter for therapists. Children, of course, were to be kept away from death particularly; here was another experience for which they were ill-equipped. Among adults, at least until advanced age, death became an unfamiliar and uncomfortable topic.[11]

Compensatory innovations arose as well, particularly in the United States. While some authorities have contended that death became a taboo subject, disturbing in all its manifestations, their argument has over reached. While death was never pleasant, new rituals arose that could allow people to come to terms with the most common forms of death. Proper insistence on increasingly expensive medical care provided assurance that "everything possible" had been done; assuming the dying person was reasonably old, this was already some comfort. Then the increasing (and again, often fairly expensive) ministrations of funeral homes provided an opportunity for parting, amid open but time-limited grief, that added its comfort as well. Funeral home directors, expert in providing a homelike and semireligious atmosphere, helped families mediate between the fact of death in hospitals and preparation for burial. New funeral practices themselves, including lifelike embalming and costly caskets impervious to decay, allowed additional adjustments to the fact of death of an older loved one.[12]

Several aspects of death and encounters with death did, however, deteriorate, despite these important developments; all had potential bearing on the wider reaches of fear in American life.[13]

- First, while individuals contemplating their own death might find some solace in the knowledge that relatives would push for expensive medical care and the best that morticians could offer, the leading adjustments to death did far more for survivors than for the person most directly involved. The loneliness of contemporary death was barely addressed. Indeed, continued emphasis on heroic medical measures, plus advances in medical technology and growing concern about malpractice lawsuits, continued to expose many dying individuals to the impersonality of intensive care units, modified at most by slightly more sensitive visiting hours for family members. There were a few palliations. Cultural changes in the later 1960s and 1970s introduced some new attention to the phenomenon of death, with people like Elisabeth Kübler-Ross urging a franker confrontation with this inevitable final stage of life.[14] The hospice movement, imported from Britain, allowed terminal patients a more supportive environment, even the possibility of dying at home. But the fact was that even by the twenty-first century less than a quarter of Americans had any contact with a hospice as they faced death, and most who did have contact engaged when it was too late to have much impact on their experience. Only a minority, as well, took advantage of opportunities to establish legal stipulations about the care they would receive while dying, and many who did venture such stipulations found their directives ignored by well-meaning relatives and nervous hospital officials.[15] The stark result: the most common goals expressed by those facing death—"having control" and "being human"—were not normally met. While claims that the contemporary United States constituted a "death-denying" society were overdrawn, it was true that the experience of death and, for many, its contemplation were rougher than necessary in recent decades, rougher than had been the case in earlier periods as well. How much this affected broader reactions is admittedly hard to determine. Lack of much involvement with death prior to later age, the absence of much relevant discussion, and an awareness of the harsh environment in which death would often be encountered could exacerbate the role death's prospect played in the formation of wider fears.[16]

- Second, the contemporary definition of acceptable death left no solace for those who suffered the loss of a loved one before older age. There was no question, here, of existential fears: the problems were far more measurable. In the twentieth century, families that experienced the death of a child were likely to experience divorce as well.[17] The strain of dealing with that which should no longer happen, and the guilt-ridden sense that someone must have done something wrong, were easily overwhelming. Ironically, though with some perverse logic, a society that had largely ended child mortality found it infinitely harder to handle the mortality that still occurred. There were few people to turn to with any understanding of the loss. Small wonder that, by the 1950s, grief groups popped up in American cities, composed of strangers whose only bond was their unusual grief, a grief that most of the population were now spared. It was also true, where deaths of children were concerned, that a lower birth rate greatly increased the value of the individual child— one scholar, studying among other things a new tendency to insure children, has aptly captured the resulting "pricelessness" of the child in contemporary America. And here, of course, the links to wider fears were quite direct. No one wanted to experience the emotions of losing a loved one prematurely, and no one wanted to face the guilt that this involvement in an unusual mortality experience would entail. Protectiveness, a desire to shield loved ones from risk, followed inescapably.[18]

- Third, Americans became increasingly uncomfortable even with the premature deaths of strangers—assuming, of course, that these strangers were also American. Military deaths, to take the most obvious example, became increasingly unacceptable, a demanding stance at a time when military engagements increased. Reporting of deaths took on a new flavor during the Korean War, in the early 1950s, as media outlets began to provide daily tallies and spiced their coverage with poignant descriptions of slain servicemen and the grief their loss caused back home (a marked contrast to the stiff-upper-lip, service-to-country approach during World War II).[19] The military leadership learned even more vividly in Vietnam that deaths must be limited for an engagement to be palatable to the American public, and began to alter basic tactics accordingly, most notably with greater reliance on airpower and bombardment. (The ironic result could be, of course, a significant increase in the deaths of non-Americans.) By the time of the invasion of Iraq, the government even attempted to limit depictions of soldiers' coffins, because of public distaste. But newspapers continued to insist on heart-rending human interest stories about individual casualties, reflecting public dismay while encouraging it as well. There was no getting away from a new level of discomfort even with (by historical standards) fairly small death totals.

Another outcropping of the need to come to public terms with military death involved the fixation on the recovery of bodies of those missing in action, where, by the time of the Vietnam war, efforts went well beyond any historical (some would also argue rational) norm. Guilt about military deaths prevented the kind of treatment of the fallen possible in the two world wars, with the many foreign graves and the considerable number of unrecovered and unidentifiable bodies.

The need to memorialize was yet another revealing symptom of this third new discomfort with death. National military monuments, beginning with Vietnam, turned less to celebration of battles and more to explicit recognition of Americans killed in the conflict. Man-made catastrophes such as the Oklahoma City bombing of a federal building now must not only be lamented, but turned into large and costly monuments to the victims. The decision to dedicate the space previously occupied by this federal building to a massive marker, of the sort usually reserved for major wars, was truly unprecedented, a sign of unusual empathy with those lost but also a real need to expiate innocent deaths. The same reaction quickly surfaced after September 11, with regard to plans for rebuilding on the disaster site in New York City. Clearly, the changing contours of death had a major impact on both military policy and collective symbolism by the final third of the twentieth century. As a public, Americans were now finding many types of deaths unusually unacceptable, requiring demonstrations of grief and concern but also generating resentments against the agents of death as well as needs to express the burden of resulting public emotion. Grief, like fear, should not have to happen. Indeed, the two reactions could be directly connected, as when fear of a deadly onslaught conjoined with the legacy of past public grief, to create a powerful push against further vulnerability.

This third set of changes helps explain an unusual American need or willingness to turn to media for cues in response to death or threat—many, aware that they are uncomfortable, do not quite know how to frame their reactions on their own. They seize on the media, which in turn are usually only too willing to preach collective grief and mourning. "Media-ization" of public emotional discomfort, visible at least from the Kennedy assassination onward, also helps link American reactions to death to their sense of public fear, where guided grief sets a basis for a more prolonged search for sources of further threat.

And the media, for their part, from whatever mixture of sincere concern and a desire to fan emotions that can boost ratings and subscriptions, have unquestionably expanded their ability to play up complex reactions to the deaths of others. In contrast for example to terse lists of names of those killed—the pattern in reaction to Pearl Harbor and World War II more generally—contemporary media, blessed with fuller information, eagerly present extensive portraits of victims, personal worthiness and family ties front and center, often complete with pictures. This not only drives home emotional discomfort with unfair death, but prolongs the whole process—as with the *New York Times'* catalog of all the victims of September 11, over an extended period of time. There was little doubt about how readers were supposed to feel.

Unprecedented contemporary changes in death, in sum, might generate new uncertainties about one's own death, and certainly produced increased anxieties about the deaths of loved ones, and particularly children, that could now be seen as clearly premature and in that sense not just inappropriate, but unacceptable. They also produced new rituals and resentments concerning deaths that seemed to be a public responsibility, and attendant fears pushed for unusual limits on deaths of this sort even in outright military engagements. The American public may not have become death-denying, but it certainly became acutely death-sensitive. And while the basic objective changes in death were not American alone—they occurred in most industrial societies—Americans reacted with decided vigor in several contexts, seeking to minimize the risks that might lead to inappropriate deaths and to difficult emotional responses alike. The result was a set of new vulnerabilities that could become closely aligned with fear.

Indeed, new concerns about death and its threat help explain why a fear-averse culture could not avoid recurrent interaction with the emotion. They also help explain why various entities, some well-meaning, others clearly self-serving, used the emotion to promote a number of different interests.

The impacts of the new American attitude toward death had wide-ranging potential. Psychologists, by the later twentieth century, frequently emphasized the complex reactions to the loss of another, for example in military combat. They highlighted the guilt than an individual was likely to feel that he or she had not been taken instead, compounding normal shock and grief and sometimes adding up to incapacitating trauma. The assumption was, of course, that this was a standard pattern, applicable to all places at all times, though obviously varying with different individual personalities—and so it may have been to some degree. But American hesitations about death, the sense that deaths of others were confusingly inappropriate and unfair, would likely compound the reaction, making guilt and attendant fear far more likely than in many other cultures. Some of this distinctiveness, furthermore, could spill over into broader public reactions to deaths of others in combat or in terrorist attack—a confusing combination of relief that someone other than oneself had fallen, a sense of connection because it might have been otherwise, an anxious concern that one might still be punished for having avoided mishap the first time around.

Changes in death and its impact also help explain the odd mixture of empathy and selfishness that emerged so often in American responses to crises, including September 11. On the one hand, outpourings of grief and a need to memorialize greeted news of the victims, involving sincere expressions of emotion toward total strangers; but on the other, the crisis was quickly personalized, turned into a threat to oneself and one's family. Clearly, new standards for encounters with public death combined with uncertainties about one's own, adding to the emotional level in both public and private forums.

Certainly, mass terrorist attacks like those of September 11 played directly on the American culture toward death. The terrorists themselves were quite aware of aspects of this, as they believed that Americans were likely to pull out of situations in which deaths of their own mounted up—in this case, in fact, the widespread assumptions of timidity were in fact exaggerated. Bombings added to emotional tension because of the time required to identify the actual victims, the days of open anguish as relatives sought more definite information—and no special American culture had to be involved in this normal, if painful, human response. But bombings in which it was difficult if not impossible ever to locate some of the victims, despite, as in the case of September 11, massive effort and investment—these played directly into the American sense that death, even in combat, must at least yield the kind of identifiable remains that would allow loved ones, and through them society at large, a sense of suitable closure. Lacking this, the emotional sores were less easy to heal than might have been the case in other cultures. The ramifications of the contemporary American sense of the strangeness of death, however understandable in terms of the altered life experience, could be considerable.

CONTEXT OR CAUSATION?

New exposure to themes of cosmic destruction and huge changes in the implications and experience of death certainly fit one of the analytical needs in dealing with contemporary American fear: to explain why reactions have shifted, for example between Pearl Harbor and September 11. It is even possible that the two big reorientations have some mutual relationship: anxieties about American overreach could heighten some of the new sensitivities about death, particularly those that involve a public setting. Why, for example, are Americans so much more firmly bent on building a massive memorial to the victims of Oklahoma City than are Spaniards for their dead in the subway attack? Both societies display a need for some immediate postevent mourning, with flowers, visits to the sites, public gatherings. But only the United States insists on more substantial, durable commemoration. Is this partly because of the sense of guilt and insecurity about national power also expressed in, and encouraged by, the cosmic destruction genre as well as the new nervousness about death itself? Do Americans have a special need to palliate national demons, which creates a special twist on the implications of the larger revolution in the experience of death?

Questions like this are valid. It would be dramatic to claim that we can move directly from the changing psychological impact of death and the concomitant worry about cosmic destruction to a set of clear conclusions about why American fear is distinctive and novel. However, it is better, in the long run, to be honest than dramatic—these connections are possible, but they cannot be proved. The two patterns may be entirely unconnected; after all, the cosmic threat theme builds clearly on the apocalyptic tradition in American culture, whereas the new challenges of death have no particular basis in earlier cultural patterns save in destabilizing them.

It's best to be cautious: Americans faced a pervasive new strand of popular media, spiced by real claims of alien sightings; they also faced large alterations in their encounters with death. Some distinctive national features attach to both these changes. But whether the changes are in any significant way linked, save by chronology, and above all whether they had wide impact in altering the perceptions and experience of fear, cannot be determined with any precision. It's safest to think of both transformations as part of a novel context rather than as specific causation, though a context that could have substantial impact on various groups and individuals. The central transformation of fear can be traced much more precisely, though it is compatible with the stresses of the new context as well. The fact was that, between the late nineteenth and the later twentieth centuries, fear itself was directly reconsidered, its socialization significantly altered. For some, this change could be enhanced by anxieties about national overreach or confusions about how to handle aspects of contemporary death.

III

The Decisive Changes

*Redefining Fear and Risk
in Life and in Media*

6

FEARING FEAR
A New Socialization

American fear has a rich contemporary past. Recent manifestations of American fear follow quite directly from earlier changes in the way fear was handled, particularly in childrearing. They may also reflect new concerns about death and the clear fascination with devastation scenarios. But it's the explicit focus on fear itself in recent decades that provides the clearest links to characteristic current reactions.

While the fears most obvious today, in public responses to dangers such as terrorism, are far different from the emotions that a few decades ago began to prompt recourses such as night-lights and parental bribes, there is a direct connection; where fear is concerned, the historical child was father to the man. Complicating the issue is the concomitant influence of the even older fear traditions that emerged from the more formative period in American culture and have endured.

This chapter identifies the very definite changes in fear culture that began to take shape early in the twentieth century; here, the contrast with an earlier, nineteenth-century take on fear is quite dramatic. This new fear culture—which can readily make contact with the more traditional components and with the wider context resulting from transitions to global power and the new experience of death—has persisted and intensified in recent decades, forming a vulnerable framework for responses to new threats.

CREATING A NEW FEAR CULTURE:
RECONSIDERING COURAGE

New kinds of worries about fear and its emotional damage began to affect mainstream American values by the 1920s, transforming recommendations about childrearing and coloring adult experience as well. These worries progressively repudiated a more confident approach to fear that had been forged in the nineteenth century, partly in response to the Evangelical subculture.

These worries surfaced at the same time as the new proclamation of freedom from fear, mentioned earlier in the Preface. The progressive hope to eliminate fear in fact helped set the standards that made fear a new concern, as groups like the Behaviorist psychologists sought to translate broader optimism into parental goals. But there was also a new perception of a fear as a problem, which complicated the optimism and led to a broader reconsideration of the emotion.

Historians of American childhood have increasingly noted how the criterion for "surviving childhood" increasingly shifted from a concern for physical well-being, the dominant traditional motif, to worries about emotional scars. We will see that health and safety concerns have endured as well despite statistical rarity; but the growing emotional focus is undeniable. Fear, furthermore, nested in the center of this anxiety. It has even been argued that adults themselves ultimately became afraid of children's fears—afraid of what parental inadequacies or future personality problems they might portend.[1]

Various scholars have worked on the contrast between twentieth- or late twentieth-century American culture and its Victorian predecessor. Plausible analysis contrasts a preoccupation with personality with earlier emphasis on character, or an eager other-directedness—checking with others about appropriate responses—replacing a guilt-based inner direction. Frank consumerism, in another ambitious contrast, supersedes a greater rhetorical emphasis on work and frugality.[2] The assessment that follows is narrower, involving a more specific change, and we need not belabor relationships to the broader characterological shifts, though some are plausible. It is important to note that the reevaluations of fear linked a larger trend toward hostility to emotional intensity of any sort—applying, for example, to grief, to guilt, and even to aspects of love and to fear.[3] Yet other elements entered in as well, including a partial redefinition of children's nature and, more widely, of the risks associated with modern life in general.

Efforts to pinpoint sea-changes in culture always court oversimplification. Not all Americans, or all facets of American life, made the same changes where fear was concerned. Victorian values continued to resonate, manifested among other things in eager participation in—or at least spectatorship of—dangerous sports where conquest of fear was a central feature. The durability of the Evangelical subculture, quite different in its approaches to fear and to childrearing, introduces yet another note of caution. Yet there was widespread change, and it would profoundly condition actual reactions to major threats.

A final introductory note: strictly speaking, cultural change deserves a neutral evaluation. After all, quite different beliefs can prove functional, and change may also validly respond to new conditions in the larger environment. A good bit of scholarly, and indeed popular, commentary on the contemporary/Victorian contrast has favored the latter, seeing in current values a decided declension from values past. Where fear is concerned, nineteenth-century culture had some definite drawbacks. It could be cruel toward the timid, and it downplayed female courage to the point of virtual neglect. Its deficiencies, indeed, helped motivate twentieth-century reevaluations. But Victorian approaches to fear had merits as well, and they created less emotional vulnerability to outside threat than the current culture encourages. This is why the change proves so important in explaining what contemporary American fear is all about. Nostalgia is irrelevant: noting the drawbacks of change does not suggest we could recover the past even if we wanted to. But awareness of change is essential to an intelligent understanding of why we are where we are, an essential preliminary to personal and social evaluation.

Victorian leaders, we will argue (though without possibility of definitive proof since the topic never came up—no Code Orange Alert for possible Confederate raids seems to have been considered in the 1860s, though the danger was real), would not have cottoned to color-coded injunctions to be more afraid. They would have done more than urge Americans to stick to normal routines: they would have railed against fear directly. For those of us hostile to the emotional implications of color-coding, and its possibilities for manipulation, the putative Victorian stance seems preferable to our own. We probably cannot get it back, but in thinking about the changes that eroded the Victorian approach to fear we can consider other alternatives to current patterns.

Currents of change became quite apparent by the 1920s. Fear became a major problem, just as the elimination of fear became a major goal, first for children but by extension for adults as well. The emotion was bad for the body, and it inhibited rational responses. But it was also tricky to handle. Children needed maximum possible protection from fear, and careful reassurance when fear did strike. Improperly handled, childish fears not only disrupted childhood, but could lead to dysfunctional adults. In the 1920s, behaviorist psychologists, headed by James Watson, stated quite simply, "The main job of the parent should be to prevent fears, since some fears are extremely difficult to cure." More permissive successors, like Dr. Spock, would change the specific advice, toward more active distraction and nurturing, but the goal was the same: fears should be banished as much as possible. Above all, children must not be told simply to get over a fear, for the emotion was too powerful to master through willpower alone. "When a child evinces fear, the one danger to avoid is repression. As long as the fear is brought into the open and discussed, little harm can be done." Injunctions of courage became not only irrelevant but positively dangerous in this new climate: as one childrearing expert, Sidonie Gruenberg, noted, "There is always the danger that the fear resulting from such methods will reach the 'overwhelming' stage and leave its mark for a long time."[4]

This new advice replaced a clear-cut approach to fear developed by childrearing experts and authors of children's literature during the nineteenth century, in which mastery, not distraction or ventilation, played the central role. Victorian standards had sought to eliminate uses of fear in discipline—here they directly attacked the Evangelical approach—but also to create children—at least male children—accustomed to thinking about fear and prepared to surmount it with courage. Gratuitous fear, directed at the very young, was bad; in this sense Victorian culture anticipated the more elaborate statements in the twentieth century. But contemplating fear from the outside world, particularly for older children, was not only unavoidable but positively desirable, a key part of character development.

The Victorian amalgam began to take shape in the 1820s. It did not erase earlier patterns. For example, racial fears certainly continued, though Victorian promptings did seek to undermine traditional Christian uses of fear, creating a new division between mainstream prescriptions and the Evangelical minority. The first reform target involved disciplinary scare tactics. In the new mainstream view, children were not victims of original sin; they should not be frightened by references to hell and damnation, or more humble folk ploys such as bogeymen. Particular care should apply to the presentation of death, so that children "do not imbibe terrific and gloomy ideas of death." Not only parents, but also maids must learn more self-control, neither frightening children nor letting their own fears show. Fear, in this new view, was not natural to innocent children, but could only come from outside influences. Imported fears could interfere with appropriate loving relationships and could "trouble" an individual on a lifelong basis.

Fear, for children and adults alike, was an "infirmity" that was "most enslaving to the mind, and destructive of its strength and capability of enjoyment....How cruel, then, purposely to excite false terrors in those under our care."[5]

This was a huge change in outlook, and, of course, it was contested. Traditionalist and particularly Evangelical authors continued to believe that children should be told that they were "not too little to die," "not too little to go to hell." Ordinary parents long persisted in using customary scare tactics, as at least part of their disciplinary arsenal. As a result, injunctions against the infusion of fear would continue to play a prominent part in childrearing manuals well into the twentieth century—until finally it became a standard element of received wisdom, requiring less emphasis. And again, the new belief in the gap between loving childish innocence and fear was a key basis for the more systematic attacks on fear in the twentieth century itself.

But in the Victorian decades themselves, the injunctions about young children were not the whole story. Properly raised in early innocence, older children should deliberately be introduced to situations involving potential fear, so that they could learn to surmount the emotion. The introduction operated at the formal level—in the childrearing manuals and uplifting stories for the young—and in informal children's culture as well. This, obviously, was where nineteenth-century standards differed not only from more traditional religious fare, but from the norms developed by the 1920s as well.

The crucial factor was courage. In 1847, for example, Horace Bushnell, while repeating the now-standard idea that children should not have to fear parents or God, also referred to a "natural state of courage" that children could rely on as well. Here, children should be actively engaged with the power of fear. T. S. Arthur, a childrearing authority and also boys' story author, put it succinctly, urging parents to "train up your children to be virtuous and fearless. Moral courage is one of the surest safeguards of virtue."[6]

Fiction for boys drove this point home relentlessly. Heroes, often including fictional boys themselves, were constantly thrust into situations where they must overcome fear, in order to rescue someone (often a sister) from danger or to deal properly with abusive bullies. Boys thus stopped runaway horses, disregarding their own fright. Even a timid lad could find "the courage to do a deed which might have made the stoutest heart tremble with terror." Fear is acknowledged, but it can be overcome. "We have seen that he felt fear. Had it been otherwise he must have possessed nerves of steel, or have been utterly destitute of the power of reasoning; but that fear did not so completely overpower

him....On the contrary, it nerved him to make the greatest exertion."
Civil War stories provided a common opportunity to praise the stout-
hearted: "A little pluck does more for a wound than a good many ban-
dages." Boys were meant to transport themselves, if only figuratively
through fiction, into situations in which their control would be tested,
so that they would learn that they need not yield to the first rush of
emotion. The last great Victorian childrearing writer, Felix Adler, put
the point this way: children could overcome cowardice and so conquer the "paralyzing effect of fear by a powerful effort of the will." This
capacity was part of character training, derived from good reading and
good teachers.[7]

The classic Victorian term for boys who did not measure up—the
sissy—drove the lesson home. The word had been coined in the 1840s
as an affectionate term for sister, but by the century's end it clearly
denoted boys and men who were spineless in the face of fear. Clearly,
of course, this same term denoted the characteristic Victorian gender
gap: women were urged not to show fear, lest children be frightened, but
explicit association of girls and women with courage was rare indeed.
Many boys' stories suggested that, while courage was essential, courage displayed in front of a quivering female was even nicer. On the
other hand, the Carnegie Hero Fund, established by the philanthropist
Andrew Carnegie in 1904, as a way to reward courage and through
example encourage good character where fear was concerned, allowed
for female recipients, so the gender distinction was not absolute; the
desirability of conquering fear trumped sheer masculinity.

Finally, standards counted in real life. Many boys did devour the
stories of courage and pondered how they would respond to challenge.
The spread of character-building sports, including boxing for middle-
class lads as well as the more durable team sports, explicitly trained in
the mastery of fear in the face of some physical danger. Cultural pundits might cluck about the wildness of boys, but they largely approved
of hearty play, and even manners columnists wanted to make sure that
no male child would turn into a "girl-boy." Actual middle-class boys
required demonstrations as well, often taunting timid colleagues with
"dares." "The deeper the water, the thinner the ice, the longer the run,
the hotter the blaze, the more certain the challenge": conquering fear
linked directly to demonstrating physical prowess. Games such as rock
throwing by competing groups or "soak-about" (which involved hitting vulnerable spots on the body with a hard ball) probed the ability to master fear and pain, with terms like "baby" or "sissy" ready to
denote failures. Hazing rituals in youth and young adult organizations
similarly tested courage in the face of fright. Many soldiers, as in the

Civil War, took pride in writing home about their coolness under fire (using the accepted rhetoric, regardless of their actual emotional experience). The Victorian culture of fear was widely advertised and, at least for public consumption, widely accepted.[8]

This, in turn, is what makes the subsequent change in signals so striking, despite key continuities from the Victorian amalgam in areas such as sports and despite some continued preference among male parents (contrasting with common maternal attitudes) to see boys able to display courage under challenge. At least two major factors triggered the change. Most obvious was a new, psychological approach to human nature and a new role for psychologists, psychology-minded doctors, and related popularizers in advising the public on childrearing, health, and similar issues. G. Stanley Hall, a commanding figure in his field and author of extremely influential work on adolescence, issued a major study on children's fears in 1897. Hall's rambling piece, based on empirical research, emphasized the frequency of fears among children, including nighttime terrors, concluding that the emotion was a huge and potentially unmanageable problem, far greater and less predictable, and less subject to rational control, than had ever been imagined. These findings, amplified by subsequent research—fear was a major item for behaviorist psychologists in the 1920s, though they were a bit more confident in their formulas to control the problem—introduced a new tone in mainstream childrearing advice almost immediately, the first salvo in what became a more systematic effort to portray children as emotionally vulnerable. Essentially, amid admittedly shifting specifics, the experts have never pulled back from this anxiety about fear, and their work has informed ever-wider spheres of activity—including, as we will see, the military.[9]

Complementing the new expertise was a growing if amorphous sense that the wider world was a more dangerous place than had previously been imagined, a point we will explore more fully in ensuing chapters. There was irony in this perception, for life expectancy was expanding rapidly, amid the huge decline in infant deaths, and the closing of the frontier ended one of the more uncertain passages in the American experience. It was as if, amid greater security, the risks that unquestionably remained became more fearsome. Yet there were some objective changes as well. Amid new machinery, like automobiles, certain kinds of mechanical dangers undeniably increased. Military weaponry became more destructive, as World War I amply demonstrated. The greater involvement of the United States in the wider world created new threats, real or imagined; it was not entirely an accident that the reevaluation of fear coincided chronologically with the great Red Scare of the 1920s, a development we will explore more closely subsequently. Threats to health, though objectively reduced from the past, shifted toward less familiar sources such as cancer or hypertension, and the changes in the management of death created anxiety as well. In various ways, many Americans became uneasy about key aspects of the modern world, even as their involvement steadily increased. The combination was murky, certainly not entirely rational, but it fed the new concern about fear and vulnerability.[10]

Explicit concerns about fear unfolded first, of course, in the area of childrearing. Following Hall's study, expertise began quickly to move away from Victorian promptings toward courage and stiff upper lips; fear constituted the first emotional area where Victorianism was revisited. Felix Adler introduced new warnings about scary stories for children in a revision of his manual in 1901. Three years later Mrs. Theodore Birney, picking up directly from Hall, devoted a great deal of space to the omnipresence of unaccountable fears in early childhood, urging parents not to dismiss or punish fears lest they "harden" into durable emotional scars. She did continue to refer to bravery, but the tone was changing. Another manual published in 1919 upped the ante: children between two and six years old were at great risk, and parents should not only avoid scaring them and conceal their own fears, but work hard to keep children away from experiences that might frighten them—don't push them to swim, for example, if they fear the water. Older children were still fair game: boxing could legitimately strengthen the boy afraid to fight and "prepare him imaginatively to face other perils, even though their exact character may be unknown."[11]

The transition was completed in the following decade with a simple expansion of the attention devoted to the problem of fear and a fuller attack on the Victorian notion that children could be urged to conquer the emotion through courage. This was the context in which behaviorist Watson argued quite simply that preventing fear was the most important single responsibility for parents. Emphasis on the need for parents to mask their own fears increased—not an entirely new theme, but the urgency added significantly to parental responsibilities and emotional complexities. Revealingly, experts no longer asked parents to be courageous, but rather to hide what they felt, suggesting a pattern of concealment that, by the late twentieth century, as comparative studies demonstrated, became something of an American hallmark when dealing with unpleasant emotions like fear.[12] New detail also spelled out why fear was bad. As *Parents' Magazine* put it in 1927, "Fear is essentially an unpleasant and sometimes painful emotion," whose usefulness in keeping children away from danger was outweighed by its disagreeable qualities and its potential to mar adult life. Physical effects were highlighted as well, including harm to the digestive tract and the cardiovascular system from prolonged fear. "Too intense fear...interferes with biologically adequate behavior." But the key problem was fear's inhibition of the kind of rational thought that children should be urged to employ in dealing with problems. "Strong emotion interferes with the functioning of reasoning power; it is impossible—especially for a young child—to recognize the absence of danger when his intelligence is inactive because of fear." The instinctive functions of fear now seemed counterproductive. Finally, fear's impact on children risked having lasting qualities. In contrast to Victorian confidence that older children could learn to surmount fear through courage, the new wisdom urged that fear could prevent adequate response at any stage of life, and that reliance on courage was either irrelevant to deal with this kind of deficiency or capable of producing further damage. "An untold dread may become a veritable poison in the mind, bringing its evil to fullness years later." Some commentators attributed a claimed rise in juvenile delinquency and crime to inadequate management of children's fears, as wayward souls used violence to express an inner terror.[13]

But satisfactory management was immensely complicated in this same new approach. Children could not be expected by themselves to get used to things that scared them, for fear now had a life of its own. Forcing them to deal with an object of fear—the Victorian impulse, in its confidence in courage—not only would not work, but "may cause the fear to spread to other situations." So parents should shield children from anything that scared them, provide constant reassurance without reprimand, and at most deploy attractive bribes to induce children gradually to handle fear situations. For a child afraid of the dark, for example, use night-lights to dissipate the problem—an interesting new possibility—but also gradually put desirable candy or some other inducement to encourage him or her hesitantly to enter a darkened room. Popular manuals, like the widely sold publications of the federal Children's Bureau, repeated these recommendations endlessly.

Fear, in these discussions, lost most of its gradations: it easily slipped into stark terror. It also lost any remaining moral stigma. Dealing with it became a matter of manipulation, not triumphant conquest. Coddling, not reproof or ridicule was essential. What once was praised as courage now more often seemed psychologically risky. Talking about fear was now positively desirable, if avoidance had failed. Even if fear must be concealed in certain circumstances, a healthy individual should have some audience before which the anxiety could be brought into the open without shame. Yet, even with some chance for ventilation, many experts continued to worry that fears were hard to cure. Prevention, by keeping children away from risky situations, and immediate and elaborate reassurance were essential. Children would have internal demons no matter how much care was lavished; they should not be burdened with additional fears in their environment. Discipline, as a result, should be softened when fears might be involved; toilet training, for instance, was far less important than removing any fears about accidents. And when fear did crop up, the worthy parent would respond with immediate affection: "This is the time for extra hugs and comforting reminders that you love him very much and will always protect him." Convincing the child that his or her environment was risk free was essential; teaching him or her to overcome risk with courage dropped away—a truly fundamental change.[14]

Fear, in this vision, became an almost overwhelming problem that children simply could not handle on their own. "Unless some grown-up helps them, each frightening experience leaves them weakened for the next assault." Obviously, the problem could be met with effort. If parents carefully reduced risks of encountering fear to a minimum, provided careful reassurance and compensatory reward, and avoided any real reference to or reliance on courage, a child might just grow up adequately healthy—but the challenge to parental ingenuity would be very real.[15]

One result of the new expertise—and a sign that it had practical implications early on—showed in the schools, in tensions between guidance counselors and related authorities and actual teachers in discussing problem children from the 1920s onward. Subject: aggressive, disruptive students and students whom they cowed. For teachers, the first group constituted a clear problem, but the second group, silent and docile, were just fine, a real relief in fact. For counselors, however, the angry students were a clear problem but no more pressing than the intimidated students around them, who in the new vision were internalizing fear in almost certainly damaging ways and who needed help. The experts, of course, prodded teachers to believe that there were unseen, harmful fears that required intervention. Here was a backdrop to the more recent concerns about bullying, which we will take up later on. Again, there is a direct link between the recasting of fear in the 1920s and very contemporary reactions.

Clearly, a dramatically new emotional culture had arrived, based on a new view of the child and an apprehensive sense of the larger environment. Did the culture catch hold? Obviously, the answer must be both complex and nuanced: it's far harder to trace actual receptivity and impact than to describe the culture itself. Certainly parents expressed growing concern. Referring fearful children for therapeutic help increased rapidly, as parental letters to *Parents Magazine* in the 1930s and 1940s began to attest. An inquiry by the same magazine in the 1940s suggested that actual middle-class parents perceived childhood fears as one of their most pressing concerns, with references (particularly where younger children were concerned) to fears of darkness, water, animals, germs, and death, along with generalized fearfulness. Parental references also avoided claims on courage, and indeed the concept itself began to seem slightly quaint, at least outside the military realm. New cultural standards, in other words, were translating into actual socialization, in ways that would affect both the evolution and the experience of fear. Parents did admit their temptation to punish children who showed fear, but they also (at least for public consumption) stated that they were aware that this was the wrong approach. Letters frequently shared successful avoidance strategies, including use of night-lights and bribes. There were variations, by individual personality, by social class, and by gender. Mothers were much more eager to shield children from emotional challenges than fathers were, and the latter frequently indicated their impulse to urge children to buck up or to use sports for character training in fear; but even here fathers tended to grant that maternal concerns should have primacy.

Older children picked up the culture as well. Polls of teenagers, including an elaborate inquiry in 1956 by Arnold Gesell and his colleagues, revealed little interest in reading about fear or imagining situations in which courage would be required. The Victorian themes of staring down bullies or stopping runaway horses, at least in the mind's eye, no longer echoed strongly. Rather, teenagers tended to associate fear with childishness, and wanted to assure a pollster that they simply did not have fears any more. Here too an intriguing redefinition had taken hold, if slightly more subtle than the changes directed toward comforting younger children. In both cases—for the young and the adolescents—fear avoidance rather than explicit mastery seemed to predominate. By age fifteen, fear had become a matter of reminiscing about childhood frights or initial sports anxieties; it did not figure (or at least was not acknowledged) as an ongoing emotional encounter.[16]

Beyond self-professed reactions by parents and teenagers, including resorts to therapy, the new fear culture showed in a variety of public arrangements—demonstrating further, though not surprisingly, that attitudes mattered. Traditional occasions for fear were either attacked or altered. Fraternity hazings were widely limited after the 1950s, partly because of the physical harm they could do, but also because they involved too much emotional stress: people should not have to master fear to become part of a peer group. Older practices like boxing lessons for middle-class boys also fell by the wayside; again, this kind of test of physical prowess and emotional courage was either irrelevant or dangerous. Halloween was tamed. While bits of emotional titillation might remain, in carefully managed Fright Nights, children were urged to see the holiday as a chance for treats and to wear usually benign costumes, not as an opportunity to face independently the spirits of the night. The same defanging applied to Christmas—to the point that, by the second half of the twentieth century, few remembered that the holiday used to evoke fear as well as piety and greed. Fearsome animal dances associated with folk Christmas had fallen away in the nineteenth century. But it was only after the 1940s that figures like the German-American Belsnickel, a fur-wearing variant of St. Nick who carried sticks for beating bad children while recording their names in a punishment book, disappeared entirely.

Images directed at children changed in other respects. Gory folk tales were sanitized, much in the fashion of the trajectory of the *Curious George* series discussed in chapter 1. Disney developed a thriving industry in turning grisly, fear-provoking stories into sugary myths. Cinderella blithely pardons her stepsisters, instead of exacting bloody punishments as in most of the original versions. The dwarfs who aid Snow White are adorable—one cute grump included—rather than mysterious. Indeed the more general cuteness enveloping childhood, about which historian Gary Cross has written so persuasively, reflected among other things a desire to banish fear from the environment, to replace it with bland frills.[17]

Fiction for children, and particularly boys, still carried excitement— lest it not sell at all—but it no longer called for probes of courage. Whether in books or on radio or TV shows, the new children's heroes were not people who openly grappled with fear and overcame it: rather, the new superheroes did not experience fear at all. In this, they served the dual purpose of illustrating an environment in which emotional encounter was not involved and highlighting a personality without emotional nuance. No Victorian lessons here, indeed no overt lessons of any sort; the new superhero was to be enjoyed, not studied. The idea of presenting uplifting models of people who grappled with fear and overcame it dropped away—much as teenagers themselves liked to assume a fear-free stance resulting from shaking off childishness. Critics, of course, worried that the violence of radio shows, comic books, TV fare, and later video games might frighten children, as well as inure them to mayhem, and this aspect of contemporary media deserves attention later on. But the heroic figure itself definitely changed. Superman, most obviously, launched a whole series of action characters—some super-human, such as Batman or Wonder Woman, some simply machine-like, as with Sylvester Stallone in the movies—notable for unbelievable physical prowess without emotional struggle of any sort. Their coolness was as remarkable as their ability to fly or brush aside scores of hap-less natives. Science fiction fare added to the settings in which chal-lenge could be encountered without normal human fear. Even real-boy heroes, like Frank Dixon's Hardy boys, popular through mid-century, participated in this new trend. Frank and Joe fly a blimp with no prior experience or survive getting shot at with no reference to surprising themselves with bravery. A new model was up for inspection; the ques-tion was, what would it inspire for people who might have to face risk with a real-life human emotional arsenal?[18]

These changes went beyond children's fiction. A study, still in prog-ress, on *Reader's Digest* articles on heroism, courage, and bravery, in the decade after 1995, showed that 90 percent contained no mention of fear or its management. Courage, in this regular series, became a behavioral phenomenon—rushing into a burning building, diving after a child into an icy pond—with emotions left out. Here too was a marked contrast with the Victorian patterns, where coping with fear was an active part of bravery. Two implications followed from the shift: first, most obviously, many Americans, even those who contemplated brav-ery, were left with few guidelines for managing almost inevitable emo-tions, which exacerbated the issues that would arise when fear emerged in real life. Second, absence of comment reflected and reinforced the new but widespread aversion to fear, implicitly promoting not only con-fusion but resentment when the emotion intruded.[19]

In this context, it was no accident that, in the wake of September 11, public fascination with superheroes reached an all-time high. After all, the introduction of Superman, in 1938, had picked up on war fears, and World War II helped indeed to solidify American fascination with the genre. (Other countries would pick up an interest as well—Tur-key, Japan, and Mexico for example; but the United States remained the center of the craze.) The Spiderman movie was in gestation before September 11, but the timing of the tragedy—eight months before issu-ance—helped assure its unprecedented success. After September 11, the floodgates opened. The year 2004 saw eight superhero movies, and nineteen were projected for 2005. Movie moguls saw the connection to post–September 11 complexities: "There is some comfort in watching superheroes who conquer world problems without significant reper-cussions." Or more simply, "Our nerves were really raw." To be sure, the superhero theme gained a bit of nuance: Peter Parker (the human version of Spiderman) and Clark Kent (ditto for Superman) became a bit more bumbly, particularly in the area of romance. But Kent had always been timid. It was the transformation into fearlessness when danger threatened that really counted, and this quality persisted. Escaping into a world where ordinary mortals were transformed into fearless paragons translated the new fear culture and moved it from childhood to wider adulthood, as the popularity of the new movies suggested. The timing of this popularity's surges showed the connection of this same culture to wider national vulnerabilities. At least for a few hours, an emotional challenge many preferred not to face could be cast aside.[20]

Schools participated in campaigns against fear, though imperfectly. Worries about children's fears, from the 1920s onward, played a role in a variety of efforts to reduce stress and competition and to replace negative reinforcements with more positive inducements such as higher grades and greater promotion of self-esteem. Attacks on corporal punishment and the marked reduction in flunking reflected, among other things, a desire to reduce fear in classroom discipline. Even more humble changes might be phrased in terms of attacks on fear: a school authority claimed in the 1930s that restricting homework and stressing daily assignments rather than all-or-nothing tests "have done much to banish the fear of semester examinations."[21]

Even the military adjusted its approaches to fear, in response both to the new general culture and the changing nature of war. Traditionally, soldiers who could not measure up in battle were treated, and sometimes punished, as cowards. Elements of this approach affected reactions to psychological problems among troops in World War I. Military heroism was widely praised—this remains a constant—but soldiers who could not perform were either labeled cowards or were partially excused on grounds of essentially physical trauma, under headings like "shell shock" or concussion. By the time of World War II, the possibility of more complex psychological interactions with battle stress and fear gained credence. New terms like "war neurosis" or "battle fatigue" covered lack of capacity to deal with fear. Even more revealingly, manuals for soldiers moved away from simple injunctions of heroism. An infantry pamphlet for the Fifth Army in Italy thus noted: "Don't be too scared. Everybody is afraid, but you can control your fear....Being too scared is harmful to you." Obviously, full adjustment to contemporary culture, in which people should be protected from fear and elaborately reassured when it occurred, was incompatible with a wartime military. But the recognition of fear's unpleasantness and the futility of simply urging people to buck up did penetrate military ranks. Programs to permit soldiers to talk openly about their fears advanced as well, and other personnel took the opportunity even when programs were not available. The frank admissions of fears to journalists, by Gulf War pilots, shows again a significant set of changes in military life, reflecting the recognition of fear as a painful problem in contemporary life—again, when it could not be prevented altogether.[22]

Civilian personnel protocols shifted in comparable fashion, moving away from deliberate uses of fear in interviews toward a more reassuring atmosphere. Human resources experts now saw fear as an emotion that could incapacitate otherwise qualified interviewees, rather than a challenge that could reveal strength of character. Here again, the impact of the new culture had concrete results, suggestive of the wider effects discussed below.

Obviously, the ramifications of the new standards for fear were widespread, affecting parental perceptions and children's self-evaluation, along with various aspects of institutional policy and cultural arrangements. The new standards were also impressively durable, signaling the ongoing role of relevant expertise about children and their vulnerabilities. The new fear culture not only persisted, but steadily amplified. Early in the twenty-first century, for example, a new flurry of concern surfaced regarding bullying in the schools. Authorities argued that many shooting incidents in schools resulted from children who had been bullied earlier in life and had internalized their isolation and hostility until it burst forth in violence. Not surprisingly, given this analysis, bullying was quickly added to the list of things that parents and school administrators should worry about. And experts had another new cause for which their knowledge and concern were essential. The goal, given the still-fashionable post-Victorian evaluation of fear, was to find ways to eliminate the bullying. The Victorian idea, of teaching children to stand up to bullies as part of their mastery of fear and positive character development, found no echo. It was up to adults to manage arrangements such that children would not face this emotional problem on their own, with the scars and resentments that would result and which, by themselves, they could not overcome. The protective impulse was still running strong.

ASSESSING THE CONTEMPORARY CULTURE OF FEAR

Reactions to the picture of a historical redefinition of fear in our own time will surely vary. Some, whether neo-Victorians or Evangelicals, will surely recoil against the obvious signs of softness and coddling, for again American fear culture is far from homogeneous. But others will find the new approach not only understandable but positively desirable: how can children be expected, for example, to stand up to bullies in the dangerous environment of today's schools? What's really important, however, is not the editorial evaluation—points can be scored on both sides—but the question of larger impacts on American reactions to fear in real life, in adulthood as well as childhood. Here too, of course, we're on somewhat speculative ground, at least until the ramifications of fear are traced more fully in the chapters that follow. But the possibilities are intriguing.

Cultures provide guidelines for actual emotional response and behavior. Individual as well as subgroup variations, the nature of particular challenges, and a host of other factors determine reality. In no sense should we assume even a mainstream American middle class marching lockstep to the latest recommendations about fear. Yet it would be surprising if no linkage existed, which is why a preliminary sketch offers more than an idle exercise. What we see—and this is hardly an original thought—is an unusually secure society (secure in terms of material standards, health conditions, educational access—all despite some obvious problems particularly associated with social inequalities) displaying two characteristic drawbacks of security: first, a vulnerability to disruptions of the status quo, for which there is little prior collective experience; and second, a tendency to invent new fears and anxieties precisely because some of the standard uncertainties of life have been largely controlled. Contemporary fear culture reflected both the advantages and disadvantages of American security, and gave further shape to the disadvantages in turn.

The new, twentieth-century approach to fear, and the clearly substantial extent to which it was widely accepted and internalized, had several probable consequences, particularly by the turn of the next century when it had been brewing and expanding for several decades.

- First, fear was a very bad emotion and people who were mentally healthy and properly raised should not have to put up with it very often. Absence or avoidance must be stressed, precisely because fear had such damaging physical and psychological consequences. This was a clear goal of the new childrearing advice, and as suggested, even teenagers seemed implicitly to agree. We have seen, of course, that these standards were historically quite unusual: most cultures have viewed fear as more inescapable, if less dire, and even in a perverse way useful (at least in moderation) in stimulating constructive response, or character development, or both. The extrapolation from contemporary mainstream American values would suggest that fear might be regarded less as a warning than as a direct attack, an emotional burden that should not have to be tolerated.

- Second, following from point one, Americans were provided with fewer cultural models and experiences relevant to dealing with fear, compared to many other societies. The pop-cultural tendency to equate bold deeds with a total absence of emotion, rather than any signs of turmoil or emotional encounter, exacerbated this gap. It is important not to oversimplify. General cultural norms and even conscientious parenting did not prevent children, in real life, from encountering all sorts of fears, and building up some responses. But they were more likely to be sheltered, less likely to ponder fear, and more likely indeed to think of fear in association mainly with the vagaries of early childhood than as a companion of adulthood. The new context might also make it more difficult to distinguish levels of threat—all fear was bad, any incursion that prompted fear was immensely menacing, gradations of danger were hard to assess. It certainly muddied the ground between the ideal of absolute fearlessness or fear avoidance and the various levels of fear that might intrude in real life: if one were not fearless, was the alternative stark terror?

- In consequence, the need to deal with intense fear would come as a true surprise, and could be bitterly resented—natural reactions perhaps to a point, but likely to be magnified in the American cultural context. Any measures possible against the perpetrator of fear could seem justified, because the emotional offense was so great—disruptions of Americans' emotional security were simply unacceptable, not only impossible to explain but extremely difficult to forget. The need to memorialize occasions of fear followed from the emotional lesion, and obviously helped maintain the rawness of feeling as well.

- True to the lessons of the new culture, Americans would find it normal to discuss their fears widely and openly and would expect a sympathetic audience. This approach could well provide solace. It certainly did not necessarily detract from effective action—the fact that military personnel now openly discussed fears did not measurably impair their subsequent performance. But the need to vent could also help keep fears alive; it could baffle groups, whether within the United States or elsewhere, who found excited chatter about fear unattractive; and it could encourage policy agencies to participate in the same sense of ongoing emotional ferment, if not to exploit the ferment directly.

- Fear, finally, demanded reassurance and protection. A society that was intensely individualistic in so many ways did not believe that individuals should have to handle fear on their own. Without again denying all sorts of individual experiences, many Americans had been schooled to believe that, if fear did occur, there would be lots of assistance in making amends and in pledging that it would not happen again.

In sum, there could be a strong tendency in substantial segments of the contemporary American public to regard the experience of fear as someone else's fault—someone who should be taken to task for causing emotional distress on top of whatever objective wrongs had been committed; with a further belief that whatever could be done to compensate and prevent would be fully justified. All this would write into public response the lessons learned from family contexts and expert advice alike.

The new culture toward fear, developing now for over half a century, served then as a major causal factor shaping reactions to emotion-laden risks and to dangers. The culture had many positive features, in easing emotional life for many people in a secure society. It arguably had drawbacks, however, in leaving some Americans less emotionally prepared than desirable for unexpected intrusions, more open to manipulations that either prolonged fear or promised decisive remediation, and unduly dependent on supportive sympathy and simply a willingness to listen to national expressions of angst. Reactions of this sort were neither accidental nor dictated simply by the terrible logic of events like those of September 11. The recent history of fear standards powerfully shaped response.

MAINSTREAM AND THE EVANGELICALS

Finally, of course, there was the odd combination of the new mainstream culture and the more durable traditions of evangelical Christianity and racial targeting of fear, with anxieties about American power and science added in. Obviously, a further peculiarity of the American approach involves its divisions into several rather different communities where fear was involved, some seeking to avoid fear, others eager to use it in discipline and motivation, and some, doubtless, attempting to merge theoretically incompatible elements. Certainly, mainstream aversion to fear could prove compatible with some traditional racial targeting, when it became important to assign blame for causing unwonted emotional challenge. Discomfort with fear of crime, for example, linked directly to racial profiling, with the emotion toward crime and toward race often both measurably unrealistic. Special circumstances might also prompt a reversal of balance between majority and Evangelical minority. Normally, mainstream Americans would tend to disparage the minority approach, insofar as they were aware of it: after all, truly modern people would not be menacing congregants immersed in threats of hell or fears of death. And some Evangelicals, for their part, were at pains to dress up parts of their message; we have seen that, while images of hell might persist, references to outright fear tended to decline.

But in a crisis, roles might shift: Evangelical leaders might prove more comfortable in dealing with a sudden emotional onset than would the fear-shunning majority, though both sides might conjoin in seeking to pinpoint blame.[23] Worries about national vulnerability or cosmic disaster could cause some bond between mainstreamers and apocalyptics. Evangelicals might even take an understandable delight in seeing Americans more generally exposed to the prod of an emotion that, in their opinion, they should be prepared to handle as part of spiritual development or as punishment for sins. Warnings of menace, familiar to one group, would simply enhance uneasiness and emotional discomfort in the other. The result would hardly merge the two approaches—a big difference remains between seeing fear as a product of evil and seeing fear as simply unfair—but some Americans, retaining their desire to avoid fear but no longer seeing a way to do so, might yield initiative to groups that could be more decisive in their response to emotional challenge.

But it's the total package which seems particularly persuasive. Some key traditions, borne with particular vigor by certain groups, proved quite hardy—possibly more persuasive than in many other societies. Their persistence helped explain a fascination with themes of cosmic destruction and some of the difficulties in adjusting to contemporary patterns of death—yet these anxieties provided an independent context for new fears as well, potentially explaining significant change. Then on top of all this came the explicit shift in socialization, which generated the most relevant kind of guidance to public and often to private reactions to fear from mainstream Americans. The combination was potent: it remains to explore its fuller impact and, to the extent its implications have proved undesirable, to discuss correctives. One ambivalent feature of historical causation—in this case, of novel fear reactions—is that it can at once be quite powerful—history can be hard to undo—but also in principle open to serious modification, precisely because its sources are ultimately human and time-specific, not natural or divinely ordained.

The significant changes in recommended socialization toward fear in the United States are both definite and clear, part of the historical record. As we have seen, they emerge at first in childrearing literature, but they show up also in school materials and ultimately in adult prescriptions, such as military manuals, and in the novel fascination with fictional fearless heroes. And their parallels with actual, recent fear reactions are striking and plausible: a troubling contemporary propensity toward public panic maps closely on the implications of the cultural shift, with its impatience over controlling fear.

Several steps are involved in sorting out the consequences of the changes in fear standards. First, not everyone had the same level of access or interest in the prescriptions. Changes in actual socialization and actual fear experiences undoubtedly varied. Several studies in the 1930s and 1940s suggested that fathers, for example, on average retained more sense that boys should stand up to fears and risks than mothers did.[24]

Variety, however, does not preclude significant change in emotional repertoire. In general, social psychologists argue that a widely disseminated set of emotional standards will impact how people express emotions—to others and to themselves—and how they experience emotions directly. This has been tested in contemporary historical settings concerning shyness, jealousy, and various aspects of anger. Changes in standards do count over time, even though not producing full uniformity, and the pattern applies to shifts in fear as well.[25]

But a timing issue is crucial too. The new fear standards just began to be enunciated between the two world wars. Only the most up-to-date, advice-sensitive parents would pick them up quickly or fully. Judging by letters to *Parents' Magazine*, it was only in the 1940s that concern about children's fears was fully assimilated, though by that point the topic was drawing extensive comments. It takes two generations, at the least, to integrate new emotional standards under normal circumstances—insofar as we can judge from the other historical cases. When the children of the first group to encounter new standards themselves grow up to express public emotion and to become parents, the changes will begin to kick in more widely and affect adult perceptions more directly. It is no surprise, in this sense, that reactions to the fear potential of Pear Harbor and World War II reflected more traditional criteria, including stiff-upper-lip responses, rather than the cutting edge fear literature. Trained experts, to be sure, were talking about the need to bolster children against wartime fears, but they did not yet have a wide audience.[26] The situation would be far different several decades later, when the new socialization standards had become routine, part of an established emotional landscape.

Finally, of course, the impact of the growing aversion to fear would be supplemented by other developments. New attitudes toward risk built in the concern about fear but also extended it. Changes in media signals also amplified the consequences of the shift in socialization, as did the prolonged experience with foreign threats and tensions that opened up with the cold war. These supplements, along with the sheer habituation to the new standards, underlie the close correspondence with actual reactions, and were fundamental to setting the larger process of change in motion.

Cumulative changes in the American approach to fear, coexisting with some persistent traditions, in no sense undermined a capacity for considerable courage. Americans did not collapse in the face of threat, even though they were inclined to display unusual signals of distress. But the new sensitivity, and the resultant capacity for outrage when fear proved unavoidable, did create a novel climate.

Many Americans sensed the change, certainly by the 1990s—even aside from the throwbacks who persisted in regarding the aversion to encountering fear as an embrace of moral weakness or simple sissyhood. During the 1990s, a spate of celebrations of World War II heroism implicitly, or sometimes explicitly, contrasted the bravery of past soldiers with the mushier resources of contemporary life. Films and television series like *Saving Private Ryan* and *Band of Brothers* drew huge audiences, and, of course, history outlets had long privileged past war stories of various sorts. There were several reasons for the surge. Half-century memorials coincided with the realization of the rapid attrition of the veteran generation; many adults were marking the achievements of their own fathers and grandfathers as well. In a post–cold war decade, there was also some oversimplified envy of an earlier war when goals seemed clear and incontestable. But there was also a nostalgia for a past ability to stand up to danger, to surmount fear, that, many sensed, may have weakened in a more materialistic and psychologically edgy America. Newsman Tom Brokaw's book, *The Greatest Generation*, first published in 1998 and endlessly celebrated on his newscasts, made the claim simply, though without real analysis: contemporary Americans lacked the challenge but also lacked the fortitude of their ancestors. And all this, of course, before September 11 raised its own new questions about the national capacity to handle fear. This contrast with apparent British ability to recapture World War II courage as an explicit guide to contemporary emotional response, rather than a cherished but regrettably somewhat distant museum piece, is tantalizing. Despite an eagerness to seize on both past and current examples of heroism, it seemed brash for an American leader simply to urge people to be brave—and there were decades of socialization behind this hesitancy.

For, at risk of oversimplification, it can be suggested that many contemporary Americans, and American public culture, face severe challenges where fear is concerned. And while it would be an oversimplification to attribute major aspects of American foreign, military, and budget policy to emotional signals shaped by American culture, it is no distortion to see the connections, in the policies themselves and even more in the public support they receive. The linkages apply both to the more traditional holdovers and to the anxious contemporary approach as it has emerged over the past several decades.

Thus many Americans harbor remnants of the old fear culture about racial strangers—open to reactivation in crisis. A durable minority of Americans is, in all sincerity, quite ready to invoke fear as desirable social discipline in a world full of sin, eager to use fear as both explanation and target. Elements of this minority are highly placed, in the military among other sites. Its assessment of fear also links to wider cultural expressions, for example in science fiction and the fascination with the apocalypse.

Finally, for the majority, reactions to fear—including fears transmitted via Evangelical promptings—are shaped by the changes in fear's estimation, changes most Americans have grown up with and for which they assume responsibility as watchful parents. In this new culture, fear is unacceptable, an emotion that, if it cannot be prevented, legitimizes both lament and retaliation. In this new culture, as it has solidified and amplified since the 1920s, lie clear contours of reactions to tragedies like September 11. Faced with genuine threat and a legitimate need for fear, Americans have been unwittingly but thoroughly socialized to overreact, from a combination of inexperience, learned resentment, and a quest for reassurance. Small wonder that, as many of the September 11 accounts directly suggested, Americans respond to fear as a highly individual emotion affront—translating the public to the personal—which someone, somehow should both punish and assuage.

7

NEW APPROACHES TO RISK
Lawyers and Bicycle Helmets

Prevention of fear logically involved efforts to reduce danger. Emotion—or more properly, emotion prevention—lay at the heart of a growing intolerance of risks: here was a key link between the changing emotional culture and new policies and behaviors. Legal and corporate factors joined in the resultant attack in the unpredictable and the accidental. The result, however—since there were limits to accident prevention—could ironically increase emotional anxiety and heighten a desire to seek specific responsibility for mischance. Redefinition of risk, in a climate of emotional reassessment, helped translate aversion to fear into a variety of public and international policies.

The sensitivities to fear that developed from the 1920s onward, and their causes, in new openness to psychological evaluations and concerns about the hazards of modern life, go far toward explaining American reactions to threat by the turn of the next century. They exemplify that kind of behavioral history essential in evaluating contemporary patterns, making these patterns at once understandable but also neither simply "natural" nor inevitable. It was no accident—granting the problems of perspective on recent events—that contemporary reactions to fear crises have mapped so closely the potential implications of the earlier shift in emotional culture.

The relationship between the changes in emotional culture and the shifts in approaches to risk was complicated, however. Initially, the increasing desire to avoid fear led quite logically to attempts to minimize risk: there seemed to be an easy harmony. Over time, however, the pressure to shun risk took on a life of its own, creating new opportunities for fear of uncertainty—all the more unsettling in that the discomfort with fear continued to grow. The risk's tail began wagging the emotional dog, as media leaders quickly discovered. In dealing with changes toward risk, this chapter also prepares a chronological crossover, in which fear avoidance unintentionally produced new vulnerabilities.

For the new approach to fear was increasingly intensified by a concurrent pattern of warning and manipulation, in which a variety of practitioners—some well-intentioned, some simply on the make—used a growing aversion to risk to sell goods and services. The result built on but also amplified the contemporary culture of fear. It encouraged the sense that, in order to avoid fear and anxiety, arrangements should be available that would minimize both risk and its emotional concomitant. Worries about children captured much of this climate, but there were worries about self and other loved ones, and even strangers whose service might create emotional demands, as well. Not surprisingly, accidents, pain, and death organized many of the new anxieties, which formed something of an unrecognized undercurrent amid the more obvious cheerfulness and hedonism of mainstream consumer culture. Avoidance of fear, in other words, led to unusual efforts to avoid risk or to assign human agency for risks that occurred nevertheless. American approaches to the environment changed substantially, beginning in the later nineteenth century but accelerating greatly in the middle decades of the twentieth century and beyond. Chance and accident yielded to precaution and liability.[1]

Safety and security were the new watchwords. Safety concerns created all sorts of sensible protections—like bicycle helmets or seat belts—that it seemed foolish (and sometimes illegal) to scorn, but that also signaled a timidity inconceivable just a generation back, when kids and adults had pedaled away in blissful ignorance of the dangers they faced. (It was also true, of course, that more crowded streets and faster vehicles objectively changed the safety situation; the roots of change were not simple.) Again, a comparative measure is relevant: the United States, proudly scornful of the security-mindedness of other societies in social and environmental matters, became unusually obsessed with safety, whatever the implications in terms of real security and peace of mind. A rocky park or a monument of any height is far more circumscribed by dire warning signs and fences in the United States than its counterpart in Europe or China.

A specific contrast drives the point home. Even as Americans protect their fragile heads when cycling, the Dutch, among the more devoted bicycle riders in the world, have almost uniformly abandoned the helmet except for racing. It was, for them, a passing fad, soon annoying and unattractive—not the emblem of conscientious good sense it became in the United States. Whether or not Americans are actually safer or not in these venues and situations, they are measurably more anxious where risk and fear conjoin.

This chapter focuses on the new approaches to danger, and particularly physical danger, arguing that the new anxieties about childhood fears, and the pressures on parents to prevent fear-inducing situations and to reassure when defenses broke down, along with heightened demands for personal security, directly relate to a pervasive set of safety concerns that made further inroads on the public culture. They also relate to changes in American legal culture and expectations, where movements toward identifying individual responsibility for unsuccessful responses to risk virtually redefined the meaning of the term. Even insurance companies, aiming obviously at reducing the monetary losses entailed in risk, participated in further redefinitions, additionally constraining the idea of the accidental.[2]

The new experience of risk was at the heart of the matter. Historians have shown that ideas about risk began to change in Western culture around 1700, when new actuarial findings led scholars to calculate risks mathematically, rather than assuming that chance was entirely blind. This cultural shift set the basis for new risk procedures, including insurance programs, but they did not immediately lead to popular reconsideration of chance, or to assumptions that risk could be eliminated as opposed to recalculated. This wider change awaited the American twentieth century. This was the point at which chances for death and serious premature illness diminished steadily, as we have seen; despite some new challenges, particularly in the area of vehicular accidents, and even despite growing military involvements, the most awesome risks dropped measurably. This meant, however, that the risks that remained could seem more unacceptable, quite literally scarier; and in this context it became easier to exaggerate some of the remaining risks as well.

With sensitivities to fear increasing as well, a growing array of players had a stake in magnifying risk to discipline behaviors or sell new products and services. The same context also encouraged the new search for responsible agents of risk: with risk rarer and less palatable, and with expanding ranks of lawyers and insurance actuaries devoted to finding cause, it became easier to assign fault. One way to limit fear or express the turmoil that fear now generated was to assume individual responsibilities such that risk could either be prevented or punished. Two key changes occurred, then, which can be traced in several specific contexts: (1) risk became less tolerable, and (2) the idea of real chance or accident lost favor. The first change could generate heightened anxiety despite growing safety. The second change led to the growing impulse to retaliate when fears emerged.

What was happening—and it had direct connection to the changing experience of death discussed in chapter 5—was both odd and very real. A society that was becoming increasingly secure, by all reasonable standards, began to perceive its environment as more menacing, with greater resultant need to protect from risk and to determine culprits when protection broke down. Even as people became less likely to die prematurely, even less likely to become involved in physical fights, the surroundings seemed somehow less secure. There were new dangers in fact—cars, for example—though they did not overturn the larger gains in life expectancy. There were new imaginings, sometimes linked to reality but often not, of rising crime or menacing foreigners. Above all, there were new standards: so much progress in personal safety made middle-class Americans yearn for still greater perfection. They came close to expecting, or being told to expect, no accidents, no germs, nothing that could not be controlled. And, of course, their expectations could not be realized, so they sought cover, not only trying to minimize risk—the bicycle helmet approach—but often assuming the worst of the world around them. Here, along with the more fabled stresses of modern life, was why Americans, to so many observers, often to themselves, seemed so anxious amid success.

THE REGULATED LIFE

A recent reminiscence, if perhaps overly nostalgic, captured the sea change. The subject: what parents now check on, before sending their kids to play with others, compared to the greater latitudes in remembered childhoods past. Once upon a time, nobody checked on much of anything; kids were simply sent out to play. But now: Have the child safety seats in the transporting vehicles recently been checked? Are electric outlets in the home protected by childproofs covers, and do the oven controls have kid guards? Is there a foam bumper pad around the stone fireplace, purchased from an outfit like Right Start? Is the toilet lid locked down so the child cannot accidentally fall in and drown? Is there enough soft rubber around any outdoor play equipment? Safety rules, obviously, have multiplied, replacing divine guidance or sheer injunctions of obedience in controlling children's behaviors. And the rules and related protective equipment get stricter with each passing year. Even simple roughhousing is discouraged, where it was once part of the child's life at the playground or at camp.

Camps themselves have massively changed. Counselors are carefully briefed on definitions of physical and sexual abuse. Swimmers as well as nonswimmers must wear life vests, and beach areas are carefully fenced off. State requirements dictate detailed reports on any accident, in case of future lawsuits, and camp managers must attend a risk management session in the off-season. Staff parties, which once included beer, are now outlawed as too risky.

Historians of childhood can add another contrasting vignette. Into the 1960s, children might break a limb with no particular commentary—they did something imprudent or simply had bad luck, their casts were signed, healing eventually occurred, and that was it. By the 1990s, a broken arm was much more worrisome, almost surely a badge of some parental irresponsibility, complete with anxieties about whether some permanent dysfunction might result. Here again, risk became unacceptable, though frustratingly it would not be entirely banished.

The high school atmosphere massively changed. In the 1960s, court decisions limited school interference with children's lives, and the dominant assumption was that kids should be allowed considerable breathing room, even with regard to parental control. Now the prevalent wisdom—as suggested in reports like the National Longitudinal Study of Adolescent Health in 1997—is that adolescents' well-being depends on steady parental involvement. Thus parties must be carefully chaperoned, with kids ideally signing pledges about their restrained behavior. Children must be watched for telltale signs of incipient violence or psychological disorder. The world, again, has become a dangerous place, and children, even older children, are not by themselves prepared to cope.

And for children not easy to regulate, we increasingly offer drugs. As is well known, American reliance on calmants like Ritalin has massively raced ahead of practices in other parts of the world. We want sedate children, and where rules don't work, we sedate.

How is all this to be viewed? Is the new concern for regulation and monitoring simply an objective response to increasing danger? (The answer is almost certainly no, though certain risks have increased with new levels of technology and urban/suburban congestion.) Do we simply know more than we once did, and so respond responsibly? After all, we blithely look back at past ages in which accident potentials were ignored—for instance, no covers on wells, into which children could and did fall fairly easily—and wonder at the neglect. Can we do the same for the 1920s or 1960s and congratulate ourselves on our growing knowledge, which has schooled us, for example, on the possible head injuries that can result from bicycle rides? Or is there an additional subjective element, which has made us (not only parents, but many contemporary children as well by all report, who become increasingly eager for less undefined freedom and space) more timid, less willing to rely on common sense, less interested in training in courage and self-definition? Obviously, new problems and new knowledge are involved, but the national protective mania has wider roots and implications as well. And while controls have tightened measurably in the last two decades, the core of the risk-reassessment process started even earlier.[3]

LEGAL APPROACHES TO RISK

Many changes in the law provided early signs of a modern reassessment of risk, and encouraged not only legal but popular reevaluation from the nineteenth century onward. Evolution of the concept of torts, and accompanying changes in the importance of tort litigation, were at the heart of this development. Changes in tort law are much debated—as to their meaning as well as their desirability; and regardless of interpretation, the changes reflected a variety of factors, and not the evaluation of risk alone. Nevertheless, the central theme involved a redefinition of causation, so that misfortunes once shrugged off as chance were now imputed to human causes and attendant liabilities.[4]

All societies look for human responsibility for certain kinds of misfortune. Various tribal groups, for example, long ago established traditions of compensation, whereby if a hunter from one group was injured while hunting with another, the other would provide some support for the hunter's family. In the main, however, in American society until the later nineteenth century, primary responsibility for most accidents lay with the injured—either imprudence or sheer fate lay at the root of the problem. Life, in either perspective, involved risk, and there was not much to do about it. Children, in early factories, according to the prevailing wisdom, were constantly imprudently sticking their fingers into unguarded machinery. Their resultant loss of digits, or worse, was either their fault, or plain bad luck—just part of life. More than business callousness was involved in this approach, but broader attitudes as well. Historians have long wondered at the nonchalance of many early modern parents in Western society where accidents were involved that we would view as eminently preventable, as in the case of the uncovered wells.

Carelessness (by modern standards) does not mean that emotions, including fears, were not present as well; it would be misleading to generalize about fatalism too glibly. The very unpreventability of environmental mishaps could increase a sense of fear. But there does seem to have been a degree of passivity involved in the premodern approach to accidents that may have muted emotional reactions, save perhaps grief after the fact.[5]

Whatever the traditional emotional equation, the thinking behind the legal approach to accidents began to change in the United States toward the middle of the nineteenth century, with the reconsideration and then the rapid expansion of tort law. As one scholar has put it, during most of the nineteenth century, catastrophe was an everyday occurrence, but recovery of damages was not: there was no expectation what anyone was really responsible for accidents, or certainly that anyone should be required to pay for them (other than the injured party, where possible). Verdicts, concerning disasters such as deadly steamboat explosions, characteristically came back: "Nobody to Blame." Risk was largely a matter of individual choice. As one legal scholar noted, concerning accidents at work: when a person "fully cognizant of the particular service, voluntarily enters thereon, his undertaking of service is interpreted as an assumption of those risks, and a waiver of any right to complain of an injury there from."[6]

It was this thinking that began to change. Legal scholars like Oliver Wendell Holmes devoted considerable attention to the previously untended area of tort law, and while the new ideas were often complex, even contradictory, they moved clearly toward a belief that many risks had legitimate legal consequences, not only when malice or outright negligence was involved, but also when conduct fell below objective standards. The new question began to be, not whether someone deliberately harmed another, but whether an accident happened as a result of conditions a prudent man should have foreseen. The "principle of foreseeability," indeed, signaled a massive alteration in conventional thinking about risk, not only widening legal responsibility (the main change in tort law) but also shifting the view of the daily environment from randomness to predictability.

The famous *MacPherson v. Buick Motor Company* case, in 1913, shows the new thinking and its consequences in court. MacPherson bought his Buick car in 1910, and drove it for about a year without mishap, storing it in his barn during the winter. The following summer, the car's left wheel collapsed as he was driving, pinning him under the vehicle, in turn breaking an arm and damaging one eye. Over time, his sight deteriorated, seriously affecting his work and life. So he sued, claiming defective wood in the wheel's axle. The first trial ended with charges dismissed, but a later jury awarded damages; confirming this verdict, an appellate judge argued that Buick "owed a duty to all purchasers of automobiles to make a reasonable inspection and test to ascertain whether the wheels purchased and put in use by it were reasonably fit for the purposes for which it used them." Despite the fact that various factors might have affected the wheel between the time of purchase and the mishap, this was no mere accident, but a condition that the manufacturer could have and should have anticipated.[7]

Several principles were converging in this expansion of tort law—an expansion signaled, by 1900, by a massive growth in the tort sections of legal textbooks. First, of course, with industrialization and urbanization more of the environment in which people lived was explicitly man-made. New tort law reflected this change by insisting, increasingly, that the people who created the environment, like automobile producers or (where work accidents were concerned) factory owners, maintain maximum standards of safety, and not hide behind older ideas of random accidents. Early tort law had strongly reflected the importance of landed property in preindustrial life, seeking to protect property owners from lawsuits from people who were injured when wandering onto their land. Increasingly, shops, roads, and assembly lines were replacing the land as the framework for most people's ordinary activities. This meant, according to the new thinking, a need for a duty to care, and a shift in beliefs about causation of accidents from chance, or contributory negligence of the injured party, to conditions attributable to bodies like corporations. The expansion of science and social science, and the growing acceptance of scientific thinking, also affected tort law, by providing specific explanations for developments that once were attributed to fate or divine whim. All this added up, quite obviously, to a sea change in the idea of accidents, toward a belief that most accidents had specific causes and that these causes did not usually lie in the behavior of the victim but rather in some action—not necessarily malfeasance; possibly only lack of foresight—on the part of other human agents. The new thinking, clearly, paralleled the ideas that, as we will see, would increasingly inspire safety officials in the twentieth century: accidents were not usually accidental.

Buyers, according to these standards, no longer had to beware, for product manufacturers were the agents responsible for quality and safety. Workers, by the same standards, were not usually negligent in on-the-job injuries, for it was the duty of factory owners to protect them. The environment, where the individual was concerned, should not be random.

The expansion of the idea of responsibility took many forms in the twentieth century. A man tried to commit suicide by jumping in front of a subway train. He subsequently sued the city's transit authority, arguing that the train's operator had not stopped it fast enough. He received a large settlement. Another man had a heart attack while trying to start a lawn mower. A jury ordered the lawn mower company to pay him $1.75 million. Yet another man was injured when a drunk driver crashed into a telephone booth he was in. A judge ruled that the company that designed the booth was liable. Yet another person was robbed and killed on a street near his hotel. His family successfully sued the hotel and the city in which it was located.[8]

These examples show that the growth of tort litigation entailed more than a reconsideration of risk. In a nation in which class warfare was massively discouraged, on the whole successfully, litigation, and attendant jury deliberations, became a key means of allowing ordinary people to sock it to their masters—big business particularly, but also increasingly powerful individuals like doctors and also public agencies. During the twentieth century, judges specifically noted that corporations had both deep pockets and the possibility of buying insurance, beyond the capacities of most ordinary folk; so fining them was the best way to pay for the consequences of accidents regardless of real blame. But new ideas about causation remained central. In the nineteenth century, medical malpractice suites were virtually unheard of; if something happened following a doctor's care, it was simply bad luck. The casual approach shifted massively during the twentieth century, in a society that became notoriously litigious.

There were several specific surges in tort litigation, after the fundamental rethinking among jurists in the later nineteenth century. Progressive-era politics pushed for new restraints on corporate behavior, particularly in the area of workplace safety. Less should be left to chance. More activist courts after 1960 pushed the boundaries still further.

The main point, following from the new popular as well as legal thinking about risk, was the sheer expansion of tort cases in both number and range. In California, tort activity constituted only 1.2 percent of all filings in 1903–4, but it had soared to 24 percent by 1976–77. Tort action constituted 6 percent of the cases before Superior Courts in 1890, but 27 percent by 1970. Barriers against tort action crumbled. A classic 1960 case, again involving automobiles, limited the capacity of corporations to defend themselves against suits by specific contract disclaimers. Individuals could not sign away their ability to claim causation for accidents. Special status also did not provide immunity. Rulings increasingly embraced public agencies, including charities: there was no backing off the need to control the social environment.[9]

The most interesting later extension of tort law occurred in the famous asbestos cases of the early 1980s. Here, manufacturers were held accountable for not warning victims about risks that could not have been foreseen when the damage occurred. The environment, apparently, should be so predictable that manufacturers could be made responsible for anticipatory prudence. Other interesting extensions further reduced the role of accident victims. In 1970 the National Commission on Product Safety acknowledged that automobile drivers often make mistakes, but noted "a craftsworthy vehicle can make [driver] failures failsafe."[10]

There is no need to exaggerate. Most accidents did not result in litigation—only one per 320, to be exact, during the later twentieth century. Either a sense of personal fault or the workings of chance, or the costs and burdens of legal action, or some combination, limited the tort approach. It is also true that the conservative surge of the 1980s, bent on greater protection for business and possibly a more individualistic approach to risk, rolled back tort opportunities in some key areas. Drug companies, most notably, were largely protected from unforeseen consequences of medication. Efforts extended also to protect gun makers and food producers (this last against liabilities for obesity), and there was abundant discussion of greater protection for physicians.

Still, fundamental assumptions about the range of human causation and attendant responsibility remained unchallenged. Even drug manufacturers could not maintain immunity. A classic Texas case in 2005 further extended the innovation in tort law involving the "duty to warn." The manufacturer of Vioxx, a pain medication used for arthritis, was held liable for not providing warnings of a possible slight increase in the risk of heart attacks, among individuals taking the pill for more than eighteen months. It is possible that the manufacturer did ignore a study, though ironically the successful suit occurred on behalf of an individual who had been taking the medicine for only twelve months and died of a different kind of heart ailment; his lawyer argued that his problem might have been caused by an earlier heart attack that left no trace, and the jury bought the argument to the tune of a $253 million-dollar award. Modern tort law was alive and well, with reports of up to twenty thousand suits, each with an eager lawyer attached, lined up to take their shots at the makers of Vioxx.

The evolution of modern tort law and its use offers both a generous opportunity for amusement, on the vagaries of lawyers and juries, as well as a serious commentary on the odd channeling of social tensions and resentments in the United States. But the core assumption—that some human agency must be responsible for a host of mishaps and that most accidents were in fact preventable if only causation were more systematically attended to—remains crucial to the larger approaches to risk. Many Americans, including, surely, many who did not bother to sue, came to share a belief that many mishaps, that once would have been attributed to accident, were clearly a matter of someone's fault, that in a better world would be anticipated and that surely should be punished in the meantime.

The result, clearly, was an increase in the emotions surrounding many accidents. Grief remained, and sometimes predominated still. Even a certain degree of fatalism might persist—the idea that accidents will happen was hardly eliminated. But the evolution of tort law clearly reflected a reduction in the emotional cushion of fatalism. For now, thanks to the expansion of the American legal apparatus, an unprevented risk could far more readily than ever before turn into anger and resentment, into a focused desire to pin blame and win compensation. At the same time, the thinking behind modern tort law might also, in encouraging increased intolerance of risk, promote a greater degree of fear. For torts and attendant manufacturer compliance did not necessarily keep pace with the growing desire for elimination of risk and environmental predictability. While the mania for safety most directly expressed continued and sometimes increasing anxieties about the lived environment, the desire to use law to express concerns about risk was important in its own right.

The tort frenzy had another angle, familiar enough but immediately relevant to the context for fear: just as it was intended to do, it promoted an obsessive, sometimes explicitly fearful security consciousness among those responsible for public or individual safety. To be sure, there were corporations who continued to game the system, calculating the costs of lawsuits against the expense of providing maximum feasible protection. But tort law, and the attitudes behind it, not only increased the costs of failure to protect and anticipate, it also increased anxious awareness. The familiar result, the doctor ordering batteries of probably unnecessary tests to guard against a later suit for malpractice, had interesting analogies in other areas. American agencies of various sorts developed a passion for warning, hoping that even when they could not actually prevent every mishap, they at least could claim they had the foresight to call attention to danger. In some cases, warnings might reduce public concern about the environment: if one heeded the sign, one should be all right. But the approach—including, of course, the batteries of precautionary medical tests—could also increase anxiety, joining public and officialdom in a common sense that the environment ought to be risk free but maybe was not. No high emotions here necessarily, save for the paranoid, but some shared tension over the gap between expectations of security and the reality that not all mischance could be controlled.

INSURING RISKS: INNOVATIONS IN RESPONSIBILITY

A few decades after the beginnings of the redefinition of torts, changes in the dominant approach to risk by insurance companies signaled a similar effort to reduce the realm of the truly accidental in favor of pinpointing a new precision in individual responsibility. The process was interesting in further supporting the whole transformation of thinking about chance and accident. It also drove home, to many individuals, the importance of risk assignment, for the new approach involved substantial new costs and, for some, the possibility of losing insurability altogether.

Insurance has always had a complex relationship to risk. Insurance systems began to develop in the Western world from the seventeenth century onward, based on the desire of customers—initially, mainly businesses—to limit the costs of accidents like fires or lost ships and on the ability of insurance providers to calculate probabilities so that, from their standpoint, risks could be sufficiently distributed to make client costs reasonable. Popular use of insurance started in the United States only in the nineteenth century. Life insurance was directed toward burial costs. It provided some protection against premature death expenses but did not have huge risk implications.[11]

The advent of more widespread life and home insurance and, even more, car insurance (the first American policy was issued in 1898) introduced risk complexities more clearly. Ordinary policy holders saw insurance as a means of protection against chance—an unexpectedly early fatal illness or a car crash, for example; the possibility of limiting the financial costs of mishap was new, and welcome, but the idea of mishap or accident itself did not have to be rethought. Insurance companies, however, began to introduce greater subtlety. For, with growing actuarial precision, risks could be calculated not only for whole populations, but also for subgroups. Life insurers could thus determine that certain weight categories had lower life expectancies than others, or even more obviously that those who suffered from diseases like diabetes were far poorer insurance risks than the population at large. Here were the seeds of a quiet conflict between what most people expected from insurance—a hedge against incalculables, such as the possible advent of diabetes—and corporate interest in limiting the incalculables by assigning more specific causation or responsibility, thus allowing lower rates to certain groups, fewer unexpected claims, and more secure profit margins.

The tipping point in this tension occurred during the 1950s, but with accelerating impact thereafter. Predictably, the corporate approach increasingly prevailed, along with growing masses of data about the

characteristics of individual insurance applicants. Several developments coincided. Knowledge of special risks led to increasingly differ-
entiated policy rates or even denials of policy. It was between 1950 and
1954, for instance, that insurance companies began to single out male
drivers between the ages of twenty and twenty-four. Though decisions
stretched out over several years, many companies began to refuse to
insure this group outright unless parents also had policies or unless the
men had taken special classes or were married. Later, similar distinctions would be applied to older drivers (less likely to have accidents but
more likely to suffer severe physical consequences—another cost danger). State legislation sometimes limited this kind of discrimination, but
the basic message was clear. Accidents might still be accidents, but some
groups were particularly responsible—such that mishaps for them were
less accidental than was once imagined. The same thinking applied to
subcategories where health or life insurance was involved, save as cushioned by group policies that distributed risk more blindly.[12]

Soon thereafter, thanks to increasing automation of data, individual
experiences began to be monitored, where they affected actuarial cases.
Driving offenses, most obviously, began to be tallied against the costs
of insurance or even against outright insurability. The National Criminal Information System began to computerize local records, making traffic violations (and more serious crimes) available across state
lines. Records were and remain imperfect, thanks to vagaries of local
reporting and state policies, but the trend was clear. Certain individuals displayed behaviors that made it more likely that they would have
accidents—that therefore suggested, once more, that what happened to
them was less than truly accidental. Even more clearly than with age
categories, individual fault, not chance, governed many mishaps.

Most interesting of all was the increasing tendency to raise rates (or,
again, deny insurability) on the basis of prior accidents, even when the
driver or owner was in no sense responsible. The State Farm company,
for example, was raising premiums for car insurance after any accident that required the firm to pay more than $750 in damages, even
when the driver involved was entirely exonerated. Or, a house burns
down, as a result of electrical wiring failure—fire marshal investigation
revealed no malfeasance on anyone's part; the insurance company pays
the claim, but immediately cancels the policy. Here, quite clearly, was
a self-interested, and no doubt actuarially sound, insistence that accidents were not really random at all, in suggesting patterns of behavior
that required some kind of sanction.

To be sure, many states sought to limit company freedom in the
name of the more popular conception of risk and accident. Several

states banned insurers from raising premiums in no-fault situations. On the other hand, trial lawyers blocked most consumer group initiatives to encourage no-fault insurance that would protect the insured on conditions of restraint in suits for damages. A few companies found it useful to forgive a policyholder for one no-fault accident, but to apply pressure when other, though equally blameless, accidents occurred, on grounds that despite all the signs of blind chance there must be "something hazardous" about the individual's behavior.[13]

Shifts in insurance behavior are, admittedly, farther from standard emotions than the changes in tort law; anger at corporate indifference might result, but there was little measurable fear involved. But the direction of change did have important, and intriguing, implications. It coincided with, and doubtless encouraged, the sense that responsibility, not chance, governed human events. Paradoxically, the result was to increase risk for certain people—those denied access to insurance. But this could be justified on grounds of their particular liability. Paradoxically, given the goals most ordinary people maintained for insurance, new policies drove many to cover the costs of minor accidents themselves, rather than risk changes in rates—which added complexities to the meaning and impact of certain kinds of accidents.

The main point, however, was the massive revision of the balance between unassignable chance and explicit human failure—again, the same revision prompted by the changes in tort law. The overall goal, with which insurance companies and the public could agree, despite different vantage points, was to maximize the prevention of risk, rather than rely on the workings of chance or Providence. When prevention worked, the results could be splendid. But the redefinition added emotional freight to the whole topic of risk and arguably exaggerated the extent to which the course of events was or should be under human management.

By the early twenty-first century this new thinking had important additional consequences. Where dangers accumulated beyond apparent control, as with political risks after September 11, insurance became almost impossible to acquire at any price. More sweepingly still, government agencies in the United States began to be held politically responsible for failures in risk management. As devastating hurricanes in the summer of 2005 revealed, the American public was unwilling to tolerate significant human suffering on grounds of chance: some agency must be responsible, and no amount of invoking unprecedented disaster would get the government off the hook.[14]

In fact, perhaps partly in responses to insurers' stickiness, and certainly reflecting the widespread desire to bypass risk, many Americans increasingly viewed the government as insurer of last resort. This, despite growing proclamations of resistance to state intervention and certainly to taxation. Reliance on police and public health institutions to obviate the worst effects of automobile accidents increased, with impressive if costly results. Smaller numbers of Americans—admittedly, far from entirely risk averse, but goaded by eager real estate agents—built homes in risk-prone areas, on the sides of mud-caked hills in California or next to rising tides on many erosion-prone beaches. Their assumption, often realized in fact, was that if accident did strike, the government would pick up the pieces—literally—and often facilitate rebuilding in the same imprudent spots. The insouciance was uncharacteristic, but the assumption that risk could be controlled was part of a wider expectation.

More generally, whether the venue was a court of law or an insurance carrier, the reassessment of risk had powerful implications. Most obvious, however—and eagerly supported by insurance companies where self-interest and public image overlapped—was the connection between the redefinition of chance and the implications for personal responsibility for safety. Heightened emotions accompanied the redefinition as well: fear, where the cushion of fatalism was reduced, and certainly guilt or anticipated guilt when anticipation did not suffice to prevent.

A MANIA FOR SAFETY

Overall, the most overt translation of the new desire to prevent risk at almost all cost showed in attempts to curtail household and highway accidents, while phrasing key safety campaigns in terms of fears. To be sure, there were genuine new threats, from the 1920s onward. The campaigns were not simply manifestations of anxious psyches. Neither cars nor the growing array of chemical and mechanical domestic devices were people friendly. But with one glaring exception the American safety mania was unusually intense, the desire to limit risk unusually ambitious—and, arguably, the underlying fears were unusually great, then to be compounded by the rhetoric of safety itself.[15]

Concern about car accidents surfaced vividly in the 1920s. In 1922, New York City unveiled a Child Memorial to the thousands of children killed by cars. The city's Health Commissioner underlined the theme: "We are here to dedicate a monument to the martyrs of civilization—to the helpless little ones who have met death through the agencies of modern life." Speed limits and other traffic control measures were introduced early in the United States, compared to Western Europe where limits even today tend to be sketchier. Later, mandatory seat belts and other restraints enveloped young children while riding, with safety clearly superseding freedom of movement. Only in the provision of driver's licenses to adolescents did the United States prove relatively lenient, where the need to provide children with mobility in rural and then suburban contexts trumped the accelerating concern for safety.[16]

Playgrounds provided alternatives to the street for urban children, and here too safety measures mounted progressively, with the more unfettered equipment replaced by tamer options and with concrete or earthen platforms giving way to cushioned mats. Games were progressively reined in. By the 1990s a school staple, dodgeball, was under attack because children might be hit too hard, and the balls themselves were softened.

The National Council on Safety began to issue annual reports on children injured in the home soon after its formation in 1914. Insurance companies provided their own prods, combining concern with self-interest. It was hard to avoid the conviction that new parental attention was essential. By the 1930s the Federation of Women's Clubs proclaimed "the responsibility that rests on the shoulders of women for the elimination of home accidents." A host of conferences and government agencies produced dire figures on deaths in the home, and again homemakers were put on notice that it was their job to safeguard. Accidents, in other words, were not really random, but resulted from adult deficiencies—a huge move away from earlier attitudes that had combined surprising nonchalance with a belief that bad things could happen with no one to blame. As one authority hammered home in 1922, "By analyzing some of the accidents to children, the mother's responsibility is clear enough. None but she could have prevented them." A White House conference in 1960 went a step further, arguing that parents should be legally as well as morally accountable for mishaps.[17]

By then, to be sure, emphasis was shifting from parents to manufacturers, now obligated to provide all sorts of protective measures for toys and household equipment. "Childproof" devices for electrical outlets and medicine bottles, along with car seats, might reduce risk and parental anxiety alike. Warnings and restraints cropped up everywhere. A country normally insistent on its individual freedom generated far more caution signs in parks and public buildings, far more railings and guardrails, far more requirements for safety gear like bicycle helmets, than its counterparts elsewhere. And the trend intensified with every passing decade.

Several points emerge. In the first place, safety hazards were real, and most countermeasures made sense. Bicycle helmets might seem wimpy, particularly to adults who had survived their own childhood uncushioned, but they did protect against rare but dreadful head injuries and they did respond to increasing traffic hazards. In the second place, however, the safety movement in the United States proceeded at a pace that suggested both the unusual anxiety about children and their survival and the belief that risk needed to be eliminated at whatever cost to resources and freedom of movement. It followed, in other words, from the same denial of the truly accidental that showed in law and insurance. And third, when mishaps did happen—precisely because risk should in principle be banished—someone must be responsible. It might be parents, it might be manufacturers, but it could not just happen. The same point reverberated in discussions of traffic: there was always a fault. Insurance materials in the 1940s put the bulk of the blame on drivers—"driver failure or poor judgment." A bit later, manufacturing defects might move center stage. But chance or unattributable mishap must not enter the mix—both because of the ways most Americans now thought about risk, and because, for legal reasons, the notion of fault was crucial. Catching the basic point, the U.S. Department of Transportation revealingly insisted outright, in 1997, that car crashes should no longer be called accidents: "If you call something an accident, you are saying it's fate, it's an act of God, it's something you can't foresee....It's not accidental that one person survives a crash wearing a seat belt and one person goes through a window and dies." And the ensuing public awareness campaign was duly headed, "Crashes Aren't Accidents." There was always a human cause, always something that could be better regulated—and more often than not someone who could be sued.[18]

Risk concern, and the desirability of assigning human cause, went beyond the arenas of safety and accidents, and well beyond childhood. Fed, admittedly, by some changes in the nineteenth century itself, including germ theory, ideas and behaviors related to disease shifted in two crucial aspects. First, obviously, the environment became more dangerous. The United States led the world in a new mania for hygiene and sanitation, even down to the frequency of personal bathing. Along with bicycle helmets, perhaps no development in the later twentieth century so captured American obsession with protection than the ubiquity of plastic gloves—never had a people been so worried about the ominous potential of the human hand.

The second change focused on assignment of responsibility. Disease—not in all cases, to be sure, but in many—increasingly became a function of human fault. With huge gains in infant survival, the deaths of children that did occur were readily seen—by outside commentators and by anguished parents themselves—in terms of adult negligence. As attention shifted from contagious to degenerative diseases, another crucial twentieth-century transformation, again the emphasis on personal responsibility increased. The responsible individual, with appropriate discipline and self-restraint, should be able to avoid practices like smoking, overeating, and excessive alcohol consumption—and this in turn could mean, in the eyes of some physicians and public health authorities, that a sizable percentage of the leading adult killers, heart disease and cancer, really resulted not from risk or bad luck, but simply from personal failure. As a Harvard University School of Public Health report put it, in 1996, about 75 percent of all cancer resulted from lifestyle choices and therefore could be avoided: the individuals involved did not simply "get sick." Even the increasingly popular concept of addiction, though potentially partially absolving the victim, was double-edged: after all, ultimately the only cure for addiction was a new level of self-control, which meant that the addict himself could be blamed. All of this was a matter of some debate, of course—more than where safety and accidents were concerned. But the notion of removing part of the explanation of disease from the area of chance or environment, to relocate in terms of individual capacity, added considerably to the larger shift in views about risk and the external world.[19]

One quite specific disease fear contributed to the national emotional climate as well. During the 1980s, news about AIDS—the first reports emerged in 1981—generated what turned out to be excessive anxieties, with many magazines trumpeting a latter-day Black Death. Surveys soon suggested not only wide awareness of the disease, but also inaccurate beliefs about resulting mortality rates and particularly about the methods and risks of transmission. For a time, substantial majorities favored significant restrictions on AIDS patients, to limit or prevent any contact with the general public. Attitudes toward behaviors more conducive to exposure—homosexuality, nonmarital sex, and drug taking—not surprisingly strongly influenced reactions, a key instance where attributions of personal responsibility could affect both levels of tolerance and policy recommendations (including recommendations about mandatory testing). Large majorities, for example, favored compulsory testing of immigrants, even though this was not a group disproportionately suffering from the disease. The AIDS fears declined somewhat by the turn of the century; indeed, some authorities now worried about insufficient caution and anxiety. But the episode provided a reminder not simply about disease fears and a potential for excessive concern and media exaggeration, but about particular resentments associated with beliefs about levels of personal responsibility. Certainly, and to a point realistically, AIDS fears added to the sense of an uncertain environment even as the passion to reduce risk persisted.[20]

PERCEPTION VS. REALITY

Finally, and not surprisingly in the fearful desire to eliminate risk, campaigns frequently pushed beyond the facts, beyond the real hazards of modern life. Occasional kidnappings, horrible to be sure but quite rare, could become widespread obsessions. National news readily translated an isolated event in one part of the country into a new need for parental monitoring and restrictions. The milk carton campaigns, featuring pictures of lost children, began in 1979, after an appealing New York City boy was abducted (he was never found). Soon, campaigns were claiming that fifty thousand abductions by strangers took place each year (the actual figure was between two and three hundred). Well-intentioned warnings created a problem where, statistically, almost none existed, simultaneously building on and escalating fears about children's vulnerability. Similar panics in the later twentieth century targeted sexual predators of children, with greatly exaggerated accounts of pedophile rings. Again, inflated figures were intended to drive the point home, with virtually no controls over publicity-seeking scholars eager to gain attention amid an adult audience ready to believe the worst. New methods of labeling convicted sex offenders who had completed their prison sentences—a very broad category, also reflecting extended definitions of offense—provided yet another worry for parents, who would easily be convinced that their very neighborhood was a source of acute fear. One mother noted that she and her suburban friends had "to watch for dangers that lurked in every shadow."[21] For parents bent on elimination of risk for their precious charges, statistical reality was in some sense irrelevant: two hundred or fifty thousand, what if it happens to my child, on my watch?

The dramatic conversion of Halloween, from a traditional evening of modest childish revelry and some deviltry into a highly regulated parade of children with parents in tow, showed the growing range of fears—including fears of neighbors. Reports spread widely in 1982 about poisoned candy and apples filled with razorblades and handed out to trick-or-treating children. In fact, poisoning reports were never verified. And while there was documentation of three candy bars with pins struck in them, distributed on Long Island, the razorblade scare was false as well. But here too, accuracy did not matter: risk reduction did not depend on facts. Increasingly, city governments limited trick or treat hours and places. Merchants provided alternatives to children going house to house. And parents trudged wearily behind the kids, incapable of letting them out on their own and nervously jettisoning any unwrapped item in the trick-or-treat postmortems that continued faithfully into the twenty-first century.[22]

While activities relating to children brought out the most systematic rigor against risk, adult environments were also drawn into the mix. In the 1920s and again in the 1980s and 1990s, adult fears about crime in general routinely exceeded reality, sometimes encouraged by scholars, like the Chicago School of sociologists in the 1920s, who mistakenly believed that crime inevitably mounted with modernity. Lurid accounts of actual crimes, particularly those committed by feared minority groups, and by the later twentieth century at least the ubiquity of convincing crime shows in the media persuaded many Americans that problems were far worse than they were in reality. In the 1990s, when crime rates were declining quite rapidly, surveys suggested deep commitments to an alternative vision, based on fears of modern life and, sometimes, the blandishments of politicians eager to gain law-and-order votes. It was hard to persuade American majorities that crime was not increasing, even amid clearly contrary data. Not only votes, but gun purchases and warning equipment by homeowners responded to problems that, while real, were far more modest than many people deeply believed. Fear, not for the first time, could create durable realities of its own.[23]

Two or three American ingredients stand out in the campaigns for safety and against risk, for, as noted, the broader context, including the changes in birth and death rates and the new threats from cars and appliances, mirrored developments in advanced industrial societies more generally. Americans were not confident of their communities, easily convinced that they were surrounded by unreliable strangers who could turn menacing. They were not confident in the reliability of basic institutions, to whom children might be entrusted, for example, or who were responsible for urban protection. (Unsurprisingly, middle-class Americans remain much less willing to enroll children in day-care centers than their European counterparts, at real cost to parental ease.) Mistrust was compounded by the zeal for attribution. As is well known, American culture encouraged an extreme form of individualism, in which every occurrence must be connected to some responsible agent—such that accident cannot be chance, even illness in many instances must be pinned to flaws in personal behavior. The combination could be menacing: convinced of the importance of protecting one's own against mishap, eager to believe that risk could be eliminated because it derived from human agency, or, where it could not be eliminated, that someone could be sued or punished for the resultant misfortune, many Americans also faced a social environment they found extremely uncertain. Small wonder that, at times, they were fearful, and fed their fears by exaggeration. All this, finally, in an American setting in which (again to an unusual extent) fear itself was resented, a challenge toward reassurance and redress.[24]

A WEATHER REPORT

Few recent changes are more revealing, where American attitudes toward risk and fear are concerned, and where these attitudes intertwine with external manipulation, than the transformation of the humble weather report over the past three decades. Most of us are accustomed to the present, where a looming storm is announced often days away, and then treated to ominous announcements by television meteorologists—and, even more, by the publicists who invite viewers to stay tuned to the local newscast—as it nears. It may be a bit harder to recall the prehyperbole days, say in the mid-1970s when the weather reports were shorter and, above all, far more matter-of-fact.

One veteran weatherman puts the change this way: when he broke into the business about thirty years ago, he worked in a region where tornadoes were common. If one loomed, a brief program interruption announced the fact. But the larger newscast was rarely bent to emotion-stirring storm warnings. Weather descriptions were normally short, descriptive summaries. Now, he works in an area where tornadoes are far rarer, though two have hit in the past five years with significant, and much-remembered, damage in one case. But the amount of coverage given to the possibility of tornadoes considerably surpasses his previous experience, and the emotional overtones are far starker.[25]

Another commentator notes the American fascination with storms, which drives television to seek new disasters to quench viewer appetite—even sending reporters to foreign hurricanes where they can brave the winds just as they do back home. And where nature fails to oblige, movies and then television mount surrogate efforts, like the new television series in 2005 called quite simply *Category 7*—another special effects bonanza.[26]

Even summer weather can be recast. The introduction of the heat index and heat advisories turn the prospect of sweating some into a more ominous prospect. Numbers are introduced, like the discomfort index, that can add 10 percent to the reading on the thermometer. Again, a variety of factors are involved. Warnings that go beyond the obvious—that there will be some unpleasantness—may be essential for some vulnerable groups in the population, like the elderly (though the ones most at risk may not watch the news). But there is little question also that new ratings like wind-chill factors can add to a sense of dangerous environment.

Part of the change is technological. With Doppler radar, storms can be tracked earlier and somewhat more precisely. Home videos provide records of local damage that remain in memory. More parts of the nation, indeed the world, can be quickly described when a weather disaster hits, allowing viewers to "experience" more storms than was once the case. We're accustomed to seeing cars skid off the roads in Minnesota gales and to watching weathermen bend with the wind as hurricanes approach the Gulf Coast, as if it's all happening next door—and this may condition our reactions when we're told that a snowstorm or hurricane is actually nearing our own neck of the woods.

But more of the change has to do with media calculations and public reactions. The simple fact is that weather is the number one reason most people watch the local newscasts. As a result, the temptation to make a weather item seem far more menacing than it is really likely to be, in order to gain prominence, is almost overwhelming, and only the most experienced meteorologist, with the greatest bargaining power, can reduce the impulse. We're given anxiety-laden forecasts, in other words, to induce us to tune in and stay tuned. Not surprisingly, the current media approach is not only different from the past, but also distinctive in an international context; European weather reporting remains far more matter-of-fact, and far less extensive, than the American version.

At the same time, this is not simply a case of media manipulation. Why are we so fascinated with weather in the first place, and why do we not simply refuse to put up with the new hyperbole? It is possible, of course, that weather has objectively worsened in the past three decades—global warming may justify some disaster-speak, as hurricane frequency, for example, seems to be increasing; but to date this is not a major factor. There is particular irony in the growing interest in warnings about summer, for air conditioning reduces weather vulnerability for more Americans (though admittedly, not all) than ever before. One aspect of American life may have become more weather-dependent, and this provides a clearer if partial explanation for more ominous forecasting: the daily commute. (The citizens who heedlessly build homes on eroding beaches or mud-slid hills also, admittedly, have additional reasons for anxiety.) Overall, however, we are far less weather dependent than our forefathers were, when agriculture loomed larger, which makes the fascination, and the willingness to have our anxieties needlessly aroused by exaggeration, truly intriguing.

For surely—granting the very real commuter concerns—the basic reason for our perverse and increasing delight in scary weather rests squarely in our unavoidable fascination with one of the few elements in normal daily American life that represents risk pure and simple. It's not so much that weather matters greatly—we shield ourselves far more completely than in the Mark Twain days when Americans simply complained—it's that it defies our control. So we want to know about what's coming, almost obsessively, and we readily accept distortions of the real magnitude because they help convey the fact of risk itself. We fear this traditional category of risk more than people did when weather mattered more; and in the process we sometimes manage to get needlessly excited about weather prospects themselves.

We are, in sum, guided in weather anxieties by commercial media, but we open ourselves to this guidance by more basic anxieties. We far more frequently think that weather events are going to be worse than they turn out to be, than the reverse, partly because scare tactics have led us to the newscasts in the first place, under compelling labels like "stormtracker," but partly because this category of risk seems to anomalous and unsettling. Weather is one of the reasons contemporary Americans, despite a more secure existence than in the past, recurrently perceive themselves surrounded by dangers.[27]

CONCLUSION: RISK AND FEAR

The considerable shift in Americans' attitudes toward risk, over the past century, is obvious, important, and multifaceted. It shows in law, in accident prevention, in insurance policies, and even in weather reports. Of course attitudes vary, and there are important subcultures that differ from mainstream thinking, among other things with regard to religious or even magical causation. In the main, however, Americans have steadily heightened their commitments to predictable safety and security, reducing their willingness to accept explanations based on chance and increasing their fears and guilts when their expectations are contradicted. The result, without question, has been a host of measures that have in fact reduced unpredictability and limited the range of accidental mishaps, sometimes in the process protecting individuals from their own folly as well. While contemporary American attitudes and policies toward risk are partly shared with other advanced industrial societies, there are also some national peculiarities, including the extent of safety mania and the litigious approach toward the assignment of responsibility.

Yet, even as efforts to limit risk successfully reduce certain hazards—for example, work accidents—rising expectations can outpace reality, creating if not fearfulness at least some anxiety about the environment despite improved safety overall. There is a tendency to constantly expand the quest for absolute security. Anxiety is compounded in domains such as meteorology, where predictive capacity has improved but controllability falters.

Hopes for safety and worries about continued vulnerability to risk certainly open Americans to commercial appeals in which fear is an implicit or explicit component. Rising uncertainty about risk, because of expanding expectations, has generated new commercial exploitations and some outright misperceptions in recent decades, as the following chapter will further suggest. Again, what began as an effort to harmonize risk with the growing aversion to fear could turn into a new emotional sore.

Attacks on risk, and particularly the growing penchant for assigning responsibility for security breakdowns or inadequacies in disaster management, create a circle of concern, joining governing and governed alike in American society. The consequences of not doing everything possible to prevent risk—at times, even at a level of expense or monomania that might otherwise be questioned—and of not warning where controls remain uncertain, draw many elements of American leadership into shared fears. The political or litigation costs of failures to anticipate have arguably increased beyond reasonable bounds, creating excessive pressures and distorting balanced policy. Here, through the assignment of responsibility for risk, is where fear can grip leaders even more than the public at large. There are pitchmen in this area as well, eager to use intolerance of risk to claim political or commercial advantage. But the shared assumptions about responsibility, where leadership and public agree that nearly absolute security is a reasonable expectation, are actually more important. And where risk cannot be entirely prevented, the dominant assumptions press leaders to issue regular, exculpatory warnings to make it clear that, if something does happen, they cannot really be held responsible—increasing mutual fears in the process.

Risk aversion, finally, has had significant implications for American approaches to diplomacy, at least in the past few decades. Efforts at litigation designed to hold foreign governments responsible for risks incurred by American nationals constitute an intriguing, if rather imperialistic, argument that, ideally, international activities should be as risk-free for Americans as other activities, and if not someone should be held accountable. American courts have shown increasing willingness to sue other states for mischances befalling American citizens. But international affairs are not so neatly predictable, which is one reason that, as American attitudes toward risk hardened, a desire to isolate from foreign entanglements frequently resulted. No more than litigation, however, did isolationism really work. By no means did risk aversion prevent successful American international action on many occasions. It did however reduce the capacity for nuance, increase sensitivities to otherwise minor initiatives by hostile elements abroad, and increase a penchant for precautionary interventions that could turn out, however, to prove counterproductive.

Arguably, the mainstream approach to risk would make Americans particularly vulnerable to terrorist threat, designed precisely to heighten a sense of risk on grounds of inherent unpredictability. Any society would react to this kind of threat by seeking protective measures. Americans, leadership and public alike, were particularly likely to invest massively in order to reduce the gap between terrorism and predictability and to seek to retaliate for the violation of security. It is in this domain also, where predictability could not be achieved, that the temptation was particularly great to issue recurrent warnings that would seek both to diffuse responsibility and express the outraged feelings of a society thwarted, at least for a time, in one of its major goals. Terrorist incidents frighten any group directly involved. But they, arguably, loom especially large in a society in which risks of almost any sort, unless undertaken voluntarily, have become virtually unacceptable.

8

SELF-SCARING AND ADVERTISING
The Commerce Factor

Discussion of increasing American anxiety about fear and risk would be incomplete without serious attention to a concomitant national delight in self-scaring, through watching frightening films and TV shows and participating in terror-inducing rides (with greater abandon than people in places like Great Britain; the nation led the world in death-defying amusement park attractions from the early twentieth century onward). The national propensity reached such proportions by the turn of the twenty-first century that movies might simply be entitled "Scary," with the only justification a set of scenarios designed to cause chills; and one of the most touted of the "reality" TV series was called *Fear Factor*, though it seemed to deal as often with disgust, mainly around the consumption of worms, as with fear itself.

We deal here with entertainment patterns far more varied and ubiquitous than the apocalyptic genre discussed in chapter 4. Though cosmic destruction and alien invasion might be part of fear fare, the tremendous range of scare items did not mainly relate to the apocalyptic tradition or to unspoken anxieties about national power or the role of science. Many items indeed were much more old-fashioned, however sophisticated the special effects technology: stalking murderers, hauntings, ghosts, and demons, with targets mainly individuals or families, with no real implications for society at large.

What makes this larger genre interesting, in context of our overall argument, is its juxtaposition with so many efforts to limit fear and risk. Here's the central question at hand, after a brief description of this aspect of popular culture more generally. Of course, there were efforts at consistency, with well-meaning child psychologists and parents' groups seeking to restrict even vicarious fear exposure. Disney and other child-conscious entertainers ventured their intriguing sanitizations of older folk tales, like Cinderella, to reduce fear content (though Disney also provided a decent ration of fear even so). Attacks on violent comic books and later television and video games followed quite logically from the larger campaigns for emotional safety. But these attacks, interesting as they are, largely failed: the thirst for fear-soaked entertainment, and the commercial interest in producing this entertainment, simply could not be curtailed. Rating systems provided the only real constraint, and they had limited impact. Revealingly, attempts to regulate sexual content, though also porous, gained greater success than attacks on appeals to blood thirst and fear.

A second angle, applying to another facet of commercial culture, is also intriguing, and though harder to pin down actually more important than recreational fear: how, if at all, was fear used in the nation's burgeoning advertising industry? Advertising gurus frequently discussed fear and occasionally acknowledged its explicit use to sell goods. But it was also obvious that fear was used sparingly, and rarely reached any serious emotional pitch. American advertising may indeed have been particularly restrained in this regard, though comparisons must be somewhat speculative. Aversion to fear actually helped define American advertising for many decades. At the end of the twentieth century however, floodgates opened as growing sensitivities to fear provided irresistible opportunities to sell goods—in a pattern that could intensify fears in turn.

This chapter deals, then, with fear in mainstream American popular and commercial culture. Open enjoyment of fear is the most obvious aspect here, but more subtle commercial messages need attention as well. How do these two facets connect? Given the pleasure many Americans took in artificial fear, why did the emotion not loom larger earlier in the otherwise frenzied interest in selling goods? And if there was a hint of a distinctive American approach to fear in popular culture, how did it relate to the deeper-seated anxieties about the emotion and about risk more generally?

Ultimately, it was not entertainment fear that added significantly to the reshaping of the emotion in American public life. When the less heralded commercial approach to fear, long respectful of the larger emotional standards of the twentieth century, yielded fully to more blatant exploitation—just a quarter century ago—commercial fears became a key element in increasing emotional sensitivity along with the socialization standards and the aversion to risk.

As Americans spent more and more time with movies and then television it was not surprising that they became increasingly accustomed to taking emotional cues from media. Engagement with fictional emotions could easily bleed over into a reliance on media for emotional guidance in real life, particularly when public events were involved. This chapter deals with the impact of the "media-ization" of emotion in terms both of artifice and of reality.

CHOOSING TO BE FRIGHTENED

People in various cultures—most cultures and possibly all cultures—have scared themselves, at least partly voluntarily, since human societies with language capabilities developed. They've told stories about monsters, dangers, macabre deaths; they've organized rituals and dances that are designed to provoke anxiety if not outright fear in their audiences; sometimes of course they've gone farther than that, and done directly terrifying things like offering human sacrifices. These activities presumably have various functions. They help socialize groups, like young men, who need to think about fear in order to prepare for later life activities, including initiation into adulthood. They acknowledge but also perhaps provide some sense of mastery over the uncertainties of the physical environment. They represent efforts to conciliate divinities, spirits, and other forces outside normal control. And the frights they generate, though quite real and surely often troubling, correspondingly provide some sense of perverse pleasure. They certainly can help different members of the society bond together, through the shared experience and the satisfaction derived from dealing with difficult emotions without collapsing. This latter also helps explain why many societies use fear occasions as part of childhood socialization, though there is probably some outright sadism involved as well from adults burdened by children without wanting to say so directly.[1]

Point one, then, admittedly pretty obvious, is that our penchant for scaring ourselves in contemporary America is not just a recent invention requiring entirely novel explanations. The longstanding motives for self-scaring obviously still apply, overriding (at least for some people—contemporary self-scaring is not a uniform delight) any constraints that might result from newer discomforts with fear.

Point two, self-scaring took a new turn in Western society, including the United States, in the late eighteenth to early nineteenth centuries. This was the time in which Gothic novels, the early mystery story under the pens of masters like Edgar Allan Poe, and new kinds of literary monsters like Frankenstein began to gain wide popularity.

Part of this efflorescence reflected growing literacy and also the decline of traditional villages and attendant oral cultures of fright—in other words, aspects of the new mechanisms did not involve real innovation so much as replacements for older sources of cultural fear. But most authorities—and this is a field full of interesting analysis, for it is not self-evident why such elaborate devices for voluntary fear prosper so—believe that certain modern needs also explain the upsurge of literary outlets. First, for many middle-class readers, expectations of fear in real life declined; there was less probable exposure to actual terror. With better policing and more residential segregation, for example, likelihood of experiencing violent crime went down—for the types of people who provided readership for the new genres. Fictional fear, in other words, helped provide some pleasant spice in lives that were otherwise fairly secure and, perhaps, a bit boring. (It is worth noting that the concept of boredom developed at precisely this point: artificial scares were and are one of the antidotes to this modern malady.)[2] Further, most analysts continue, new interest in fictional fear followed from the growing official emphases on science and rationality. It became harder really to argue that the environment was populated by monsters and ghosts, but fictional counterparts helped preserve some needed balance against excessive predictability and regularity. This motive could relate directly, of course, for the need for some alternative to growing security. Fiction might, finally, have expressed some real new fears, about potential excesses of science and technology, which could not be explicitly voiced lest one seem backward and antimodern. New kinds of imaginings (like Frankenstein) easily suggest this further extension.

So, extending point two: current American self-scaring builds on some new motivations that are at least two centuries old in Western culture, including a need for some imaginary antidotes to undue security and rationality. Here too, we are not dealing with entirely novel factors, but with some functions that have survived and, for certain Americans, have modified or overridden the twentieth-century distaste for fear. Many twentieth-century fictions have reused themes and creations from the burst of fear imaginings that developed in Victorian times, including, of course, the Frankenstein monster itself.

Thus, contemporary American popular culture, where fear is concerned, displays some intriguing inconsistencies. The very real innovations about shunning fear and risk simply do not entirely conquer older impulses—both human-in-general and modern Western—to expose oneself to fictional but undeniable fright. Many Americans accept the innovations, and really do work on real-life fears in new ways compared to their Victorian predecessors, but they also indulge some more traditional quirks that have their own explanations. This is not simply an abstract contradiction. In the later twentieth century, as we have seen, many conscientious parents worked hard to eliminate any exposure to fear in their children's Halloweens—organizing cute costumes and parties that would keep kids off the streets and away from potentially scary "tricks"—while also indulging the same kids in frightening amusement park rides or movies. Really consistent parents, of course, often worried as well about bloodthirsty films or comic books, which sober experts warned against; but more parents concentrated on reducing real-life fears for kids without worrying quite so much about fictional exposures that tapped into the older traditions of self-scaring.

But there is a third point: the use of fears in popular culture changed yet again in the early twentieth century—the changes on the whole intensifying as the century wore on. We now can scare ourselves in ways unavailable in traditional societies of an earlier day, although there is some real continuity with themes and needs of the past. This is a really surprising change: just at the time when concern about fear was developing in new ways, popular culture introduced new mechanisms for voluntary or semivoluntary fright. We're not, then, simply identifying inconsistencies between contemporary fear standards and some older, atavistic traditions, though this is part of the story. We're faced with some deliberate intensification of cultural fear opportunities just at the point when, logically, one might have expected some retreat. This poses the real analytical problem.

We begin, if briefly, by examining the evidence for the escalation itself. Entertainment thrills increased in several ways around of the turn of the century, further expanding in the 1920s. In amusement parks, the roller coaster first arrived in the 1880s, a distinctively American ride though building on Russian and French precedents. The 1920s formed a classic decade for this ride, whose deliberate appeal to fear and overtones of plunging disaster differed from the mechanical rides introduced in British beach parks in the same period.[3] Sites like Coney Island enhanced the challenge of the roller coaster itself by taking some rides through "hell"—adding visual frights to the physical plunges. American themes doubtless reflected the nation's more religious atmosphere, in which amusement park rides might help express some transcendent fears that had declined on the other side of the Atlantic. World War I disasters were far closer to home in Britain, constraining the motif in amusement parks, in contrast to a blander American environment in which mechanical challenges might seem desirable spice.[4]

The 1920s also saw the increasing introduction of the horror film. Fright movies often built on nineteenth-century literary themes—

Frankenstein was a famous case in point. But they disseminated fear both more widely and more graphically than ever before.[5] Certain horror film stars, like Boris Karloff or Bela Lugosi, developed huge reputations by the 1930s through their concentration on this genre. The Depression decade also saw steady innovations in special effects. By 1940, after a slightly slow start, scary films had taken over from literature the primary role in frightening people; in the words of one scholar, they "owned the place."[6]

Literature itself, however, was not stagnant. The advent of horror anthologies in the 1920s showed the capacity of this field, as well, to innovate and to legitimize. A pulp magazine, *Weird Tales*, debuted in 1924, full of bloodshed—and horror stories generally became increasingly graphic. The advent of horror comics, soon afterward in 1940, again represented further popularization and a growing penchant for the disgusting, as they filled with pictures of disembowelment and putrefaction.[7]

And the major genres continued to develop greater capacities to terrify. Roller coasters declined in popularity for a bit, but then revived after 1959 with Disney's Space Mountain. From then on into the early twenty-first century, amusement parks competed with larger, faster, more challenging rides each year. Disney and others enhanced the fear by running rides through special scenery. Space Mountain, with its futuristic scenarios, could give riders the sense not only of surviving a spectacular ride, but of conquering the future. Top Gun, based on a movie, gave riders the impression of aerial combat, again adding a realistic-seeming (if entirely artificial) assignment in courage to the challenge of the ride itself. Several rides employed NASA crews to inaugurate the trip, helping early riders to associate their achievement with the courage of space flights. At Six Flags, riders on the Great American Scream Machine received a red badge of courage.

A similar intensification occurred in films and, increasingly, on television. From the late 1950s onward, the use of color to demonstrate copious quantities of gore and blood became standard. Special effects ran rampant in films like *The Texas Chainsaw Massacre* of 1974. Acts of violence increased, and older hesitations about showing death agonies vanished. By the 1980s "slasher" films multiplied the number of incidents of mayhem: an average of ten victims per slasher movie in 1980 had risen to fourteen by 1989. Monster movies also escalated, with increasingly repulsive and terrifying invaders. Young children, used in 1930s horror movies to provide an innocent contrast to violence and villainy—the child sitting next to Frankenstein, playing with flowers (1931)—now themselves become creatures of evil, possessed of death and corruption. And while many horror films were low-budget and fleeting, classics like *Psycho* and *Jaws*, and some of the blockbuster apocalyptic offerings, demonstrated the potential for massive audience and box office success.

By the twenty-first century, the wave of scare media began to command increasing attention on the major television networks. Creatures from outer space, menacing invasions, hideous insects, all often conventionally complete with bloodied female victims, dominated the new show list in 2005, for example. The surge was additionally interesting because the intended audience went well beyond adolescent males. As with movies earlier, observers wondered if this frenzy reflected the growing fears in the American public, allowing indirect venting of hostility to outsiders but veiled through the space alien motif, or whether the presentation of such ridiculous frights actually eased real life anxiety. One thing was clear: the networks had become fear factories.

By virtually every measure—availability of audiences, sheer numbers of rides and productions, escalation of themes, and enhancement of deliberately provocative special effects—Americans gained increasing opportunities to frighten themselves during the turn-of-the-century decades, building on the acceleration already launched by the 1920s. And while not all of this was distinctively American—roller coasters ultimately spread to Europe, the Japanese proved inventive in violent and scary films and effects—the United States was the epicenter of this fear production.

The contrast to the new fear standards spreading during the same period could not be more striking. A bevy of critics, of course, sought consistency. Attacks on violent comics, films, and later video games featured abundant claims about the psychological damage inflicted by deliberate fear. Experts who urged bans or at least restrictions on popular culture tried valiantly to bring it in line with the fear criteria applied to other aspects of limited life. And, through Production Codes, occasional voluntary restraint, and age-graded rating systems, they periodically won some limited success.[8]

Obviously, however, they did not win the war. Fright-based popular culture advanced steadily, which returns us to the question of causation. Indeed, the advance may pose the further question of primacy: did the pious fear standards matter, when entertainment filled so extensively with images and experiences designed to frighten, indeed to terrify? Even granting the power of earlier traditions—age-old and Victorian alike—why the intensification in precisely the decades when, judging by official socialization standards, it should not have occurred?

Several factors intertwine, and some of them significantly modify the apparent inconsistencies. First, some authorities have claimed that fictional fear actually helps audiences overcome real fear, making dangerous environments seem less menacing because of the mastery of fright in artificial settings. Terry Heller makes this claim for terror literature, particularly with regard to fears generated by advancing science and technology.[9] Stories, and presumably films, that show scientists themselves fleeing from monsters, but whose fears readers and audiences can themselves survive, assist adjustment to genuine threats with less fear than would otherwise arise. In this case, for some people, and despite the clucking of the experts, there may be no inconsistency between a desire to limit fear in real life and a certain passion for cultural opportunities to hone self-control.

Four other explanations are more plausible for American audiences generally, and while they do not erase some possible inconsistency they ultimately, in combination, do explain the simultaneity of new levels of distaste for fear and the contemporary intensification of fear fare in popular culture.

First, of course, is sheer technological capacity, outstripping standards of any sort. Faster and higher roller coasters, graphic spurts of dazzling red blood, and devastating earthquakes before your very eyes happened partly because, for the first time, their production was possible. Audience response was not inevitable: the technology card does not work by itself. But some appeal, despite fear norms, may have resulted from the steady changes in capability, drawing in certain participants almost in spite of themselves.

Second, and more significant, are new needs, some of which related to the growing distaste for fear, some of which might partially supersede the distaste. Fear in entertainment resulted, first, from the growing convergence of gender socialization. For boys and girls attending the same schools, participating in similar activities, a felt need, however atavistic, for new ways to demonstrate gender identity clearly fed the escalation of fears in entertainment. Boys could show they were boys by sneering off fear, going to the bloodiest movies possible, riding the most challenging items amusement parks had to offer. Girls were girls because they could show their greater anxiety, depending on their manly escort to cajole them onto the roller coaster or to tide them through a blood and guts film. And the fictional fear gamely fed the gender imagery by multiplying the number of female victims of slashers and monsters, thus confirming the femaleness of vulnerability.[10]

Fictional fright and violence also had some relationship to changes in the actual experience of death: the chronological overlap here was no accident. People for whom death became more remote, in some ways scarier, needed to see death represented, often fearfully, as a means of acknowledging the new terrors of death but also, in the process, possibly lessening them. Here again, popular fear fare and aversion to fear could actually go hand in hand, albeit in complicated ways. Watching death on the screen was undeniably scary—a seeming contradiction to the larger mantra to avoid fear—but in fact served to reduce anxiety over death—an ultimate if tense consistency.[11]

Finally, entertainment fears responded directly to the growing security of real life aside from death, and even to the careful aversion to fear in childhood socialization. Here too, there were new needs, though the connection had begun a century earlier. Many people found fictional fear an essential spice because of the blandness and caution of their daily lives. They did not contest the removal of fear from real life, but they needed an artificial counterpoint. As one scholar has noted, fictional terror in this sense responded to the "absence of risk."[12] It may in this sense actually have helped people accept their secure daily routines, because they had a safe but dramatic alternative when they caught the latest horror film.

Many teenagers, most specifically, reacted directly to the emotional constraints they had sensed as children, particularly around fear, using commercial culture to declare their (partial, and often temporary) independence. Courage as spectators might be a lame response (which a minority of teenagers supplemented by more flagrant acts of daredeviltry), but it did allow some sense of defiance against adult anxieties.

But here, fear-provoking entertainment demonstrated important divisions in the American public, who responded both to the entertainment, and to the new distaste for fear, in different ways. Gender was part of this—males flocked to fear sites far more frequently than females. Age was another key element. The fact was that a fundamental cause of the scope of fear fare was commercial discovery of the buying power of teenagers, particularly teenage boys. Here were the main occupants of the more daring roller coasters and the basic audience for the endless round of summer horror specials. For this group, clearly, a cultural alternative to the larger efforts to control fear and to reassure was part of the establishment of identity and independence. A few went still further, and participated not only in spectated fear but in real if foolish challenges, like daredevil automobile driving or bungee jumping. Larger numbers were apparently satisfied by watching movies that adults disapproved of. In some cases, interests continued into early adulthood. By the 1980s and 1990s sociologists had identified a hardcore group of "horror mavens"; subscribers to such new outlets as the *Gore Gazette*, who were overwhelmingly males aged fifteen to forty-five.[13]

Fear fare, in other words, simply has to be approached in terms of differentials. People who did not care for it, whose standards most literally echoed the larger campaigns to control fear, simply did not participate—particularly large numbers of adults and other females. A component in this group managed actually to ridicule the culture. Humorous takeoffs on horror movies began to emerge by the 1950s, in films like *Abbott and Costello Meet Frankenstein*, and spoofs of later gore movies appeared as well. A subculture also emerged, however, not necessarily rejecting fear control standards in real life but delighting in a spicy contrast.

A few people, amid these differentials, were undoubtedly adversely affected by the culture. Experts noted that many young children encountered some fearful media item that had lasting impact—even when they seemingly volunteered for the viewing. Whether this damaged them, or simply lingered in memory, could be debated. One study of Midwestern college students found 90 percent who remembered a media fright reaction from childhood or adolescence, with 26 percent reporting a "residual anxiety," including prolonged sleep difficulties or finding oneself horrified at the sight of blood. For some of this group, clearly, whatever their intentions in watching fear fare (or being cajoled into watching), there was some real inconsistency with the larger fear standards in American life. Here, in fact, fear fare might actually increase resistance to fear and difficulties in handling fear-provoking situations.[14]

The surge of fear-inducing entertainments, in sum, relates to the mainstream socialization concerning the emotion in complicated ways. For many who learned to avoid the scary movies, or who actively fought the dominant media, there was little inconsistency. For others, exposure to media fright, at least for a period in life, actually helped train in mastering fear (including fear of death) or served as a harmless cultural option that allowed acceptance of cautious fear controls in real life. For still others, the culture complicated fear control—while possibly enhancing the desire for it and contributing to a sense of the dangers of the contemporary social environment.

But there is a final point that applies to most groups as well, in context of the larger socialization standards. Media fear was, ultimately, controlled fear in itself. It might provoke classic somatic fear reactions for a brief time—faster heartbeats, clamminess, even shrieks—but this was a finite, spectator experience, not the real thing. The largest lesson it might teach, even for many of the adolescent boys who seemed so eager, was that one should always be able to end fear, by turning off the video or getting off the ride. There were no real risks in media fear, no fundamental contradictions to a risk-averse society—indeed, in many respects, the notion that risks should be limited was ultimately confirmed. Here was the greatest potential impact for the same society when real dangers did emerge, when fear and risk could not simply be switched off. Aversion to actual fear, the impulse to expect limits and reassurance, could easily survive the admittedly dramatic American addiction to simulated emotion.

FEAR IN SALES: COMMERCIAL STANDARDS

Media fear fare was only a part of the larger commercial context that surrounded Americans during the twentieth century. Fear also played a role in selling products of other types. Here, however, there was greater harmony with the standards applied to socialization, for many crucial decades. With one category a partial exception, fear was used gingerly in advertising until very recently, and commercial messages largely reinforced beliefs that risk could and should be controlled.

Overall, historians of American advertising have noted a pronounced turn toward greater emotionality around 1900. To be sure, there are a few examples of print ads as early as the 1860s that depicted early, tragic death as a result of not taking the manufacturer's health pills, but these are exceptional. Fear may have been much more widely used in oral solicitations, for example in urging poor people to buy insurance policies with warnings about the indignity of pauper's graves and bereft orphans, but records here are sparse.[15]

As advertising expanded, with increasing pictorial content, fear undoubtedly played some role in the commercial emotional arsenal. One study of magazines in the 1920s and 1930s, for example, finds fear appeals, of some sort, in about 15 percent of all advertisements (somewhat over one-third of all emotion-directed efforts); magazines aimed at a lower-class audience, where fear may have been more common in any event, could go as high as 42 percent (the case for *True Story*), whereas high-toned periodicals avoided fear altogether. A particular target, especially for the lower classes, involved threats to the safety or health of children. By the 1920s advertisers readily referred to "scare copy" as one of the emotional directions available and, at times, effective. It was also true that some cheaper advertising media, such as direct mail advertisements, long showed a greater willingness to use fear to sell—and this continued through the twentieth century and beyond.[16]

Certain products were prone to some use of fear: insurance was an obvious example. Hygiene items also indulged in a certain amount of fear-mongering. Germs and social ostracism could easily escalate into jobs lost, romances ended—unless the product in question was purchased as soon as possible.[17] A Lysol disinfectant ad, in the 1920s, depicted two women murmuring about a third, as she passed with her husband, that "she looks old enough to be his mother"—because her hygiene was inadequate. The Depression prompted even greater emotional vigor, from manufacturers increasingly desperate to sell products. A dancer collapses on stage, in one ad, because of "closed pores"—readers should quickly buy a new soap—"In the meantime, don't take needless chances." A Listerine mouthwash ad, describing "her last party," featured a woman who died because she forgot to rinse after catching a chill. Scott tissues played up the disease angle as well, with an operating room scene: "A single contact with inferior toilet tissue may start the way for serious infection—and a long, painful illness." In another motif, women in story ads periodically lost their husbands because they failed to purchase essential beauty products, or a couple, entertaining the boss, failed in the crucial first impression because their furniture was so out of date. Between 1929 and 1933, a series of companies played up possible deficiencies in children: mothers who didn't serve Campbell Soup might be losing their chance for connection with their children, whose characters were fully formed in such a brief period. Poor foods—remediable if one purchased Postum—could also caused failures at school. Insurance notices hit the same theme, clearly reflecting Depression fears: fathers who failed to buy life insurance risked depriving their sons of education.[18]

Most of this, however, was fairly tame stuff. Few efforts really tried to evoke graphic fears. Even when television came on the scene, with its greater visual potential, there were almost no literal appeals to fear as emotion. Rather, what "scare copy" usually involved was an appeal to anxieties, to reasonably rational worries about health issues or not measuring up to social standards—a particular issue for women. Advertisers largely heeded the developing culture, in not trying to use visceral fear lest it backfire. Agencies on occasion even disputed their clients' more exploitative wishes: the writers for the Scott tissues ad objected to the material about infection and hospitalization, though in this case they were overruled. The basic emotional emphases in American advertising had far more to do with positive fantasies, with invocations to join in the American dream, than with appeals to fear. And this common dissociation from fear occurred despite the growing psychological sophistication of the advertising community, its increasing reliance on scientific research. For whatever reason—and an implicit understanding of the distastes of modern American culture was generally a key element—fear was not seen as a useful way to sell goods.[19]

Here, of course, advertising fare differed greatly from entertainment trends. Graphic violence routinely shown to titillate could not be used to sell goods—even goods directed at target audiences like teenage males. Clearly, ads hewed closer to the standard norms that were developing around fear, and the less-voluntary composition of their audience-imposed constraints as well.

Indeed, again with a few exceptions such as appeals for smoke alarms or other products inextricably associated with disaster, scare copy if anything receded in American advertising in the middle decades of the century. The expansion of middle-class standards, and these standards' embrace of the goal of avoiding fear, undergirded this modest shift. In this respect too, commercial advertising largely confirms the advancing hold of the mainstream culture toward fear. Periodic articles in advertising journals, from the 1940s onward, speculated about fear as an untapped commercial resource, but the musings generated little forward motion. And—though the subject deserves more attention—some national distinctiveness shone through as well. Contrasts with foreign advertisements could be striking—where television, for example, more commonly displayed graphic heart attacks or pictures of a Grim Reaper in the aid of a particular product. It was simply not constructive to evoke fear so directly in the United States—at least where commerce was involved, at least until the century's end. Even in 2000, referring to older Americans brought up in the more genteel decades of advertising, industry authorities urged promoters to avoid scare tactics, because they were simply counterproductive.[20]

It remains true that modern advertising could enhance the fear culture in two respects. First, while scare copy did not seek to strike terror, it could depict a dangerous social and physical environment. The steady increase in hygiene standards, so often noted in American commercial culture, did this quite deliberately. Practices not long before regarded as perfectly normal, like spitting or sweating, now became not only unacceptable but positively dangerous. People were surrounded by germs, odors, and potential social disapproval. None of this was deeply frightening, but the representations could enhance anxiety and further a sense of one's own or one's family's vulnerability.[21]

But further, of course, these environmental risks could be resolved. The newest breath mint or nutritional product would do the trick. The conscientious consumer, observant of advertising, not only sought new pleasures; he or she also sought security. With rare exceptions, there was nothing that could be depicted that could not be remedied: risk was the result of buyer ineptitude. Indeed, another scare copy mantra insisted that any fear evoked must be explicitly resolved, or the ad could have no impact. Here, quite clearly, a vital plank of contemporary American culture was both confirmed and furthered.[22]

Additionally—for even commercials had their complexities—one distinct category of advertising conventionally took a radically different tack, and appealed to fear very directly: the public service and political category. Here there were no products to sell, with rare exceptions, but a set of behaviors to modify, or a particular candidate to vote for. And in this domain, which increased in salience with new political tactics and new public service communications rules by the later twentieth century, no holds were barred. It was perfectly legitimate to scare people silly about smoking, or teenage driving, or unsafe sex. Even the nuclear threat could be fair game, as in a powerful though controversial 1964 ad for Lyndon Johnson that showed a child, picking daisy petals, suddenly replaced by the mushroom cloud of an atomic bomb—linking the atomic menace to Johnson's opponent, Barry Goldwater. George Bush (senior) would have similar luck with a different but similarly dramatic fear ad in 1988, a menacing black man who seemed to threaten rampant crime. Public service and political emotional appeals were direct, backed by increasingly sophisticated psychological research.[23] Experts like Howard Lowenthal and his associates demonstrated that the greater the fear, the more likely the behavioral modification.[24] Mild fear, or even great fear not accompanied by specific instructions about successful responses, would simply not work. Here too, risks could be accepted if the advertisement promised remedy; there was no contradiction to the idea of avoiding risk. But in contrast to product notices, high emotion could be justified precisely because it was unsettling, with the goal of modifying behaviors. Efforts to persuade women to obtain mammograms, for example, worked much better when the subjects were threatened with cancer if they did not oblige, than when they were told that most likely the test would confirm their good health. Here, one might argue, is a constructive use of fear as caution, but a sign also of public exploitability through the emotion. This type of advertising explicitly, and quite possibly justifiably in many instances, not only increased a sense of risk, but baited American distaste for fear—which is why the ads might work so well.

Finally, and this is the most important point, the linkage between fear and advertising more generally began to shift decisively in the 1980s and 1990s. More heated competition amid new product lines; new latitude in advertising items like prescription drugs all encouraged new tactics. The increase in public service and political notices, and their shrillness, factored in as well. But there was also the audience side: many Americans were becoming edgier, easier to scare and ever more eager to escape their fears. While continuing to promise a world safer from risk, if only the right products were purchased or candidates voted for, advertising began to contribute more directly to fear culture, and to exploit this culture, than it had in previous decades. Its impact, in promoting fright, began to rival entertainment fare, and it might reach a broader audience, an audience with less capacity to opt out of the message. Even the industry staple of not evoking fear without a precise remedy was increasingly violated.

Straws in the wind began to accumulate in the late 1980s. Growing health concerns triggered change in the media. The AIDS scare allowed toilet seat manufacturers, new to the mass advertising racket, to take advantage—as one candidly noted, "It was a tough sell, at first, before the scare was in the air." Citing a poll that showed 79 percent of Americans believing that diseases can be transmitted by sitting on a toilet seat—beliefs that were erroneous—advertisers found fear to be money in the bank. "We don't capitalize on the fears"—one guru disingenuously claimed—"but they're very powerful." Rising fears of crime—even as rates were actually falling—provided another spur. Graphic TV ads featured masked intruders racing through suburban houses, in the interests of promoting home security devices. Pepper sprays and antitheft devices on cars also used fear techniques and implicit exaggeration of the problems involved. It's important not to overdo the innovation here: the goal was still to claim that risks could be reduced, if not eliminated, with the proper product. But the emotional overtones were stronger than before, and the desire to point to vulnerabilities more explicit. One safety purveyor noted, in 1994: "People I've done programs for feel very out of control."[25]

Home safety products became increasingly direct in their appeals. A carbon monoxide detector was promoted, on TV and in print media, by showing snapshots of people felled by the gas: "Get the new First Alert...before it's too late."[26]

Somewhat less predictably, ever more heated competition in the computer field encouraged references to fear. IBM became known for "fear, uncertainty, and doubt," or FUD campaigns. The goal was to show situations in which people risked dangers like job loss if they did not rely on a time-tested provider like Big Blue. One observer speculated that worry about losing out in the dot-com boom prompted e-business advertisers to use fear—here, of loss of business—simply out of desperation, and the unfamiliarity of the product field made many consumers a willing audience.[27] Advertising experts claimed that not only rivalry, but also growing consumer skepticism about standard commercial claims prompted the turn to more fear-based messages.

And while some worried about generating yet additional skepticism, the need to capture attention seemed compelling.

The increase of direct mail appeals contributed to change as well, in both commercial and public service sectors. A consultancy firm might tout, in huge letters, the need to "protect your firm against federal fines of up to $7,500."[28] Health magazines tried to lure subscribers by pitches along the following lines, again in bold headings: "These prescription drugs recently killed nearly 70,000 Americans in a single year." Apocalyptic overtones might even creep in, in what one authority called "the world is ending (but don't tell Neiman Marcus)" approach.[29] Imminent economic depression, the more personal threat of job loss, concerns about the environment embellished for fundraising—all could feed advertising that more blatantly appealed to fear. By 1998 an advertising industry publication claimed quite simply: "Forget *Profiler* and the *X-Files*, the real terror on TV right now comes at commercial breaks." Culprits ranged from the census bureau, stating that communities would lose schools and firehouses if people did not turn in their forms, to Lysol ads that raised the specter of "more aggressive" bacteria living in toilet bowls, to car manufacturers that began to show wreckage footage as a means of touting their safety features.[30]

A final contributor was the increasing opportunity to market prescription drugs, where dire health issues could be legitimate subject matter, the emotions enhanced by the obligatory list of awe-inspiring side effects. In a society already intensely nervous about health, the drug commercial, sometimes with graphic details about the erosion of stomach walls or arterial blockage, built on and enhanced fears quite directly.[31]

Then, of course, came September 11, which did not create the new advertising mood but unquestionably intensified it. Revealingly, articles evaluating the new industry penchant had referred to commercial terrorism well before the attacks: but now the link became explicit.[32] An ad for a mental health drug featured a woman admitting, "I'm always thinking something terrible is going to happen. I can't handle it." Insurance companies, bottled water producers, providers of medical devices, even private plane companies could refer to vulnerability and the need to escape fear more directly than ever, and all could profit as a result. "FUD" became an advertising mantra because the emotions were so pervasive in the public already. Public service ads grew more blatant as well. As one commentator noted, "If you're going to spend cash money trying to persuade (i.e., terrify) voters, why waste it on fairness and context. The whole idea...is to present an issue in stark terms, and never mind if the starkness exaggerates the threat."[33]

And the subject might be remote from terrorism, the link being the emotion involved. A phone company in Chicago, warning that making a wrong decision about a service provider was dangerous, illustrated by showing an office that changed cleaning services and encountered a mad floor waxer whose work caused people to slide across the office, crashing through glass, flailing and screaming loudly. The link, fanciful enough, was purely emotional: be really scared of change. A new sanitary napkin claimed that rival products "cause many kinds of cancer," along with birth defects and toxic shock syndrome—claims whose blatant factual inaccuracy was masked, presumably, by the emotions roused.[34]

Again, new e-technology contributed as well. The dramatic increase of advertising through spam created the need for attention-getters, and once more fear could serve well. As one industry observer put it, "This shift toward a calculated attempt to frighten consumers into making purchases is very well timed."[35]

Contemporary advertising had long relied on emotionality. What was changing was the willingness to explicitly evoke fear as a core part of the emotional pitch, and the growing range of products willing to join this particular bandwagon. It was hard, amid this barrage, and particularly as environmental anxiety increased in any event, not to worry that one had forgotten to buy several of the huge number of products now crucial to safety.

All of this combined, of course, with the growing surge of so-called reality television that also tended to magnify risk and fear. In 2006, for example, ABC dramatized a presumed bird flu epidemic, using the most extreme figures for death and destruction and noting explicitly that this, not global warming or terrorism, was what Americans really had to fear. It may be hoped that the fear-inducing themes of the contemporary media will someday seem just as strange as the idyllic family imagery of the 1950s, for the current fad is no less laden with artifice and manipulation.

THE CHANGING ROLE OF THE MEDIA

Commercial culture, in sum, confirmed and enhanced the contemporary socialization toward fear in many ways. The admittedly difficult combination of fear fare and advertising justifies this conclusion. There was considerable hesitation about rousing impassioned fears *unless* they could be quickly resolved or ended, or launched with the knowledge of fundamentally secure environment that would not be rocked by a slasher film or a gravity-defying amusement park ride. At the same time, the commercial culture—again, both standard and public service ads and the knowledge of a fear fare—might exacerbate a sense of risks in the environment and a belief that they could and should be resolved. This proclivity increased as the twenty-first century loomed, even before September 11 and certainly afterward. The emphasis on risks challenged the fact that, in reality for most Americans, most of the time, the environment was becoming more secure. Commercial culture taught many Americans that mild fears might be assuaged because they could lead to resolution: the ad-induced anxiety that prompted the comforting purchase of a better disinfectant or the slight edginess about seeing a horror movie that could be calmed by the knowledge one could shut one's eyes or at most sit through the 105 minutes until it was definitively over. Commercial culture could, however, rough up the socialization toward fear around the edges—the few people really deeply unsettled by horror entertainment or those jolted by a too-graphic public service notice that failed to say how the danger could be ended.

At the same time, the recent shift in approach, to more extensive emotional manipulation, demands emphasis in its own right. During most of the twentieth century, commercial outlets for fear in entertainment, carefully hedged through a realization of ultimate safety, combined with a level of restraint in advertising that harmonized easily with the growing aversion to fear in larger socialization patterns. But then the harmony snapped. In fear as in sex, advertisers increasingly grasped that they could get by with more than their predecessors had ventured. The temptation to sell goods by exploiting fear, the temptation indeed to guide public emotions through media signals, became too great. But the shift involved more than this. What the media increasingly understood was that the aversion to risk had itself forged a new relationship with fear. The desire to avoid fear remained; but the need to master risk heightened vulnerabilities—which the media became all too ready to utilize. At this point, only buying a particular product or selecting a particular candidate might square the circle, reducing risk once again, and reviving the capacity to escape an unacceptable emotion. In the process, of course, the larger environment might be perceived as newly dangerous, despite the absence of much by the way of objective deterioration.

Not surprisingly, by the early twenty-first century, some observers were adding exploitation of fears of epidemics to the list of media intensifications and manipulations in American life. One author criticizes the Centers for Disease Control and Prevention for what he calls "public displays of worrying that always made us worry more," while also castigating the media (yet again) for their faddish pursuit of one disease outbreak after another in a shameless pursuit of ratings. Thus in

2002 the nation was encouraged to agonize over West Nile virus, which took less than three dozen lives—yet in the following year four times that number perished with very little commentary since the media had found a new darling, SARS, with which to belabor public anxieties (SARS has yet to kill a single American). These alarums—the current one is bird flu, where estimates over probable risk vary considerably—deserve evaluation. Whether warranted or not as a spur to appropriate precautions—in the short run, they seem to serve mainly to encourage panic buying of drugs of dubious utility—there is no question that the pattern adds to the escalation of fear messages in recent years.[36]

Commercial and public service culture worked within the new fear paradigm, though in the case of scary entertainment in somewhat complicated ways. It could confirm or enhance the paradigm in several respects, particularly with regard to risk avoidance. It could encourage people to seek escape from a dangerous environment and the emotions it generated—by buying particular products or by trying to calm the nerves after a movie that roused more tension than anticipated. But advertisements and fear fare could also produce some divisive responses that revealed important nuances in the contemporary emotional paradigm and its reception. Finally, both sides of the commercial culture, the entertainment fare and the advertising side, sharpened their promotion of fear over time—fairly steadily in the case of entertainment, with more deliberate innovation in the case of the pitchmen. The culture suggested that more Americans were getting scared by the turn of the century, with predictable resentment about facing the emotion; and the culture intensified the fears.

These developments operated within a broader context in which more and more Americans took serious emotional cues from media presentations. We have seen the importance of media signals in dealing with public reactions to death. National shock and mourning, whether over an individual tragedy like the Kennedy assassination or a collective incident like the Oklahoma City bombing, combined spontaneous sentiment with media orchestration that guided the outpourings of grief and outrage. Sympathy for victims could always be roused with a reference to young children. A hurricane strikes the Gulf Coast, television fastens on a crying baby (who, as child experts cynically noted, probably would have been crying at that time of day regardless of the storm), and Americans know they should respond emotionally. A fascinating kind of national community was emerging by the later twentieth century, giving Americans a sense of immediacy with the sufferings of strangers, as presented in the media, so long as they were co-nationals. This was why something like a child abduction in California would seem almost a backyard event in New Jersey, providing an exaggerated sense of threat with emotions at the ready. Disasters abroad, even in Canada, did not participate in this imagined community.[37] But given the size of the United States, there were tragedies aplenty to provoke emotional response. It was easy to believe, as many Americans did, that the social environment was deteriorating, because there were so many news items, albeit geographically scattered, to be taken to heart. Media involvement was always manipulative to a degree in this emotional setting, but it was not usually malicious. Media nevertheless added a novel factor to the construction of emotion. And where not just grief or sympathy, but outright fear was involved, the media input might take a more dubious turn. As one authority argued, fear risked becoming not simply a response to threat, but a larger cultural expression of a sense of uneasiness with the modern world—a steady diet of expectations of impending calamities, both man-made and natural. Developments in the past two decades suggest, indeed, that fear stimulation has become an overwhelming temptation for media in a variety of sectors, from commercial pitchmen to the fine arts.[38]

IV

The Exhaustion of War

9

AT YOUR OWN RISK

Growing American fearfulness has another face—the particular fear of threats from abroad. This chapter offers one comparative vantage point on the international targeting and its political context. We then turn to the broader modern experience as it reflects, but even more obviously encourages, a sense of foreign foreboding.

For many years, and with renewed gusto since Septmember 11, 2001, the U. S. Department of State has made it clear to potential American international travelers that the world is a scary place: the Department issues periodic Worldwide Cautions and Travel Warnings. The intentions behind the Department's travel advisories are sincerely designed to alert citizens to potential risks, while also minimizing situations where the Department might be taken to task for failure to anticipate problems. But the result, to the uninitiated, can be truly intimidating. Here is a microcosm of the ways American attitudes toward fear, risk, and things foreign have developed and combined over recent decades, and a contributor as well to the sense of high anxiety.

We return in this brief chapter to the issue of comparison, as well as to the ways that distinctive American fears blend with a desire to minimize risk, or responsibility from risk, where international issues are concerned. The special uneasiness with things foreign is central to analysis.

For there is a particular form of evidence that shows the intensity of American foreign fear, and also the complex union between official willingness to exploit fear, if not to encourage it outright, and the desire to step back from any involvement, legal or otherwise, in situations that might conceivably entail possible danger. The same evidence shows how government reactions intertwine with public perceptions of targets of fear.

The case in point involves official advisories about risks to American travelers in other countries. This was a hallowed genre during the cold war, designed to discourage visits to Communist nations. Even drives or train rides from West Germany to West Berlin, through but not really into the German Democratic Republic, were actively discountenanced, with American consular officials warning travelers about the horrors that might result from Communist interference with the trip—the vindictiveness of officials, the foul quality of East German jails, and so on. (In point of fact, the passage, while it involved a bureaucratic border crossing, was almost invariably uneventful.)

Terrorism, and resultant jumpiness back home, have amplified the cautionary impulse. Late in 2005, the State Department was specifically warning against travel to twenty-seven different countries, lumping countries as diverse as Iraq, the Philippines, Israel, and Colombia in its official travel advisories. Americans were not, to be sure, banned from travel to these areas, but they were urged not to take the gamble.

The presentation of Israel—where violence had, in fact, greatly receded—was an interesting case in point. The Department "urges U.S. citizens to carefully weigh the necessity of their travel...in light of the risks noted below." And government personnel were explicitly restricted within the country. The update admitted that terrorist attacks had declined, but insisted that "the potential for further violence remains high." A single incident (the bombing of a Tel Aviv night club, ten months earlier) was taken as a "reminder of the precarious security environment." The American government had "received information" that American interests within Israel could be the focus of terrorist attacks. Great danger lurked near restaurants, businesses, locations near U.S. government offices, and so on. Warnings about both public transportation and pedestrian zones made it unclear how one might get around—which was doubtless the point of this part of the exercise.

Warnings of this sort were well-intentioned. They called attention to undeniable issues, though a recent visitor to Israel/Palestine could easily dispute their tone. A clear problem was the tendency to lump unpleasantnesses over the previous two years together, as if they provided an immediate context for the present; a host of more benign recent developments were not taken into account, which confirmed the preference for exhortation and worry over ongoing risk assessment. As in many cases in the past, from the cold war onward, official advisories undeniably exaggerated the level of danger, even when there was no outright distortion. Americans who ignored the alarums rarely encountered as many problems as the worried bureaucrats had suggested. There was an element of crying wolf in the official approach that made it difficult to sort out the gradations that actually existed within an overgeneralized formal category.

And if the official travel advisories often raised questions, State Department comments on presumably safer nations were even more revealing. Take the United Arab Emirates as an example, again from late 2005. Here is a friendly state, though predominantly Arab and Muslim, with good, modern tourist facilities. But security concerns loom large, with a standard section on the possibility of terrorist attacks on U.S. citizens "throughout the world," and a highlighting of the risks of appearing in public or in any crowd situation. Or take Germany, not only a longstanding ally but also predominantly neither Arab or Muslim. Here, the safety and security section is bewilderingly peppered with exculpatory "howevers." Germany is largely free from terrorism, *however* its open borders allow terrorist groups to enter with anonymity. Security risk to travelers is low, *however* the country experiences a number of demonstrations every year on a "variety of political and economic themes." The police regulate the demonstrations, *nonetheless* the demonstrations could spread or turn violent. Skinheads sometimes attack foreigners. To be sure, Americans have not been specific targets here, *however* several Americans have reported assaults because they appear foreign. So, when in Germany, keep a careful eye out and check for current updates. At most, the State Department admits that it's safe to take the same precautions against ordinary crime that one would in an American city.

Clearly, an official culture has developed that finds threats almost everywhere, as the national aversion to risk is carried to debatable extremes. Small wonder that—in contrast to the situation in most developed nations—only a relatively modest minority of Americans even bother to apply for a passport. Or that even educated citizens often harbor exaggerated notions of danger with regard to certain whole regions.

As always, comparative assessments set the national patterns into considerable relief. French Foreign Ministry Web sites offer a particularly striking contrast, providing reasonably objective data about countries like the Emirates or Israel spiced by exceptionally rosy commentary on recent positive developments in relations with France and the latest on official exchanges of visits. The French, at least implicitly, are encouraged to look outward. Only a few extreme cases, like Iraq, command a different more cautionary tone

Britain, certainly terrorist conscious, provides a more nuanced contrast, but a contrast nevertheless. Like the United States, the British

Foreign Office singles out a number of risky countries—about the same number as in the U.S. case, in late 2005, though with some inexplicable variations in particulars. There is a more important difference: the British really isolate only two whole countries, seeing the remainder in terms of certain limited areas of danger. Thus Israel and a few parts of Palestine are fine, but stay away from the Gaza strip. The decline of violence during 2005 is carefully noted, though there are still some incidents and people should be "very careful about...personal security arrangements." Concerning the Emirates, the Foreign Office issues a general statement about the threat of terrorism and the need for vigilance in public places; here the tone is rather similar to that taken by the U.S. Department of State. But while Germany elicits some comment on threats from terrorism, the government is praised for recent counterterrorist successes and the initial Web site summary makes an unqualified statement: "most visits to Germany are trouble-free." The United States insistence on *howevers*, the dark clouds behind every silver lining, is missing altogether.

Bureaucracies are often cautious, and terrorism appropriately begets warnings. It would be unfair to make too much of the distinctive American approach—and certainly many experienced travelers have learned to take official warnings with large grains of salt (which leaves the question of more precise risk assessment sometimes up in the air, in this as in other matters of national interest).

The national approach is revealing, nevertheless. American officials are unusually eager to convey generalized worries—in comparison with greater British precision—and to find dangers even in clearly benign settings just because of their foreignness. The approach shares in the broader culture of globally oriented fears and the widespread desire to sidestep risk. Without question, the advisories encourage the same culture as well. It is easy to conclude, as many Americans have, that it's best to stay home—which helps keep the international truly foreign.

Further, the distinctive attitudes the advisories suggest spill over into distinctive policies. The United States has become measurably more timid, in recent years, than other nations afflicted with the terrorist threat, in a number of areas. The stiffening of American visa policy coincided with major intensifications of British and Australian efforts to attract foreign students, including Middle Easterners, to their universities—taking deliberate advantage of American anxiety. The immediate furor, in 2006, over the possibility that an Arab company would administer several American ports, was arguably another case in point, in which political manipulations—in this case, against the Bush administration—combined with knee-jerk emotional response to produce a debate that was not only misguided but that distracted from some very real, if less attended, vulnerabilities in the nation's harbors. Fearful excess in risk aversion offered a bad basis for reactions to international developments.

10

A DELUGE OF CRISES
Foreign Fears in the Past Century

In New York City, in 2005, a teacher asks her sixth-grade students to draw the images that they most associate with the United States. Well over half offer military scenes.[1] What they know of the nation, from their own lives, most obviously involves war. Their associations might well have been replicated by their predecessors in most decades since 1940. The militarization of the United States has been a powerful theme in contemporary history, and, not surprisingly, it has had psychological consequences.

This final source of American uneasiness, and at times outright fear, involves some familiar staples of twentieth-century American history. From the aftermath of World War I onward, many Americans encountered the world beyond their borders in terms of threats and responded often with anxiety, and sometimes with a pronounced desire to retreat into an isolationist safe haven. Some of the threats were acute, but many involved dangers undoubtedly more imagined than real. They need to be summarized, because despite their familiarity they are too rarely treated in sequence, and because they must be linked to the wider socialization about risk and fear that was developing during the same decades.

Two points are vital: First, repeated foreign threats created their own burden in American emotional life, particularly because they ran so obviously counter to the concomitant socialization against fear and risk. Second, both the prolonged experience, and its clash with expectations, help explain key focal points for fear—the tendency to move into emotional high gear when foreign sources seem to be involved. Here, of course, the exhaustion of decades of war can link with some of the oldest American fear traditions, including race and apocalyptic vision.

169

Foreign fear in one sense itself began early in the nation's experience, and some observers detect a recurrent theme emerging as early as the 1790s. At that point, tensions with revolutionary France, including French interference with American shipping, provoked the passage of the Alien and Sedition Acts of 1798. One of the most controversial laws in American history, the acts made it harder to become an American citizen and also allowed federal prosecution of vaguely defined acts of sedition, potentially allowing repression of virtually any political opposition. In fact, President John Adams implemented the acts carefully, deporting no aliens. But there was a chilling effect for dissidents and foreigners alike, and the memory of the moment, for the historically literate, has colored reactions since that time. Cynics note the propensity for politicians in power—at the time, the Federalist Party—to exaggerate foreign problems to enhance their hold on office and, more broadly, for conservative interests to use imagined dangers of revolutionary contagion to distract from social problems at home. Foreign developments, in other words, menace not so much ordinary Americans as the American hierarchy, but the issues are framed in terms of wider fears—in this case, of violence-soaked French revolutionaries well after the most radical moment in the French rising had passed. Certainly, the combination of drama abroad and domestic manipulation was to recur, particularly during the twentieth century.

There were few reasons, after the War of 1812, for significant concern about external diplomatic or military threat during the nineteenth century. The Monroe Doctrine of 1823 signaled a revealing hope that, under American leadership, foreign interference in the hemisphere could be kept at bay. In fact, the conflicting interests of the great powers, British desire to prevent major distractions in the hemisphere, and the availability of easier pickings in other parts of the world did more to limit outside intervention than did assertions from the United States. At the same time, American focus on North American expansion plus the achievement of independence throughout most of Latin America, combined with the lack of threat to United States security from that quarter, reduced apprehension as well. The result may certainly have contributed to a cocooned national culture, unusually dependent on a sense of removal from the storms and stresses of European or Asian diplomacy. But there was no reason for any particular emotional investment in larger diplomatic or military concerns.

Anxiety about foreigners, however, surfaced periodically, linking at times to the strain of racial fear that had been hardwired into American culture. Suspicion of new groups of immigrants, notably the Irish, Germans, and French Canadians, helped generate a short-lived but vividly named political movement, the Know-Nothings, shortly before the middle of the nineteenth century. The radical Paris Commune of 1871 generated another round of American bombast about foreign radicalism. Foreigners generally, and particular immigrant groups like Italian Americans, would also be held responsible for elements of rising labor strife and anarchism at the end of the nineteenth century.

Concerns about Asian immigration produced much more significant reactions in the 1880s. Worry about competition for jobs plus deep suspicion of Asian moral values, in a larger context of growing awareness of what the Kaiser Wilhelm II of Germany would dub the "Yellow Peril," prompted laws restricting immigration plus a good bit of residential segregation in major cities. Also in the 1890s, many Americans participated eagerly in the white slavery scare. Here, fears focused on the seizure of white women for sexual servitude in foreign centers like Argentina. Again, immigrants, including Jews, were widely suspected of serving as agents in the trade, though Jewish organizations quickly joined the antislavery movement. The fears were almost certainly exaggerated, in terms of the amount of actual trafficking that occurred. And Americans were not alone in their anxiety; West Europeans joined in as well. But the fears were certainly real enough in the minds of many concerned citizens, as they joined deep suspicions of a foreign menace with growing nervousness about the actual sexual proclivities of homegrown teenagers.[2]

These episodes helped keep alive a suspicion of the wider world, but they focused more on the immigrant potential to undermine presumed national virtue than on an actual, physical foreign threat. Here, it was the stress of unwonted American involvement in World War I, the subsequent desire to return to a normalcy unencumbered with foreign complexities, plus the icing of the Russian Revolution and the menace of Communism that produced a really new turn in the foreign department of American fear. Ongoing anxieties about the immigrant flood contributed, but there were genuinely new elements.

THE RED SCARE

World War I produced a wide climate of repression, initially directed against German agents and German Americans more broadly. As in other countries, wartime fears generated new restrictions on the press, as well as vigorous measures against potential spies. The fact that Americans entered the war reluctantly, having initially hoped to escape Old World contagion, may have made emotions particularly volatile.

An Espionage Act and another Sedition Act translated fears into practical police action.

What was more surprising, and more distinctively American, was the continued sense of embattled fear after the war itself ended. As is well known, despite the promptings of a more internationalist president, American sentiment quickly sought to recover normalcy defined in terms of isolation from foreign engagements (save economic activities vital to a global leader in capitalism). The combination of active labor strife—for example, a major Seattle dock strike in 1919 and other scattered violence—plus the fearsome example of Communist revolution in Russia, with threats of extensions elsewhere in Europe, generated the famous Red Scare of the early 1920s. Although there were at most seventy thousand professed Communists in the United States, leaders, headed by Woodrow Wilson's attorney general, A. Mitchell Palmer, proclaimed a nation under siege. In his essay "A Case Against the Reds," Palmer intoned that "tongues of revolutionary heat were licking the altars of the churches, leaping into the belfry of the school bell, crawling into the sacred corners of American homes, seeking to replace marriage vows with libertine laws, burning up the foundations of society." Wide popular support responded to these dramatic warnings.[3]

The twin focus of fear was social protest and foreign agents—the sense of threat from abroad was what justified a sweeping pattern of repression. The so-called "Palmer raids" began in 1919, rounding up thousands of anarchists and Communists and detaining many for long periods with no formal criminal charge. In December, in a highly publicized move, more than two hundred alien detainees were deported to Finland and later to Russia, including the famous Emma Goldman, the Russian-born anarchist, who had drawn attention by opposing the military draft and advocating birth control.

It is important to note that real if scattered violence was at hand. Several bombs were sent through the mail in this period, presumably sent by anarchists, directed at government and business leaders, causing some property damage and, in one case (at the J. P. Morgan company), killing forty people. As would be true eighty years later, there was reason for concern, but, arguably, manipulation and public emotion readily outstripped objective causation.

Palmer continued to fan the fires, claiming that May Day in 1920 would bring massive demonstrations as a prelude to revolution. While Palmer's stock quickly fell when there were no incidents, emotions continued to run high for several years. In Chicago, when a man refused to stand during the national anthem, a sailor challenged him and ultimately shot him dead, to the cheering of a crowd. More modestly, but almost as ridiculously, a Connecticut man was arrested for saying in public that Lenin was intelligent. Several labor leaders were killed by mobs, and one was castrated in addition. Evangelist Billy Sunday urged more generally that people should "stand the radicals up before a firing squad"—merely deporting them was a waste of shipping. The new Federal Bureau of Investigation, initially set up during World War I to disrupt German agents and leftists hostile to the military effort, flexed its muscles in arrests of various dissidents, including notoriously nonviolent figures such as socialist leader Eugene Debs. American fear also undergirded the arrest and ultimate execution of Sacco and Vanzetti, two Italian-born anarchists, in a murder trial widely viewed as unfair.[4]

The pattern may seem familiar. Some real violence was blown out of proportion. A variety of leaders, and a new federal agency, found it useful not just to capitalize on fear, but to intensify it with shrill rhetoric and exaggerated warnings. The American establishment more generally readily tolerated the panic reactions because it bolstered defense against even standard trade union actions and homegrown socialism, not to mention the frankly remote possibility of revolutionary fervor. Broad sectors of the American public, easily disturbed by foreign involvements of any sort and quite ready to believe in the menace of the wider world, seemed to be genuinely afraid. And finally, high emotion in turn supported a series of unconstitutionally repressive measures against freedom of speech and political action, not to mention outright violence against real or imagined subversives and foreign agents.

American fear at this point was part of a larger pattern that resulted from the exhaustion caused by the first truly modern world war and the tensions generated by the Russian revolution and the proclaimed desire to foster international risings in its wake. People in many Western countries were scared, and there were many leaders ready to take advantage of fear. In several cases, anti-Communist and antiforeign fears helped generate whole new movements, like fascism and Nazism, which helped translate emotion into political action. American fear was not so formally politicized, though the revival of efforts such as the Ku Klux Klan, directed during the 1920s more at targets such as Catholicism and urban modernity than at racial minorities, provided some outlet. In this comparative sense—in the lack of durable crystallization of Red Scare fears into some form of fascism—the American episode was relatively mild.

There remains the question of why such fear at all. The United States was not really threatened by the Russian or any other revolution. Its suffering in World War I was relatively modest, whatever the jolt to the national image of removal from the perils of foreign involvement.

Great Britain, far more war torn and far closer to potential political contagion, did not see an emotional outburst comparable to America's Red Scare. How much was the Red Scare the fruit not just of reactions to unwonted military engagement, but of suspicion of the rising tides of immigration and broader industrial changes that had been transforming the nation for several decades? To what extent was the United States, despite a normally stable political consensus, prone to periodic assertions of demagoguery, which would become possible because of volatile emotions and would promote these emotions in turn? The obvious point is that questions that would become far more pervasive after World War II can already be raised for the early 1920s. Was there, already, something unusual between disturbance/fear?

The Red Scare certainly had an aftermath, though emotions calmed somewhat. Immigration was tightly constrained by new laws in 1923. Native socialism and even a strong union movement receded amid repression. The FBI turned its attention more to crime than to foreign subversion, though it continued to use exaggerated fears to help drum up public support. Isolationism seemed to protect the United States from instabilities abroad, though at real cost to ultimate national security. Demagoguery receded for a time.

THE NUCLEAR THREAT

A far more persistent, and in most ways far more reasonable, pattern of fear emerged in the wake of the United States' tremendous efforts in World War II. The war itself did not build on widespread fears, despite the preliminary anxiety suggested by reactions to artificial stimuli such as Orson Welles' radio show announcing alien invasion, and despite a rather desperate desire to cling to isolationism as initial military action unfolded elsewhere. As we have seen, actual responses to the Japanese attack were not, at least in public, characterized by widespread emotion; resolve and confidence in the government seemed to predominate. Either fear or retribution admittedly showed in the confinement of Japanese Americans, and certainly the war took its toll on emotions as casualties mounted.[5] But World War II was more prelude than stage, where fear was concerned. Its emotional contribution lay more in reducing capacity to withstand the next challenges, than in creating a new emotional climate directly.

There were, however, some important changes even aside from the advent of the nuclear age that dawned at the war's end. First, of course, military experience, in the context of shifts in the larger culture toward fear, generated greater awareness of the emotional costs of military action amid the conditions of modern warfare. Ideas of trauma advanced, as we have seen; less onus was attached to individual soldiers who displayed fear, though this was still a transitional moment in both professional and public assessments. World War II also left a legacy of responsibility: many Americans, and most policy analysts, concluded that the United States had not been sufficiently engaged in international affairs before the conflict, that a more forceful stance toward Hitler early on, along with more foresightful military buildup, might have inhibited his aggression before his conquests required such a costly response. This was not, directly, an emotional conclusion—assumptions about the flaws of prewar appeasement were normally phrased in highly rational terms. But it could condition emotional reactions to later problems, of the sort prominent during the cold war, making it easier to add in some real fears about the potential for unbridled aggression unless checked by forceful American policy.

Finally, of course, there was the image of Hitler himself, the personification of evil, a legitimate target of fear. The dictator himself was disposed of, aside from some lingering anxieties about whether he survived in hiding and might reemerge. But the notion of modern military power in the hands of a madman lived on more directly. It was easy to draw analogies with later diplomatic contestants, and here the emotional implications were very real. The Nazi threat to American interests, in other words, left vivid memories that could color subsequent reactions. The continued American delight in reliving war experiences on film and, later, on television—a delight which persisted strongly into the twenty-first century, as offerings on the History Channel attested—kept the memories alive, cushioned by the comforting realization that this particular madman had gone down in defeat.

It was the atomic bomb, however, not the course of the war before 1945 that more directly triggered a new round of American fear. For the next big step in American emotions, international division, resulted from the advent of the nuclear age, in which suspicion of foreign threat mingled intriguingly with shock at the new potential the nation itself had unleashed. This was a new fear, based directly on a sense of threat to the United States and, often, to humanity more generally. For many people, at least recurrently into the 1980s, the fear reached very deep.

While the initial atomic attacks on Japan occasioned joy about the quick end to the war, and even some gloating about the Japanese getting what they deserved, anxieties surfaced quickly. Public opinion told a significant story, over an extended period of time. Polls in September 1945 showed 59 percent of all Americans very or fairly worried—with women leading men, as usual, and interestingly with the less educated surpassing their college-graduate peers, particularly in the very-worried category. About a fifth of all Americans believed an atomic attack would occur on a major American city within ten years. Polls into the early 1950s showed about 30 percent of all Americans (the rate increasing somewhat with time) convinced that their community suffered a good chance of being bombed should there be another war. By the early 1960s, 40 percent of all Americans rated their chance of surviving a nuclear war to be poor (comparable figures in Canada and Britain were lower by a third). Concern about personal survival seized a large minority of Americans.[6]

Newspapers almost immediately reflected profound shock. The *New York Times* noted the lack of any feasible defense against atomic weaponry and the huge cultural reversal that had to follow this unprecedented threat: "the explosion in men's minds is as shattering as the obliteration of Hiroshima." People everywhere would have to live with this new anxiety, but despite the American monopoly on atomic power at this point there was no sense that the nation was exempt. In the same vein the *Washington Post* commented that the life expectancy of the species had "dwindled immeasurably."[7] Individual reflections, reproduced in newspaper articles, maintained the same tone. Many noted their haunting visions of cities destroyed. A housewife regretted that she'd already had children who would have to face this "dreadful thing." Radio programs might refer to victims "vaporized, blown to bits, to nothingness." A *Reader's Digest* article talked about how the new weapons "can burn up in an instant every creature,"[8] while another article, in 1947, speculated on what would happen if a bomb hit New York City. A *Life* magazine piece, in a similar speculation, listed ten million killed. And the *Herald Tribune* praised widespread fear, arguing that if it led to action against the bomb "it may be the greatest benefactor of mankind." As late as 1948, a businessman could note in a public talk, "The atomic age is here, and we're all scared to death."[9]

Fear was hardly universal, of course. Majorities insisted they were not worried, though they also admitted they believed that there would sometime be an atomic war and that the United States could certainly not maintain its monopoly. Many people simply said there was "no point" in worrying, and large numbers expressed confidence that the government could organize effective defense. World War II attitudes persisted to a degree.[10]

Furthermore, the first round of intense fear began to pass by 1948. Assimilation of the end of World War II and the fact that, despite the early phases of the cold war, no actual nuclear war materialized, helped support the professed unconcern of the majority. People simply became somewhat accustomed to this new fact of life. Additionally, the government began mounting countercampaigns in favor of continued weapons development as well as peaceful uses of atomic energy. Officials had strong stakes in easing anxiety. As a result, even the Russian acquisition of the bomb, in 1949 did not occasion significant new signs of panic. Government assurances that American leadership in the weapons race would continue paid off. Upbeat religious leaders, like Norman Vincent Peale, added their own comfort: "'I will be free from fear.' Believe that and practice it and it will be so." A poll showed 69 percent of the American public favoring work on a hydrogen bomb, with only 14 percent against.[11]

Apparent calm could be deceiving, though the actual extent of ongoing fear is difficult to determine. Vigorous campaigns against the nuclear arms race explicitly sought to promote anxiety. Leadership in spreading concern and in outright mobilization of fear came from some less sanguine religious leaders, appalled by the death toll in Japan, and even more from a number of scientists aghast at their own handiwork. Physicists and others who formed the *Bulletin of Atomic Scientists* believed that only fear could produce rational policies on atomic weaponry and energy; as one noted, the only possible tactic was the "preaching of doom." Discussion of possibly larger bombs in the future featured speculation that they might ignite a chain reaction in the atmosphere or on the seas. Hans Bethe, in 1946, did demonstrate that this particular doomsday scenario was unrealistic, but other scientists remained anxious. Eugene Rabinowitch recalled how he and his colleagues walked the streets of Chicago imagining a sudden fireball, "the steel skeletons of skyscrapers bending into grotesque shapes and their masonry raining over the streets below, until a giant cloud of dust rose and settled over the crumbling city." Robert Oppenheimer corroborated this widespread concern among his colleagues about the future they had helped create: "the physicists have known sin, and this is a knowledge which they cannot lose." Rabinowitch, as founding editor of the *Bulletin*, vowed to "prevent science from becoming an executioner of mankind." Against dominant government policy, a number of scientists urged greater caution and a more internationally collaborative approach in the nuclear arena. Their views did not prevail, but they provided a great deal of information about the risks of nuclear war that periodically informed the popular press and fueled apocalyptic fiction as well.[12]

There were other voices too. A group of theologians speculated about the "possibility of the speedy end to man's life on earth." Billy Graham, after the Russian bomb announcement in 1949, insisted that the arms race was "driving us madly toward destruction," and noted specifically that the first bomb would be directed toward New York City and that Americans should repent while they had the chance. Novelists, aside from the authors of science fiction, took up the cause; even William Faulkner's 1950 Nobel Prize speech pointedly referred to a "general and universal fear so long sustained by now that we can bear it." Dorothy Thompson worried about a worldwide nervous breakdown.[13] Physician David Bradley's 1948 book, *No Place to Hide*, on the lingering effects of nuclear pollution, sold 250,000 copies within a year.[14]

Public opinion did seem to settle a bit by the early 1950s, partly because anxieties were, as we will see, transferred more directly to the cold war, partly perhaps because, as Faulkner implied, people simply got used to the dangers and managed to focus on other matters. Civil defense programs both reflected and potentially calmed concerns. Parents whose children participated in the famous schoolroom exercises, where they hid under desks to shield themselves against fallout, may have felt that at least something was being done. The more nervous could stock up on provisions or even engage in the fad of backyard fallout shelter construction, a movement more talked about than widespread. Civil defense advisors acknowledged that some fear was both understandable and healthy, but that it was important to stay in control, to be able to "get hold of yourself" by the time the all-clear sounded.[15]

It is also vital to note that concerned scientists themselves debated the use of fear in their campaigns and ultimately decided that the initial impulse, to maximize emotion, had probably proved counterproductive. Some argued that fear would quickly became numbing, vitiating any impact. Others contended that emotionalism was self-defeating in the first place. Still others, noting that anxiety was a very "questionable defense," worried that it would simply stir panic and cause undue strain. Deliberate use of fear in the first flush of the nuclear age remains interesting: here was an essentially liberal movement exploring tactics that, today, are more directly associated with the political right. But the decision against emotionalism was in turn significant, explaining in part why American liberals ultimately would have difficulties coping with fear tactics. And finally, of course, the semiofficial decision to drop emotionalism did not erase earlier public reactions, and even liberals themselves would flirt with fear potentials in subsequent campaigns over nuclear testing and, later, over broader environmental causes.[16]

Indeed, by the mid-1950s, a new emotional target emerged in the direct consequences of American and other testing programs. Expert warnings and popularized media accounts helped fuel the antitesting campaign, but there was unquestionable, deep public anxiety as well. A

Nevada test in 1953 doused residents of a Utah town with as much radiation as nuclear workers were allowed in a year. Both people and animals around the test site sickened. Government disclaimers followed the official line of optimism, but they helped create a wedge between bureaucrats and the wider public that would continue to fuel fears even after the testing ceased. Fear went international as well: a 1954 Pacific island test showered radioactive ash over a Japanese fishing boat and killed one sailor—the first known postwar victim of the nuclear age. Other crew members suffered as well.

Scientists took up this cause in turn. Geneticists demonstrated how radiation affected both exposed individuals and any progeny. Nobel Prize–winning chemist Linus Pauling estimated that ten thousand people were dying of test-induced leukemia and predicted rapid expansion of this damage in the future, over ensuing generations. A physicist translated the problem into emotion directly: fallout radiation "cannot be felt and possesses all the terror of the unknown. It is something which evokes revulsion and helplessness—like a plague." The movies and books about mutant creatures picked up on the widespread anxiety and extended it further.[17]

Wide public attention focused on the problem of strontium-90, a radioactive by-product of the testing program, found in milk. In 1958 Consumers Union published the results of milk samples in fifty different regions, noting high levels of contamination in many instances. The report was restrained, but its title, "The Milk We Drink," inevitably drew wide attention, particularly from worried parents; and the report concluded with great pessimism, that it was vital to achieve an atmosphere without fallout, milk without Sr-90, "but none of these solutions are [sic] to be had." In 1957, The Committee for a Sane Nuclear Policy, or SANE, was formed, led by a variety of noted liberal and pacifist intellectuals bent on ending nuclear testing. In a famous ad, noted pediatrician Benjamin Spock is examining a little girl, with a caption reading "Dr. Spock is worried," adding that the real danger was the damage to children and future generations if tests continued. In 1961 a separate women's group took up the cause, focusing on "mothers' issues" like contaminated milk and mounting widely publicized boycott campaigns. Even outlets like *Playboy* magazine voiced fears over the consequences of nuclear testing.[18]

Ultimately, of course, world and American opinion triumphed in this particular facet of the nuclear age, as test bans were negotiated. Here too, however, strong fears persisted near the surface of public opinion. One result was that, two decades later, widely publicized accidents at nuclear energy stations generated a level of concern that made further pursuit of this energy option virtually impossible, despite a host of rational arguments in favor. Known pollution and levels of destruction associated with the splitting of the atom created a reservoir of fear, ready to emerge at any sign of difficulty and potentially applicable as well to other sources of military or environmental danger.

With the end of nuclear testing, the most obvious anxieties about weaponry did tend to decline once again. American opinion, bolstered by the nation's undeniable military might, grew more sanguine than European, where lack of control over military destiny followed from decline in world power status and where demonstrations against nuclear weapons continued. Apparent calm, by the 1970s, did not remove an undercurrent of fear, however, though emotional tracking became more difficult.[19]

In the first place, scattered artists and intellectuals maintained active anxiety about the nuclear threat. In 1980, Alex Grey painted *Nuclear Crucifixion*, showing Jesus crucified in a mushroom cloud. Other artists offered vivid renderings of Hiroshima or child victims of radioactive burns; another painting focused concerns about government responsibility by picturing two buttons, one labeled launch, the other, lunch. Movies like *Dr. Strangelove* pilloried advocates of the use of nuclear force, and gained wide public attention. This particular film ended with the triumph of the Doomsday Machine, as the camera showed a series of mushroom clouds spreading through the sky.[20]

Formal art was echoed, of course, by the ongoing skein of apocalyptic stories, some of them building directly on scenarios announced by fundamentalists from the first evidence of the awesome power of nuclear weaponry. As noted earlier, the highpoint of doomsday science fiction accompanied the decades of most acute nuclear fears, but the genre continued and periodically revived—gaining wider popularity again in the 1990s. Here too, measuring public resonance is difficult, but without question high emotion could both be expressed and encouraged.[21]

Most important of all, however, was the subliminal effect of early fears and of widespread awareness of the possibility of nuclear conflict. Psychiatrist Robert Lifton argued that Americans could be as deeply affected, emotionally, by efforts to deny an atomic threat as by open anxiety. Psychiatrist John Mack explored what he argued were deep-seated and ongoing fears of war among American children, claiming that the emotional impact was a constant even amid superficially care-free, consumer-crazed offspring. He and others concluded that troubling adolescent symptoms, such as apparently rising rates of suicide and attempted suicide, owed much to unspoken bomb anxieties, all the more acute in that they lacked approved outlets for expression. Generalizations of this sort are difficult to evaluate, but they suggest at least a certain amount of ongoing emotional baggage, that could intertwine with the more specific anxieties associated, for example, with particular moments in the cold war.[22]

Many American adults, growing up in the decades between about 1950 and 1980, quite simply assumed that there was a decent chance they would not survive until maturity. The thought did not necessarily poison them. It could be repressed or normally replaced by the surface concerns of the day. It might affect choices in entertainment, helping to create that distinctive teenage audience morbidly interested in fear and violence. It could feed other fears: how much, for example, of the distinctive American anxieties about the advent of the new millennium were based not simply on particular religious impulses but on the widespread prior belief that personal survival past the year 2000 was unlikely? Certainly, longstanding if oft-repressed beliefs in the possibility of one's own premature death could certainly affect attitudes toward other kinds of foreign threat.

Nuclear fears were, by definition, new fears, not clearly related to earlier patterns in the American diplomatic experience. The possibility of widespread destruction naturally caused strong emotional reaction. Some of the fears—initial iterations, or the special anxieties harbored by certain groups—may now seem somewhat overblown, in light of over half a century of successful survival. But that this was a legitimate source of new anxiety is indisputable. Here was an important addition to the list of perceived threats.

People in many parts of the world shared in this nuclear concern, and emotions periodically ran high in many places—sometimes directed against the United States. But there were some distinctive American twists. The nation's service as a key early testing site raised issues directly. More broadly, guilt about American instigation in introducing the nuclear menace spurred significant reactions, including distrust of the honesty and competence of the United States government and broader worries by and about science. Formal public opinion, apart from the campaign against testing, shied away from specific admissions of responsibility, and even decades later Americans could be outraged at any challenge to the justifiability of the bombing of Japan. There was no widespread sense that retribution might be visited. But this did not mean that national involvement did not contribute to a sense of vulnerability—as the quick awareness of possible attack, even during the few years of national nuclear monopoly, suggested. Finally, and most obviously, nuclear fear fed the emotional reaction to the cold war, adding depth to the growing perception of Soviet menace.

In 1947, as the struggle with the Soviets was just taking shape, 73 percent of all Americans believed Russia already had the bomb (it did not). By 1950, 80 percent of all the Americans who had heard of the hydrogen bomb (15% had not) believed that the Soviets would use the bomb on the United States, while 91 percent thought they would use atomic weapons. Between 1954 and 1958 the majority of those who thought nuclear bombs would target the United States in case of another world war rose steadily, falling off only in the early 1960s. Nuclear fears and rising cold war rivalries went hand in hand.[23]

THE COLD WAR

Cold war fears mixed concerns about the bomb with more familiar resentments against foreign menace and related internal subversion—a kind of replay, but with greater dimensions and certainly greater visibility, of the earlier Red Scare. Soviets seemed a direct danger to the nation's territory, as their military arsenal steadily expanded its range and power. They also threatened American capitalism and social structure—even in areas such as race, when Communist leaders appealed (largely unsuccessfully) to African-American discontent. All of this readily built upon established categories of anxiety, though the level of reaction, particularly during the 1950s, was unprecedented. More specifically still, as a number of historians have shown, the domestic manipulation of the cold war flowed from the anti-Communist organizations that had formed during and after the former Red Scare, eager to use an undeniable new military rivalry to deal a crushing blow to an already enfeebled political movement within the United States.

Americans—policy makers and public alike—were clearly unprepared for aggressive Soviet moves immediately after World War II. Using but also violating allied agreements, the Russians quickly took over east-central Europe in a fashion reminiscent of Hitler's aggressions less than a decade before. It was easy to believe, in a war-weary nation that had quickly and prematurely sought to stand down after victory, that another world war loomed, and many Americans reacted emotionally to the prospect. It was scary to contemplate having to engage in another world war, but one with more ominous weaponry involved. Particular crises, such as the Soviet blockade of Berlin in 1948 and the American airlift response, crystallized fears of renewed military engagement. Strong Communist surges in France and Italy added to a sense of defensiveness.

Developments in Asia exacerbated the concerns in Europe. China fell to the Communists, and many Americans, conservative Republicans and key media at the lead, took this as a major national defeat. Communist advance—and the general tendency was to view all this as a monolithic, massive threat—seemed omnipresent, and there were only a few small victories to point to for relief. The attack on South Korea, in 1950, provided further evidence of a movement on the march, and again many Americans viewed this as a prelude to an inevitable, wider war—in which, it was known by now, the nation would face a nuclear rival.

This was the context in which one of the extraordinary outbursts of American fear occurred, in the crusade against domestic Communism that ultimately, and oversimply, went under the heading of McCarthyism but which, in fact, raged from the late 1940s to the Wisconsin senator's downfall in 1954. This was the most widespread and longest-lasting wave of political repression in American history. It fed on fear; it built fear; and it created fears for the future.

The witchhunt, as it was aptly named, did not flow from some spontaneous outpouring of public emotion. A host of actors, many with personal agendas, built the campaign. A number of politicians, including Richard Nixon, saw attacks on Communists as a means of building personal careers—which does not of course mean that they were not also sincerely concerned. J. Edgar Hoover and the Federal Bureau of Investigation, picking up a role they had experimented with in the 1920s, were absolutely central to the campaign. This was not, in other words, just a cold war panic, but a top-down, often carefully orchestrated effort to attack Americans who could be tainted with Communist association and so with service to a foreign menace.

Yet the campaign depended on fearful public support. Opinion polls consistently revealed widespread anxiety about Communist subversion and direct support for the McCarthy campaign and the House Committee on Un-American Activities. Only in 1954, when McCarthy's smears and excesses were under open attack, did polls show an erosion in the public at large, to under 50 percent approval ratings for the investigatory crusade. And there was real passion involved. Each individual singled out for government investigation received hate mail and death threats. Crank calls, with heavy breathing and open epithets, pursued the same people. Parents forbade their children to play with the offspring of the stigmatized. "Commie kids" were taunted and beaten up as well as ostracized. All levels of American society participated. The daughter of diplomat and China specialist, John Carter Vincent, found herself red-baited by fellow students at prestigious Goucher College, even though she had no role in the investigations whatsoever. Almost every survivor of the McCarthy years, whether former Communist or political innocent, had stories of friends and family cutting ties and of acquaintances crossing streets to avoid eye contact. Small wonder that a number of those under attack committed suicide.[24]

Even for those who tried to carry on, punishments were extensive, again with extensive public support. People lost jobs—not just former policy makers, accused of nuclear espionage or participation in the "loss" of China, or top figures in the entertainment industry under the glare of publicity, but public school teachers, technicians, and others. Thousands suffered directly.

Beyond this, the McCarthy era seemed to authorize new levels of intolerance and self-assigned monitoring in elements of the larger public. In Texas, for example, a group called the "Minute Women" sent "agents" into high schools to ferret out subversive teachers. It was not hard to see a siege mentality fanning out in American society.[25]

Public passion was partly, of course, maneuvered and manipulated. Political leaders and media gurus like the Luce family, which headed the *Time-Life* operation, had a great stake in keeping hatred and fear burning brightly. There really was a conviction that not just the United States, but Western civilization more generally was under attack from a powerful and coordinated menace, and the American establishment, having reached that conclusion, successfully persuaded the public as well. Worries about potential attack, about the possibility of renewed war in Europe and wider conflicts in Asia, concern about loss of the nuclear monopoly all contributed to a desperate effort to pin blame on subversives at home. Fear, in other words, sought and found targets. The campaign was coordinated, but this did not mean that the panic was any less real—which is why most people supported such severe and prolonged disruptions of the normal judicial process.

There are still debates and dark corners in this episode. It is generally agreed, however, that whatever the sincere conviction at the time, domestic Communism was no longer a serious threat at any level. A movement had existed, it had some impact particularly in labor activities during the 1930s, but it had long since lost vigor. There was no objective reason for this degree of panic save for the combined orchestration and public fear. As others have noted, a number of societies experienced cold war tensions—some of them, as in the case of Germany, much closer to military threat than the United States, without a McCarthyite outbreak. Some combination of prior precedent, unusual sensitivity to the notion of foreign threat and perception of subversion, plus of course the existence of determined and skillful leadership bent on promoting and using public anxiety accounts for yet another out-cropping of unusual American response.

The witchhunt did end, of course, which means that the level of fear declined somewhat, and a certain degree of embarrassment set in at least in some quarters. Yet the emotional impact lingered, in several ways. In the first place, a variety of groups, small but persistent, continued to believe in gigantic plots and internal conspiracy bent on turning the nation over to the Communists or to some other globalist operation that would suppress national freedom. The existence of extremist fear groups, some of them developing paramilitary capabilities, continued to affect national life and provide at least an occasional goad toward wider fears. At the other extreme, the McCarthy episode created both fear and constraint on the political left. It contributed to a decline of elements on the left, including trade unions, but it also left many residual liberals fearful of further government attacks—a reaction that would surface, legitimately or not, as many contemplated disciplinary measures like the Patriot Act taken in response to September 11.

For the majority, willing to abandon McCarthyism though not to apologize for it, but also not driven into fringe militia groups, fear may have subsided but it did not end. Worries about Communist subversion persisted, if at a lower level. The sense of outside threat continued even more strongly, in policy ranks as well as in the public at large. The war in Vietnam, for example, maintained the sense of a monolithic Communism, where any regional victory would privilege the movement as a whole—with the added concern, particularly on the part of leaders in the Democratic Party, that an abandonment of Vietnam might ignite the same divisive accusations that had followed the "loss" of China, this last a direct legacy of the memory of McCarthyism.

Cold war fear drove many strange decisions. By the 1960s, Nike Hercules missiles and fighters at bases at least in and around Washington, D.C., were armed with nuclear weapons, designed to destroy incoming Soviet missiles in seeming disregard of the probability that the impact on civilian populations, exposed to resultant fallout, might be even greater than the results of the attack itself. Disproportionate anxiety about Soviet might and intentions, combined with a desire to seem vigilant at whatever cost, drove some convoluted policy as the cold war continued.[26]

Most important of all was the fact of recurrent war scares and related crises. In a context in which many Americans saw a precarious balance for national survival, even small incidents could be emotionally magnified—and there were a few objectively menacing confrontations as well.

The cold war's birth pains, amid specific confrontations such as the Berlin airlift, Communist takeover in China, and the Korean War itself, yielded in the later 1950s to another set of dramatic moments, some with war-threatening potential. Risings in east-central Europe, and particularly Hungary, in 1956, prompted some saber-rattling on both sides of the iron curtain. The downing of an American spy plane over the Soviet Union provided a troubling moment, as did the construction of the Berlin Wall.

The Cuban missile crisis, opening in October, 1962, brought Cold War threats and fears unusually close to home, and many people concluded quite reasonably, at least for a few days, that at least a local war was likely. The crisis erupted after the Soviets established missile bases on the island, and the Kennedy administration publicly revealed their presence and insisted on withdrawal. A variety of hardliners, in Washington and in the public at large, insisted that no concessions be offered, that war was preferable to this kind of intimidation—and this bluster added to widespread anxieties. While the focus was on a possible invasion of Cuba, or at least bombardment, there was widespread speculation about the possibility of a wider, nuclear conflict or of a simple miscalculation that could lead to real catastrophe.

A host of groups, both established anti-nuclear organizations and ad hoc operations, sprang up to urge a peaceful solution. Many church leaders appealed for peace. Because the crisis was relatively shortlived, it was difficult to calculate how extensive or profound the fears of war were, but a high level of anxiety was undeniable.

And while the episode was cleverly resolved, and while Kennedy himself privately recognized that missiles in Cuba did not really add to the Cold War dangers to the United States given Russian capabilities elsewhere, a sense of insecurity lingered. A variety of commentators, of many political stripes, were eager to insist that basic vulnerabilities remained. The *New York Times*, for example, editorially trumpeted that "the threat to national and hemispheric security embodied in the Castro regime...will remain as long as Castroism endures." The editor was at pains to disillusion any American belief that Kennedy's success in getting the Soviets to back down has "opened a wide, new prospect of international peace and the imminence of a stable world order." Here, quite clearly, the perpetual and perpetuated sense of Cold War threat shone through.[27]

The assassination of President Kennedy, in 1963, showed the continued rawness of American emotion. The event was tragic, and certainly media orchestration of a weekend of mourning provided additional signals to the American public. The majority of Americans was deeply affected, comparing the occasion most commonly to a death of a family member. Suspicions stirred along with emotion, suggesting cold war tensions generally and the legacy of the McCarthy era: the work of Communists was widely cited, and a majority of the public persisted in believing that the killing resulted from a larger plot, and not the work of a single individual; government efforts at assurance on this point were widely discounted. Worries about international impact, and freer-floating concerns about personal safety "these days when the President himself can get shot," affected a majority as well—though fears of this sort did not match expressions of grief and simple confusion.[28]

The Cuban missile crisis and the spate of political assassinations were soon succeeded by the mounting intervention in Vietnam. The intervention was inspired by the same domino theory—give Communists one win and they'll gain the world—that had motivated the Korean War and much of the cold war in general. As the intervention proceeded, other fears surfaced—fears of being sent into combat in a bloody war, fears of the protesters and their defiant culture. But fear was only one of the many high emotions that unfurled during the later 1960s and early 1970s. Still, Vietnam certainly reinforced, for many Americans, the belief in a dangerous international environment.

The aftermath, as the nation briefly reconsidered its interest in foreign conflict, led to a brief lull, though airplane hijackings and other instances of what would soon be called terrorism, associated sometimes with the cold war, other times with tensions in the Middle East, provided reminders of continued threats. The Soviet invasion of Afghanistan, in 1979, constituted a more vivid crisis, in which cold war tensions came flooding back. President Carter—ridiculously, at least in retrospect—proclaimed the invasion "the greatest threat to peace since the Second World War." He thus maintained the longstanding tradition of presidential hyperbole when it came to international problems. Carter's administration (and even more under his successor, Ronald Reagan) tried to respond to threats with assistance to Islamic resistance fighters in ways that would come back to haunt. Actual fear levels in the wider public did not rise to the levels of official rhetoric. But combined with the Iranian seizure of American hostages that soon followed, which was widely exploited for its emotional value by politicians and media alike, Soviet action easily renewed a sense of the apparently inescapable dangers of foreign involvement.[29]

Even as the cold war wound down, finally, a new round of fears surfaced in the 1980s—a reminder of the continued dangers of great-power confrontation and the sense of vulnerability among portions of the American public. The strident rhetoric and increased defense spending introduced by President Ronald Reagan reactivated scientists and others genuinely worried about the heightened threat of nuclear war. Reagan's willingness to bait the Soviets with terms like "evil empire," and his commitment to sponsor a military buildup to the tune of $1.5 trillion while reducing arms control efforts, led to considerable outcry. Scientists returned to the description of the consequences of atomic warfare, reviving fear tactics that some had questioned two decades earlier. Astronomer Carl Sagan and four colleagues wrote an article (that appeared in the Sunday supplement of *Parade* magazine) about a nuclear winter, following from bombs exploded in the atmosphere, which could generate an "epoch of cold and dark" and possibly lead to the extinction of the human race.

Other popularizers picked up on this theme. Jonathan Schell, in a series of *New Yorker* articles, wrote about a "Republic of Insects and Grass" that might well result from nuclear war. "What happened at Hiroshima was less than a millionth part of a holocaust at present levels of world nuclear armament." In a piece called "Second Death," he contended that "every person on earth would die; but in addition to that, and distinct from it…unborn generations would be prevented from ever existing." Physicians for Social Responsibility revived, and along with the Union of Concerned Scientists urged the danger of nuclear warfare. Thousands of people demonstrated, in Ground Zero Week, portraying the devastating effects of nuclear conflict in over six hundred cities and communities across the United States. The Reagan administration, while pursuing its own technological dream of a missile shield which might reduce fear from one angle (though the idea was vigorously disputed), found that it also had to reengage in arms limitation discussions as a response to widespread public emotion.[30]

The persistence, or at least recurrence, of fear was matched by the willingness of various camps to invoke it. Reaganites, eager to justify new expenses and technological experiments, emphasized the power and ill-intent of the Soviets—a cold war staple. Opponents, no less fearful, worried more about the possibility of miscalculation and the potential irresponsibility of American policy. A right-wing fringe feared that the government was too soft. All sides agreed that the world was still scary, and that no one nation could really claim secure control over military dangers. Not surprisingly, even in a country notorious for its preoccupation with domestic problems, a third of all Americans rated the fear of war to be the nation's most pressing problem by the mid-1980s. An undercurrent of fear, and occasionally panic, had been a fact of American life for at least forty years.

Even before it ended, the cold war was subject to various interpretations, and debate continues. Revisionist historians have emphasized a considerable degree of American responsibility for escalating tensions, and not merely Soviet aggression. A related point is more directly germane to the discussion of fear and threat: whichever side bore greatest responsibility for various stages of the contest, it is clear that Americans—certainly the public, probably many policy makers—consistently exaggerated Soviet power and threat. Some leaders may have exaggerated knowingly, eager to promote military expenditures or personal political position; far more probably shared the fear itself. Excessive reliance on historical analogy, which moved from criticizing the failure of appeasement prior to World War II to insisting that only advancing military strength would deter monolithic Communist advance, helped distort responses. Belief in the so-called domino theory convinced Americans at many levels that any advance of Communism, anywhere, constituted a clear and present danger to the United States. An accurate estimation of the destruction possible in nuclear war made it easy to avoid a more subtle analysis of actual Soviet motivations and capacities, and also of divisions within the Communist camp. It was revealing, in this context, that virtually no American analyst, in the government or outside, realized the extent of Soviet decline by the 1980s, so mesmerized had the nation become by American assumptions about the power of their foe.

The result—far easier to discern in retrospect—was a series of calculations born in fear and often productive of additional fear. As the Korean War broke out, for example, the American joint chiefs purportedly believed that the invasion was a feint while the Soviet prepared an all-out attack—a clear mistake. The launch of the Soviet Sputnik satellite, in 1957, elicited another administration reference to "grave danger," while the CIA issued a report that Soviet economic output might be triple that of the United States by the year 2000. Castro's 1959 victory in Cuba raised fears of Communist contagion throughout Latin America, another nonstarter. American loss in Vietnam was widely held to portend global strategic retreat and immediate Chinese hegemony in Asia. Threat exaggeration also applied to the prospect of nuclear disaster. Every decade saw hosts of pundits and defense groups proclaim that—without some innovation, whether decisive American military superiority or global disarmament—a cataclysm was unavoidable, that the world would never reach the year 2000 intact, or that the species would be annihilated.[30]

Virtually none of this proved correct. The Russians did not aggrandize at every opportunity, having trouble simply maintaining the territory they had gained. Asian and Russian Communists were usually at odds, not in cahoots. Nuclear disaster, however predictable given the power of the weapons and the fallibility of human leadership, did not occur. How often the exaggeration of threat was deliberate, by people who should have known better, how much it followed from a widely shared sense of panic can be debated. Whatever the judgment here, and it is important to acknowledge that American countermeasures and arms negotiations doubtless played some role in reducing risk, it is clear that many Americans spent many decades periodically more afraid than they needed to be. A tradition of edginess about the outside world not only persisted, but greatly expanded.

AFTER THE COLD WAR

By the end of the twentieth century many Americans, at various social levels, had developed a set of emotional habits, concerning international challenges, that proved hard to shake off. Among other things, the habits made it difficult to distinguish between foreign problem and foreign menace. It also made it difficult to calculate degrees of risk.

Judgments about the 1990s and the early twenty-first century are far more speculative than those about the cold war, but several points can be suggested. First, a few observers thought that history would massively change with the cold war's end, and while they did not phrase this conclusion in terms of emotion, it might have been reasonable to suggest that fear of the wider world would progressively become less necessary. Attractive generalizations gained some public attention, like the comforting notion that democracies never declare war on each other (in a decade when democracy was indeed spreading) or that no society with a McDonald's would ever embark on a war of aggression (the notion being that advanced consumerism, symbolized by the beloved Golden Arches, would inhibit military threat).

But the more important fact was the capacity of many Americans, including many leaders, quickly to reinvent threats and hyperbole, as if the emotional and rhetorical habits of long years of hot and cold wars could not be cast aside. Complicit media, eager to sell crises and blessed with new technology that facilitated instantaneous images from almost any hot spot, pushed exaggeration as well. Thus an Iraqi dictator—an undeniable nuisance who arguably needed some attention—became a latter-day Hitler or Stalin. Serious, unfortunate, ethnic conflict in the Balkans, which again arguably demanded some response, might, in the judgment of some, lead to nuclear war or threaten to spread endlessly around the world. The concept of rogue states, applied to Iraq but also several other societies, provided yet another target for familiar anxiety. These states admittedly could probably not launch a nuclear holocaust, and that particular memory did fade a bit, but they could possibly send a bomb or two, and that was fearsome enough. American leaders seemed bent on moving from prudent watchfulness to the identification of cosmic foes, deserving all the worry that once was devoted to the Soviets and nuclear Armageddon. The term "weapons of mass destruction," rarely used during the cold war when such destruction was a more active possibility, now served to escalate anxieties during a period when one might otherwise have expected greater calm. As one observer put it, the United States was bent on going abroad "in search of monsters to destroy." To be sure, actual public fear did decline somewhat for a decade, with regard to foreign threats, among other things because American coverage of international news receded in favor, for example, of greater attention to crime and health concerns. But both language and apparatus were amply available to revive recent emotional memories.

It was unsurprising, then, that fears of terrorist attacks began to rise before September 11, based on the 1993 World Trade Center bombing, plus assaults on American embassies and military equipment, along with the more general emotional volatility born of a long diet of crises. A poll taken six weeks before September 11, 2001, revealed that about 90 percent of all Americans were actively afraid of international terrorism and weapons of mass destruction. Foresightful, one might argue; but also a possibly flawed basis for assessing what was about to happen.[32]

CONCLUSION

The United States was not the only nation to develop patterns of fear regarding foreign threat in the twentieth century, not the only nation to respond at times irrationally. One need only remember France's famous Maginot Line, built in the aftermath of the nation's trauma in World War I, designed (and incompletely, at that) to repel the kind of German attack that had occurred then, rather than the one more likely in the future: the product of genuine fear, and a totally misguided reaction. While cold war fears mounted particularly in the United States, they were shared elsewhere, and doubtless on both sides of the famous Curtain. Nuclear anxieties were even more widespread, as the global campaign against testing demonstrated. The twentieth century was a difficult time internationally, not just because of military crises but because local control tended steadily to erode in favor of larger global corporations and forces. In some areas—for example, responses to diseases or to new types of food imports—Americans were less agitated, or at least no more agitated, than their counterparts elsewhere. American reactions even to September 11 were not entirely unique. People in countries such as Great Britain also showed signs of panic, and the government had to move quickly to reassure. Columnists, for example, discussed the relevance of British "Blitz spirit," arguing in terms reminiscent of American reaction that terrorism presented a more fearsome, because less identifiable, target than Nazi aggression had done—and that new emotions were therefore unavoidable.[33] A number of nations, for example Australia, quickly instituted stringent new immigration or arrest policies, not totally dissimilar to those adopted in the United States (though Australia also of course actively wooed Middle Eastern students to its universities).

It remains true that the United States had a longer sequence of real and imagined foreign challenges in the twentieth century than did most of the societies with which the nation normally compares itself. This follows from the nation's emergence as a great power, for with power comes challenge; but it deserves attention even so. The withdrawal of Europe and Japan, for example, from aggressive international roles, while it could lead to concerns about loss of control, reduced this category of high emotionality, just as American fear increased. Latin American nations faced many problems, but were far less often exposed to a sense of foreign threat. Distinctive experience accompanied the American construction of a distinctive socialization toward fear, and added important ingredients to the context in which the terrorist threat was encountered.

The brief review of the United States' foreign policy fear crises over the past century, familiar enough in itself, yields several important findings. First, the nation—policy makers and public alike—have displayed a propensity for high emotion in the face of real or imagined foreign threats. Repeated persistent tension created possibilities of assertively dramatic response to new threats. The capacity to feel menaced or violated seems undimmed by repeated experience, indeed was enhanced by it. On some occasions—not necessarily all—the result has been a considerable exaggeration of what the threat was all about. There's an emotional tradition here, fed by suspicion of foreigners, by a deep desire for immunity from the normal storms and stresses of world diplomacy and, no doubt, by the growing discomfort with fear and hopes for reduction of risk that were developing in the wider culture during the same decades.

Some observers even argued that Americans became so accustomed to the idea of crisis that they grew disoriented when none could be manufactured. Fear, to some, was a moral galvanizer, providing a sense of larger purpose as well as a welcome target for media attention at a time when the competition for ratings grew more complicated. It was even argued—cynically? realistically?—that the fear that followed September 11 was "a cleanser, washing away a lot of the indulgence of the past decade." Here was an emotional routine that could ensnare policy community and guard public alike.

Reactions to September 11, in this sense, fit into a recognizable sequence. This is all the truer in that, ironically, almost every new menace seems to obliterate historical memory, appearing as an unprecedented assault on the national fabric. It was striking, as reactions to September 11 emerged from people not directly involved, how rarely historical precedent was mentioned. Pearl Harbor came up a few times. The threat of nuclear obliteration—the most ominous of the long sequence of military and diplomatic issues—came up almost not at all in any direct sense, though references to "ground zero" for the World Trade Center site made the connection obliquely, and subsequent references to "weapons of mass destruction" linked to nuclear fears quite directly. But specific reference to actual prior fear patterns, and how the nation had weathered them, was striking by its absence. The United States was a virgin, its illusions shattered for the first time by terrorist rape. The attack seemed so awful that it eclipsed any historical sense, and its horror might have been dimmed if people were urged to recall that, just a generation before, it was global destruction, not the more finite horrors of terrorism, that had clouded the national future. It is this very lack of historical memory, of course, that allows each generation to claim that its threat is the first time the nation has been so directly menaced. This is part of the tradition as well, even if, arguably, not a very useful one.

The long list of fear-laden crises, and the fact that, in sober retrospect, it turns out that many were more emotionally intense than reality dictated, that resultant policies were adopted that turned out to be excessive, raises the legitimate possibility of analogies with the present moment. John Mueller, for example, in a provocative article, reviews the persistent tendency, in United States and allied policy, to exaggerate Communist capacity during the cold war. [34] The result was massive expenditure, dubious military engagements, and sometimes truly frightening policies such as the notion of blasting Soviet rockets over American skies with nuclear warheads. This same kind of fear-induced excess began to turn to Middle Eastern crises during the 1980s, with relatively minor incidents, like the Iranian hostage taking of over sixty Americans in 1979, turned into national catastrophes that threatened the nation's whole position in the world. Then, of course, with the cold war entirely over, fear generation turned to threats of nuclear proliferation—the dreaded weapons of mass destruction that became virtually a household term—and terrorism. Careful discussion of the reality of threats—for example, the actually quite limited destructive potential or feasibility of many so-called weapons of mass destruction—consistently yielded to emotional hyperbole: somehow it seemed important to keep the nation under threat. Terrorism bade fair to replace Communism as an amorphous, monolithic, international force against which the nation would do well to survive.

A variety of reactions closely duplicated earlier cold war and nuclear responses, to an extent almost uncanny save for the realization of the deep grooves the responses had carved during the previous half century. Post–September 11 references to the survival of our civilization and war to the death abounded, along with the notion that terrorism might "do away with our way of life." [35] A few innovations simply compounded the already familiar notion of massive threat. Thus color coding provided even more obvious invitations to fear than the halfhearted schoolroom defense drills had done a half century before. The introduction of the concept of "homeland" security probably reflected and encouraged the sense of personal risk that emerged so prominently in response to September 11—again, a poignant innovation compared to the more neutral term "civil defense."

Why did such a large minority of the American public—30 percent according to some polls—continue to believe Iraq had weapons of mass destruction as late as 2003 and early 2004? It was quite clear by then that the claim was groundless, and even the Bush administration had grudgingly changed its tune. Sheer ignorance and momentum, no doubt. But the error's persistence also reflected an easy sense, born of decades of foreign fears, that the world was a dangerous place, that menacing enemies were to be expected. It reflected as well the larger combination of habituation to disaster fears and the discomfort with fear that made careful calculation of risk increasingly difficult. The mistake revealed, in other words, the several factors that elevated the nation's emotional temperature around fear.

Fact #1: even including September 11, since the 1960s more Americans have been killed by allergic reactions to peanuts or crashes into deer than by international terrorism. Fact #2: not only September 11, but also subsequent (and as it turned out, groundless) alerts generated reactions suggesting that our very national survival was at stake, that terrorism posed an "existential" threat to the United States, that (as a member of the Joint Chiefs asserted in 2003) if terrorists could kill just ten thousand people they could "do away with our way of life." Again, there is a consistent, indeed almost constant, thread in national reactions to threat, and it has only partial links to reality.[36]

Obviously, all sorts of groups have gained a self-interest in keeping the nation scared. Some of them simply want to support inflated military and intelligence budgets. Many, however, have become so accustomed to a rhetoric of fear that they are unaware of additional motives, trapped by the same emotional hyperbole that their statements nourish. And, of course, there is always the possibility that one of the jeremiads will prove correct. World War III could have occurred, though actual Soviet policies and limitations should have made its unlikelihood clearer than was the case during the scare years of the cold war. Massive terrorist disruption might also occur, though again the constraints need more attention than they have received. And the inflation of rhetoric does not mean that all precautions should be scattered to the winds. It is a question of more reasoned and careful discussion, amid the costs and drawbacks of excessive reactions, not of complete about-face. But the historical track record, of successful appeals to public emotion, does not make this easy.

The record itself is now the key problem. The tradition of emotionality and exaggeration generates its own progeny. Inability to remember the magnitude of past fears compounds the problem. But there is more: quite apart from distorted traditions, the United States is, arguably, a war-weary society, engaged in fairly steady conflict and recurrent crises for sixty-five years—over six decades of emotional mobilization. Small wonder that the hyperbole following one emergency picks up on the rhetoric of the last one: we've been told about threats to our way of life for a long time now, and the tension is contagious. The sheer number of frights, exaggerated or not, takes a toll, making it easier to view each succeeding problem as a mortal danger based on the emotions one remembers from the last one—enhanced further, perhaps, by what one's parents conveyed about the one before that. Far from being too inexperienced with threats, many Americans may be suffering from threat fatigue. Just as other fears crescendoed in the later twentieth century, from commercial and religious sources, so diplomatic tensions create further susceptibilities—almost a siege mentality. Even though nuclear and cold war emotions were rarely directly evoked after September 11, the severity of the September 11 reaction was based partly on the lingering impact of these same emotions—and there were enough official references to keep the impact going. Here is another reason American fear has changed, another reason as well that it differs from the reactions of other societies less on the front lines of the global crises of recent decades.

Even more telling is the temptation to merge crisis experiences, to elide distinctive elements in favor of a simple dichotomy between good and evil, between American safety and foreign threat. The cold war recurrently turned into the earlier fight against Hitler, simply with different specific enemies. Constant references to the dangers of Munich-like appeasement made the connection explicit. Then in the 1990s, with the comfort of familiar cold war hostilities fading, American leaders looked for a replacement target. During the Gulf War and then again in 2003, Saddam Hussein implausibly became the next Hitler or Stalin, with (it was claimed) comparable death-dealing potential. The invasion of Iraq and subsequent troubles, amid the larger "war on terror," brought another round of analogies. In a 2005 speech, President Bush specifically likened the terrorist threat to the cold war, seeing the potential for a hostile empire stretching, Soviet-like save for the balmier geography, from Spain to Indonesia.[37] Connections with earlier nuclear fears were direct as well. The question of terrorist acquisition of nuclear weapons or the ability to build a "dirty bomb" was a direct part of fear-inspired responses. The fact that a dirty bomb had very limited potential, compared to even the atomic weaponry deployed in 1945, was not strongly emphasized. (Of course, even limited damage would be quite real.) The decision to dub the World Trade Center towers "ground zero" directly called up emotions previously associated with nuclear fears, again despite the actual incomparability of destructive levels. Linkages of this sort might be fervently believed. They reflected war-weary tensions, but they encouraged belligerent fears as well. Fear, in turn, worked to muddy the lines among particular international episodes, feeding the sense of constant challenge that was so marked in other features of contemporary American fear.

The result can be near-hysteria. A CIA official, warning that we are engaged in a "war to the death" following September 11, inadvertently suggests the toll of past crises in suggesting that death levels on the scale of the Civil War or the bombing of Dresden, not to mention Vietnam, will be essential in defeating the terrorists. Only a military effort on this scale will suffice: "Progress will be measured by the pace of killing and, yes, by body counts—precise counts that will run to extremely large numbers." Many Americans, again at both policy and public levels, have lost the capacity to distinguish easily among foreign threats, seeing everything in an emotional blur that demands maximum effort. And while some of this is contrived, on the part of unit leaders eager to feather their own nests, more of it involves a shared fear between leadership and general public—which may actually be more intractable than contrivance.[38]

For it is difficult, in this spiral, to step back and ask for sobriety. To be sure, as noted above, a few politicians argued against the extremes of fear reactions to September 11, and this was refreshing. But almost no one dares put the extent of defense against terrorism itself into the political arena: argument has to be in the terms of extreme threat, focusing only on who can point out the greater vulnerabilities, who can call for greatest vigilance. Emotion, we now realize (amid undeniable disputes), misled at key points in the cold war; its hold is even greater now, in part through the accumulating effects of collective crisis fatigue.

Much ink can be spilled, not all of it totally partisan, over blatant encouragement of American fear by members of the Bush administration, and surely this has occurred—just as it occurred under earlier administrations. But the record of war-induced emotional exhaustion, in the wider context of pervasive socialization over fear and risk, makes it even more probable that political leaders and general public are often trapped by very similar fears, each sector reinforcing reactions in the other. In 2006, the Defense Department began to trumpet the concept of a "long war" against terror, undoubtedly again reflecting assimilation of the cold war analogy as well as a felt need to prepare national endurance. It seemed normal to be on edge, as the United States moved within a few decades of its own Hundred Years' War. Whatever one's views of the magnitude of the terror risk, however, the prospect of further emotional drain was itself menacing.

Finally, the string of foreign crisis that describes recent American history does more than add to the explanation of American fear through growing war weariness. We come back to the question of targeting. Partly because of the antiforeign attitudes already available when the rise toward world power began, but more because of the apparent inundation of outside threats from the 1940s onward, Americans learned that there was more to fear when foreigners were involved. Domestic terrorists occasion little of the emotion that the foreign variety prompts. The post–September 11 panic over the appearance of anthrax powder in the mail eased considerably as soon as it became clear that internal villains were involved. American leaders' fright at four-year-old intelligence from Pakistan about a plan to go after the New York financial district, which prompted a new Orange alert in August, 2004, contrasted markedly with the neglect of an actual terrorist conspiracy, homegrown and propagated by a white American citizen, to blow up the federal building in downtown Chicago in the very same month.

The larger changes in American socialization toward fear contribute to understanding why Americans are prone to misguided emotion in recent decades. But it's the specific concern about foreigners, heightened by war weariness, that explains the political priorities in focusing fear. Policy makers and public alike are guided by the decades of war-level alerts to play on the emotional vulnerability developed from the larger patterns of American socialization and media prompts.[39]

The recent record, in historical perspective, does hold out one small hope. Granting the difficulties of comparing terrorism with earlier challenges, what the nation has not (yet) done is important. It has not interned large populations—the fear reaction to World War II and the Japanese. Here, historical lessons—that it was both unnecessary and inappropriate to single out whole groups—have thus far been retained. Quick reactions of support for Muslim Americans, after September 11, directly resulted from a desire to avoid repeating this particular mistake of the past. And thus far, there has been no equivalent of McCarthyism. To be sure, arbitrary detainments and racial profiling have been troubling and deserve attention, the constitutionally dubious authorizations of wiretapping are ominous, and restrictions on foreign visitors have become positively counterproductive to American interests. The use and endorsement of torture constitute a particularly reprehensible connection to the excesses committed during earlier international crises where the government used fear to justify unconstitutional measures.[40] A segment of American society would doubtless welcome more sweeping attacks on ordinary American Muslims. Restrictions may also be getting worse; the federal government in 2005, for example, began pressing universities to buy computer systems that would be more open to wiretaps on e-mail. Some believe that constraints on freedom are now at a new high. The issues are serious, and public silence may turn out to be worse than the more open McCarthyite emotionalism. But at least a sweeping witchhunt has not yet occurred, and again the correctives of history play some role. We can and have learned from the past, if very incompletely. As the final chapter suggests, the opportunity to learn more broadly from the history of fear over recent decades invites a wider application of this achievement.

V

Consequences and Remedies

11

CONCLUSION

The Lessons of American Fear

Fear has two major consequences, derived from its primal function in readying the body for flight from danger. First, even when it does not provoke outright flight, it stimulates unusual attentiveness to the surroundings, an awareness of possible threat. Fear, in this instantiation, warns. It can be immensely constructive. But second, fear's emotional intensity—again, when literal flight is not possible—can cloud rational judgment, provoking exaggerations of the perceptions of danger in ways that not only increase personal discomfort far beyond any objective necessity but also lead to an acceptance of responses that may distract from real needs or even exacerbate danger. Fear, in this second form, misleads, sometimes quite seriously. It promotes a generalized level of anxiety that is distracting at best, positively counterproductive at worst.[1] The previous chapters have argued that the American approach to fear and risk, developed over several decades, too often veers toward the damaging results the emotion.

This distortion can be traced in several facets of American life, from parenting to race relations, as several scholars have already concluded. It certainly affects responses to terrorism which, by definition, seeks to use relatively limited attacks to stimulate a far wider, and far more incapacitating, emotional reaction. Americans are not about to give in to terrorism. There is no sign of emotional surrender. But their management of fear has distorted responses and may make terrorist threats more effective than they would otherwise be. American fear and the unusual national sensitivity to risk have consequences.

Soon after September 11, the President's National Science and Technology Council, through a Subcommittee on Social, Behavioral and Economic Sciences, issued a wide-ranging report on the kinds of scholarly inquiries essential to a response to terrorism. Understandably, the bulk of the report dealt with probing the terrorist mentality, planning disaster management, and exploring the nation's infrastructure; but a portion was, appropriately, directed toward fear. The report noted the impact of media in spreading news about terrorist attacks, and so potentially causing "nation- or world-wide trauma"; it worried about the minority of individuals who, because of prior stress or conditioning, had difficulty recovering from unsettling events such as terrorist attacks; and it wondered about the origins of a "putative" culture of fear that might be growing among Americans. The targets were both interesting and appropriate, and they deserve the kind of attention this study has sought to provide.[2]

There is, if not a culture of fear, at least an American cultural vulnerability to fear, that is not entirely new but that has been exacerbated by developments over the past three decades—even before the anxiety about explicit terrorism. Too many Americans have developed unrealistic hopes for a risk-free existence, and as such are open to excessive reactions when risk intrudes and to excessive worries about risks that may not eventuate. The ongoing contemporary socialization against fear works well when it is unchallenged—no one is advocating fear for the hell of it—but leaves too many Americans inexperienced, open both to manipulation and to public contagion, when the emotion becomes inescapable.

It is important to repeat a few reminders. There is no claim that Americans are about to collapse under the weight of fear. The nation continues to embrace many courageous and even more sensible individuals. References to a culture of fear imply no monolithic national standard. Terrorism has never won major victories, and there is no sign that it will do so where the United States is concerned. Despite the surprising emotional vividness of the recollections of September 11, even from people remote from the attacks, fears ultimately declined. Tourist visits to Washington, D.C., for example, had recovered pre–September 11 levels by 2004, a sign that many Americans, whatever their initial frights, were returning to normal. A subway warning in New York City in the fall of 2005 increased police presence but seemed to generate apathy or resignation among most New Yorkers—or cynical speculation about the mayor's political motives. By no means are most Americans viewing the world through a consistent blur of fear. Again, it is important not to exaggerate, in a field where exaggeration is rife.

A few of the growing handful of studies of fear, in fact, overdo their claims, both about past healthiness where fear is concerned and about contemporary collapse. Irrational fear episodes are not a contemporary American invention. As to current disarray, Frank Furedi points to widespread mental health impacts and an undifferentiated inability to distinguish between specific threats and generalized anxiety. The issues are real, but his claims to go too far. Not all politicians seek simply to incite fear (though too many do so). Not all Americans believe what Furedi aptly calls the "fear entrepreneurs." There's a danger in all this that fear will be indiscriminately added to the things Americans believe they have to worry about. The issues are somewhat more specific, in point of fact.

Even so, the national response to fear has been distinctive by historical and comparative standards, and its consequences, in nurturing high levels of anxiety and in promoting questionable policies, have been unfortunate in many ways. Furthermore, as several scholars have pointed out, American fears have distorted both perceptions and policies in other areas as well. There is an emotional issue here, and it deserves continued attention.

Flaws in the national character—and the current culture toward fear is one—constitute a tricky topic. In the first place, they do invite hyperbole: to drive home a legitimate concern, it is almost irresistibly tempting to pretend a degree of cultural unity that does not exist and a level of dysfunction that strains credulity as well. Hopefully, we have avoided that shore. In the second place, attention to character flaws—or cultural deficiencies, to use a more appropriate label—risks angering the very people who should be encouraged to some self-evaluation. To be sure, conservatives have had some success in attacking the sexually permissive aspects of contemporary American character. But the concern about fear, though it need not be anticonservative, comes at American culture from a different, less familiar, and—it may be—more liberal angle, and may well antagonize its audience.

In the late 1970s, spurred by historian Christopher Lasch's fascinating exploration of an arguably increasing narcissism in the American psyche, a variety of commentators, including President Jimmy Carter, grew interested in exploring the deficiencies of contemporary values. Carter even worried about a national "malaise," and invited cultural redress. Lasch himself, though his findings were not widely accepted in the relevant scholarly community, clearly hoped for change, despite his pessimistic conclusions about cultural prospects. The project went nowhere, beyond generating a year or two of interesting commentary. The American public was not interested in being told it was malaised, greatly preferring a return to buoyant optimism and cold war targeting under Ronald Reagan, the Carter successor.[3]

The present study, though not unique in calling for a serious reassessment of the role of fear in American life, ranges less widely through American character than Lasch's effort did. We're talking about one emotional component, not about some overall moral collapse. But the analysis may face similar risks of provoking either disinterest or antipathy from conationals who dislike seeing their values critically probed by intellectuals, however well-intentioned. Reactions may even be worsened by the comparative element: in arguing that some Americans have responded less well to fear than counterparts in other places, this study risks stiffening a sturdy (and I think often misplaced) national reluctance to admit the possibility of learning from foreign example. The tension may be softened by the considerable recognition, even at the journalistic level, in the summer of 2005, that British reactions to terrorism did provide food for American thought. But there is no question that, in urging attention to cultural deficiencies, and comparative ones, we're treading on sensitive ground.

Difficulties are compounded by another obvious point: it is impossible to argue that all fear is wrong. Lasch might plausibly contend that narcissism is fundamentally shallow and misguided, even if that judgment did not dispose of the problem. Fear, however, is often useful, as noted above. Fear of terrorism is not only unavoidable but, potentially, desirable, if it's properly directed to enhanced alertness. Indeed, we will be contending—again, along with others—that improved understanding of fear actually provides leadership opportunities that have been missed so far; but again this acknowledges that some fear is both essential and constructive.

This conclusion, then, undertakes a difficult task: it argues that we need to consider some serious cultural repairs around an emotion that we not only will experience—because it's inherent—but should preserve and utilize. The overhaul is far less imposing than a full national character reform, and it hardly targets all Americans uniformly. While the argument calls into question some conservative policies, and a noticeable conservative impulse to manipulate fear, it also notes liberal misuse of fear and urges, in good conservative fashion, a desirable return to certain facets of American character that were better established a few decades ago than they are now. The argument, in other words, is not even straightforwardly partisan.

The conclusion does address both an American public and the American policy-making community. One approach to the drawbacks of contemporary American fear involves a claim that it is entirely manipulated by greedy commercial elements and self-serving politicians. And there is manipulation, without any question, including some deplorable uses of fears of terrorism. But the public has its own cultural standards, developed now over several decades; it participates actively in the fear equation. And many policy makers are ensnared in the same culture, both regarding their own fears and concerns about risk and regarding their estimates of public emotional capacity. This is an area where tracing the social and cultural roles of fear as part of a broad national canvass embraces the political component as well.[4]

THE NEWNESS OF AMERICAN FEAR, AND ITS CAUSES

What is most striking about contemporary American fear—before we return to the more challenging calls for changes in character and policy—is the novelty of so many of its standards and expressions. An important element of fear is unchangeable, of course. But the approach to the emotion, its use in media, its place in key cultural divisions, its recurrent sensitivity to real or imagined international threat—all have assumed major new dimensions during the twentieth century. We can return to an earlier image, the contrast between American military personnel in World War II and the Gulf War of 1990. In the first instance (according to an officers' manual of 1943), the soldier is enjoined to "smother" his fear through his pride and his "desire to retain the good opinion of his friends and associates"; in the second instance, aviators openly discuss their fears with television reporters prior to missions. The second group was not necessarily any more afraid, in terms of basic emotional content, than the first; but they had been taught to handle their emotions quite differently.[5]

While the evolution of the fundamental socialization toward fear, from the 1920s onward, is the key point—linked perhaps to changes in the experience of death—the enhanced use of fear in media presentations and the flowering of an apocalyptic strand constitute major departures as well—the former only partially prepared by prior Victorian shifts in popular literature. The association between new standards for fear and a concerted, sometimes almost desperate effort to limit many kinds of risk formed a final novelty, reaching, as we have seen, into legal culture and business practice alike.

In fact, though it would be tedious to develop the comparisons too exhaustively, the standards and expressions of fear have arguably changed more, and in a more complicated fashion, than corresponding features of almost any other emotion in the twentieth-century United States. (Grief would be the nearest competitor.) Anger, for example, came under new wraps from the 1920s onward, but this built on hesitations about familial anger from the Victorian period and was not so massively challenged by cultural expressions designed to evoke the emotion. Traditional strictures against envy were reversed, as the emotion gained praise for its role in stimulating consumption—this was a dramatic shift, but there was no particular complexity comparable to the reproval/attraction surrounding fear. Worries about jealousy mounted, but basic standards had already developed in the nineteenth century or earlier.[6]

And this means that some of the explanations for twentieth-century emotional change do not adequately capture the new foundations for fear, though they may apply in part. A number of scholars have identified a new concern about emotional intensity underlying changing reactions to emotions from anger to love; and fear would fit here as well, save for the contradictory commercial exploitation.[7] Cas Wouters fits fear into his general pattern of "informalization," in which people become more comfortable talking about emotions without feeling they will be overwhelmed by them. Again, a plausible approach: but clearly talking out fear does not provide the relief that venting jealousy may provide—intense aversion can remain, including of course the linked aversion to risk. The informalization model also suffers, where fear is concerned, from its blanket applicability to the United States and Western Europe; it fails as a result to account for distinctive American twists on fear standards and reactions.[8]

Fear, in other words, participated in some common processes of emotional change during the middle of the twentieth century. Expert warnings against the emotion in childhood paralleled new concerns about sibling rivalry or guilt. But the commercial use of fear, the religious current that could support apocalyptic representations, the inarticulate concern about American power that could support fear-soaked movie scenarios—these elements added to divisions, challenges, and heightened anxieties that other emotions did not command.

This degree of innovation and complexity, as well as the connection to physical dangers like disease or accident, finally, help explain why fear or potential fear caused such worry and evasion in the United States during much of the twentieth century. Fear was an unusually difficult emotion to handle, unless a person managed to avoid its provocation altogether. The fact that it was tied into reactions to external threat and the weariness with repeated foreign crises added to the difficulties and linked it to the world of policy, again as no other change in emotional standards could claim.

All of this adds up to a real issue of priorities in emotional control. The disproportionate change and complexity surrounding fear create needs thus far unaddressed, at least at any general level. Americans have grown familiar with notions of anger management, around problems sometimes more apparent than fear. The desirability of comparable attention to fear is indisputable, when the modern trajectories and consequences of the two emotions are juxtaposed.

THE RECENT CRESCENDO

Innovation has been compounded by a clear intensification of fear and avoidance during the past three decades—well before September 11 but clearly adding to its emotional impact. The indications are startling. Since the 1980s, a variety of Americans have become recurrently transfixed by representations of fear and the resultant urge to protect against it. Fear's presence has increased, and with it a greater measure of unease.

Fear found a new place in the political vocabulary. As early as the 1990s, Judith Shklar wrote revealingly of a "liberalism of fear." Boiled down (perhaps unduly), she contends that some of the classic liberal definitions of human rights have become too fuzzy—for example, invocations of an abstract natural right. Then, developments in the twentieth century, with the arbitrary actions of powerful governments and the reintroduction of torture into Western society, demonstrated how important it is for liberalism to begin, and possibly end, with a defense against cruelty. This is indeed a fearful liberalism—worried about attack rather than claiming new progress through wider individual rights—compared to some of the more ringing hopes and pronouncements of the eighteenth and nineteenth centuries. It reflects, as well, new levels of anxiety about government power—the need for defensive reactions. The liberalism of fear may reflect the spread of the emotion in modern (not just American) society, and Shklar's arguments suggest the newly broadened scope for fear references.[9]

Clearer, more directly emotional intensifications occurred in other arenas. The symptoms are varied. We have seen that advertisers found a new commercial vein in fear that they had largely downplayed or avoided in previous decades. It became fashionable to try to scare a public into buying a variety of products. Less surprisingly, media presentations of entertainment fear increased in number and, even more, in graphic quality; this included the expansion of the end-of-the-world scenarios in movie fare.

It was also from the 1980s onward that weather reports began to take on their more dramatic qualities, turning, wherever possible, from factual reports to dire warnings. By 2005, some commentators worried that "the undeniable tendency of every network and local TV station to go haywire over each tropical storm and minor-league hurricane" had reduced the capacity, on the part of responders, to distinguish between real menace and run-of-the-mill challenges. Fearmongers, in other words, might cry wolf too often; though for the wider public, every indication was that weather commentary simply added to a climate of recurrent fear, with penchants for behaviors like panic buying undimmed by repetition.[10]

The past quarter century saw repeated indications that many Americans were attaching fear to perceptions of danger that were not reality. Barry Glassner, in his superb 1999 study of fear culture, argued persuasively that Americans had become deeply afraid of a whole host of nonexistent threats. Why, he noted, as crime rates plunged during the 1990s, did two-thirds of Americans believe that they were soaring? By the middle of the decade, 62 percent of the population claimed to be "truly desperate" about crime, twice the figure of a decade prior despite the fact that rates had been higher at that earlier point. Glassner draws similar conclusions about drug use—declining, but amid rising popular fears and alarums.[11]

Glassner and others also point to the startling increase of health anxieties despite, again, improving longevity rates. In 1996, a magazine writer surveyed popular articles about the numbers of Americans claiming to be afflicted with dire disease like heart ailments, cancer, and obesity, and found that they added up to 543 million individuals—in a population of 266 million. Specific data were equally revealing: a Dartmouth survey found that American women in their forties believed that one in ten were likely to die of breast cancer, while the real figures were one in two hundred fifty.[12]

Clearly, the media were striking more fear chords than they had in the past, and finding a ready audience. The capacity to distinguish between fictional representations—the ubiquitous police shows on television—and reality deteriorated simultaneously. Americans also repeatedly magnified one or two horrible events—school shootings, for example—into a sense of omnipresent danger, increasing fears and installing safety screenings that simply maintained the emotional intensity. If by some chance fear dropped in one category, another moved in immediately to take its place.

With all apparent sincerity, experts and media combined to introduce new menaces whose only real novelty was a catchy label. "Road rage," another darling of the 1990s, was a case in point. Ignoring the fact that highway aggression changed very little, and that the more shocking instances of roadside shooting violence had occurred a decade earlier, police officials used the undeniably compelling new term to imply that driver behavior was veering out of control. And, characteristically, there was more than labeling involved. Popular tests urged drivers to probe their own propensity for road rage, claiming that feelings of anger against other motorists, or unheard curses, were symptoms of an ultimately murderous affliction. Mounting fears involved others, but, as with health, they could involve the self as well.[13]

Growing anxiety and risk aversion fed a spiral of reliance on professional therapists. Even moderate disasters brought a bevy of experts ready to offer comfort and to identify potential trauma. The trend itself may have been salutary, though there were few careful studies of the outcomes and little attention to the extent to which therapeutic gestures might encourage the articulation of fears that could otherwise have been privately managed. But good or bad, the phenomenon was new, and added to the evidence of emotional change.[14]

There was another angle, though this one became clearer after 2000. A new demographic cohort, the echo of the baby boom, was born between 1982 and 1995. The parents, from the original baby boom, displayed astonishingly protective behavior—hence the ultimate label, "helicopter parents," for their ever-hovering qualities. Careful supervision and constant organization of activities were designed to keep the new brood of kids out of danger, away from undue exposure to violent media, secure and confident. Safety devices multiplied, as part of this parental approach: not only bicycle helmets, but baby-proof bottle caps, electric socket protectors, even devices that automatically closed toilet seats against the possibility—had it ever happened?—of accidental drowning. This coddled, middle-class "millennial generation" was not only protected against fear and danger—there was also encouragement to self-esteem and other presumably positive qualities. But parental fear, and a desire to protect against fear, played a strong role in new generational behavior.

This whole panoply of intensification and protective reaction involving fear occurred, finally, as a host of threatening international risks subsided. The cold war wound down and finally ended. The threat of major nuclear war dropped to a lower point than at any time since the late 1940s. One might have expected, though not an end of history, at least a reduction in the emotional perception of threat. But precisely the reverse seemed to be occurring—even before September 11 added legitimate fuel to the fire.

What was going on? Glassner, in his pathbreaking study, suggests two factors. He notes the possibility of end-of-millennium and end-of-century angst. This was of course widely discussed during the 1990s, with some historians reaching back for what turned out to be largely mythical instances of widespread fear the last time a millennium had rolled around. The absence of extensive millennial fears in Europe or Asia also argued against this explanation—planning elaborate parties and superb fireworks displays seemed to take precedence over fearful cowering, and some countries, like Italy, did not even bother to worry much about the dreaded Y2K computer failure—with no dire consequences ensuing. In the United States, the rise of religious fundamentalism did expand a group alternatively nervous and gleeful about millennial forebodings and a coming Rapture, so the millennial factor in this one case existed, though more as symptom than as basic cause.[15]

But this left, for Glassner, a clear villain in the contemporary fear stakes: the media. And there is no question, as we have seen, that media were finding fear an increasingly successful emotional goad, amid growing competition for readership and viewership. It was striking, for example, that as foreign news declined on nightly telecasts during the 1990s—a fruit of the cold war's end—health news increased, catching American fear where it now seemed to live. No question, further, that growing numbers of Americans had become accustomed to taking media presentations for reality, blurring the line between entertainment and news and accepting an ever-mounting diet of fear in the process.

Yet surely more than media saturation was involved, for what the media explanation does not fully account for is why Americans found fear so mesmerizing. Media saturation is clearly part of the picture: we have seen Americans increasingly take not only data (real or imagined) but also outright emotional cues from media promptings, using presentations for guidance not only in public fear but also public grief. Media manipulation has been heightened, of course, by irresponsible political posturing. It was no accident that the most fear-soaked television channel, after September 11, Fox News, was also closest to the Bush administration. But viewing the relationship simply as a one-way street, media and politicians manipulating and Americans sheepishly responding, is implausible. Among other things, as all the major advertising histories have shown, media gurus not only study public culture, but are part of it. Larger cultural change alone makes the new directions of the media, and the new public receptivity, fully comprehensible.

And here, we have seen, there are several crucial factors, beyond the media. Religious change is obviously one, though there's a chicken-and-egg issue here. Americans became more religious toward the end of the twentieth century, as measured both by church (or equivalent) attendance and professed belief, and, of course, the surge of evangelical commitments was an important part of this. Religious enthusiasm left more people open to older traditions of apocalyptic thinking, and as we have seen this could have a spillover effect on a larger public as well. It is also possible—the which-came-first issue—that a rise in fear contributed to the religious turn.

Increased parental anxiety—the generational change associated with more hovering parental monitoring—was also intriguing: surely it reflected reaction to the more freewheeling behaviors of the 1960s, in which many parents had participated during their own youth. Did the baby-boom generation—raised among other things amid intense nuclear anxiety—harbor fears that would blossom further as they reached middle age?

Other changes, studied in different venues, may enter in. The strong indications that American community and associational ties have declined, with more people living alone, "bowling alone" rather than participating in wider social activities, have obvious implications for fear. So does the related decline of confidence, as measured by polls over the past two decades, in political and professional leaders and government institutions. Religion aside, more people may feel they're facing danger alone or at most with families—the kind of personalized orientation that shone through so clearly in post–September 11 stories, but that surely took hold well before this particular crisis.[16]

But the primary impetus for the spike in fear involves the long-term effects of trends that had begun earlier and were displaying a cumulative power by the century's end, in combination with media pressure and religious appeals. Even voluntary exposure to fear fare in entertainment might have wearing effects, increasing a sense of danger in the surrounding environment and leaving people less able to distinguish between perception and reality where fear was involved. This was media impact in a sense, but over a longer term, in association with the intensification of fear-based entertainment that began some decades back. Even more important was the long-term redefinition of the appropriate socialization for fear, urging avoidance and reassurance over emotional confrontation. Here, as we have seen, a cultural shift began in the 1920s, reaching wider parental attention by the 1940s and 1950s, and affecting still wider venues, such as military manuals, by the 1970s. In a real sense, hovering contemporary helicopter parents were merely putting into fuller practice, in protecting from fear and risk, standards that took initial shape three generations earlier and gained greater impact with each passing decade. Join with this the effects of five decades of crisis fears—the war scares of the confrontation with the Soviets, the anxiety about nuclear destruction. Join, finally, the clear escalation of media signals from the 1980s onward. The result was a pattern of fear expectation and discomfort that made many Americans easy game for scare headlines or terrorist threats, fearful of their surroundings even when, as in the 1990s, many dangers objectively receded.

During the decade, observers recurrently mentioned how some Americans missed the cold war. They usually meant a longing for a clear-cut enemy, an indisputable target for moral outrage. And indeed, efforts to find a new Hitler- or Stalin-like antagonist—Saddam Hussein was the most common choice, however stretched the analogy in power terms—suggested that the nostalgia was quite real. But it may be that fear, as well as legitimate targets for anger, were somehow missed, as if some people had grown so accustomed to worrying about danger and protecting from its emotional discomfort that, with real threat reduced, they sought alternatives.

It is never easy to disentangle a chain of historical factors, beginning with the new psychological expertise and the sense of the irreplaceability, but also the fragility, of precious children. Complexity was enhanced by the time it takes for new emotional signals to take wide hold—a process of two or three generations, and by the tension added by the concomitant recalculation of risk. War weariness, and the blending of new crises with older examples, provided the further opening toward particular fear of foreigners. The chain became intricate, effectively overdetermined by the early twenty-first century.

This means, of course, that redressing the fear nexus will be difficult, even aside from the obvious challenge of resisting media dominance. There are a number of pressures to unravel, from anxieties about children to frequent frenzy in the face of apparent foreign threat. The causal package needs to be addressed, however, because the present climate of public emotion is not only unpleasant, but counterproductive.

The whole combination has been enhanced, finally, by deliberate manipulation, including increasing commercial exploitation and, to a lesser degree, by the ubiquity of fear themes in a variety of entertainment forms (this last, however, more symptom than cause, save for a few overexposed individuals).[17]

The acceleration of fear and protective reactions, in advance of September 11, set the stage for the distinctive responses to the terrorist attack—in combination with the agony of the attack itself. Media guidance, but even more what was by this point a considerable historical experience with an aversive culture toward fear and risk, crystallized an emotional pitch that would affect policy makers and public alike. The emotional response in turn, though explainable, was in many respects unfortunate, not only extremely painful but in some measurable ways counterproductive.

THE DOWNSIDES OF AMERICAN FEAR

In the wake of the London subway attacks in July 2005, an Internet-based organization, Wearenotafraid.com, formed, and quickly drew wide support from people in many countries, including the United States. The rhetorically fearless response corresponded with the dominant public mood in Britain. It picked up interest from many who were tired of terrorist braggadocio and who felt that levels of fear and uncertainty manifested on other occasions, including September 11, needed a corrective. The site won eighteen million hits in a single week, showing that it met a need to provide clear options for some of the earlier models of fear response. Inevitably, some observers quickly objected, not to advocate incapacitating fear but to urge the salutary importance of some fear in stimulating alertness. The discussion was mature and appropriate. What is needed, against terrorism, is to clarify that emotional intimidation will not win through, while retaining a sufficient stimulus to prompt watchfulness. If there could be agreement that these goals, admittedly not easily combined, describe the desirable emotional range, prospects would be good for this aspect of public preparedness.

But elements of American fear do not thus far fit within that range, because of the emotion's complex history, and its involvement in the exhausting sequence of international alarums during the later twentieth century. Excessive fear—the kind to which many Americans have become susceptible as a result of twentieth-century trends, the kind that surpasses constructive motivation—has several measurable drawbacks. These drawbacks apply in personal life, concerning, for example, misplaced fears about health or children. And they have come to have serious consequences in public policy as well.

- Fear can worsen the quality of life. That's an inherent aspect of the emotion, particularly when experienced over any period of time, and we've shown that the discomfort has expanded, in recent decades, given the growing range of targets fear commands. While some individuals may revel in fear as an opportunity to test courage—and many more may muster courage in fact—this is not the culturally dominant approach. Excessive health fears affect well-being, sometimes more than the objective health problems do. Excessive fears about children's security and welfare have demonstrably reduced the enjoyment of parenting: polls between the 1930s and the 1980s reveal a steady decline in parental pleasure, the only exception being (somewhat ironically, given their characteristic lack of involvement) divorced fathers. It is even possible that certain fear-based disorders, such as panic attacks, have increased, in response to the growing discomfort with fear.[18]

Pronouncements about trying to reduce excessive fear in the interest of contentment risk sounding hollow. Certainly, there is no precise proof of the extent to which pervasive American anxieties affect the quality of life. But specific examples, like health and parenting, show a clear relationship. And as fear has extended, during the cold war and again more recently, even frightened concerns about foreign dangers color and damage the daily existence of many Americans, and where they are exaggerated or misplaced, thanks to strong emotion, they deserve attention on these grounds alone.

The same strictures may apply to excessive anxiety about limiting risk, though the boundaries between what is constructive, what simply tension-producing may be even harder to draw. Great advances have occurred on the strength of refusal to accept preventable mishaps as risks, and the whole evolution of the tort concept has played a significant role in disciplining unruly corporate behavior and supporting appropriate regulation of product safety and the like. But many Americans suffer, as well, from an inability to assess risk accurately: their desire for security prompts a sometimes wildly overblown view of jeopardy—which returns many of them to fear and its consequences to their equilibrium. We know that many traditional societies overdosed on fatalism, failing to work to prevent eminently preventable mishaps. But American society, arguably, has moved too far in the other direction, worrying about dangers that either cannot be reasonably prevented or are sufficiently remote that undue anxiety is simply misplaced. Some rebalancing is essential to enhance peace of mind, reducing emotional tension, without measurably increasing real vulnerability.

- Excessive fear distorts. One of the most troubling concomitants of the spike in public and private fears over the past two decades is the extent to which emotionality replaces fact. Examples, as previously stated, include misperceptions of the risk of breast cancer and the long confusion about actual crime rate trends. This is no mere scholarly fussiness about accuracy. Personal decisions and public debate can be immeasurably damaged by the obstinate insistence on inaccurate data. Arguably, the intensification of fear following September 11 contributed further examples of the phenomenon, in the willingness to believe inaccurate information about Iraq's weapons program, not only in advance of invasion but well after initial administration claims about weapons of mass destruction had been disproved and abandoned (though not apologized for). Fear and distortion feed each other, in contemporary American discourse, and the result is deeply dangerous.

Distortion hits personal as well as national policy: immediately after September 11, sales of home protection devices went up massively, as people rushed to buy burglar alarms and the like. The reaction was understandable, given the level of anxiety, and it allowed people to "do something"; it also reflected the high degree of personalization in the reactions to the attack, as Americans somehow merged terrorism with other concerns about family security. But the response was entirely irrelevant to the actual terrorist threat, harmless perhaps but a clear sign of the ways American fear can mislead. Bin Laden was not going to be deterred by a better home security system.

- Excessive fear can lead not only to misguided decisions, but to measures that are actually counterproductive. The same studies that reveal wildly exaggerated fears of breast cancer show that many of the most fearful women refuse to get medical check-ups because of their conviction that only dire news will result. This means, of course, that they actually enhance the possibility of developing cancers that pass the point of safe treatment.

Though the connection can be debated, emotional reactions to September 11, operating at the policy level but with substantial public support, have displayed precisely this counterproductive tendency. Fear, and a desire to avoid risk and blame at any cost, prompted rigorous new measures to oversee immigration. Countless potential friends of the United States, including businessmen, students, and scholars, have been turned away or antagonized as a result. The number includes many moderate Muslims, precisely the group a more balanced, less risk-averse national policy ought to be encouraging. World opinion, initially highly sympathetic to American suffering, has been repeatedly antagonized by measures justified in terms of the narrowest kinds of reactions to the terrorist threat. Abuse of prisoners? Vice President Dick Cheney brushed aside a Republican-sponsored bill to assure humane treatment on grounds that it might interfere with the war on terror. And, of course, there was the invasion of Iraq itself, undertaken in defiance of the largest international demonstrations ever launched, justified on grounds of preventing risk and expressing fear—at a cost to effective national policy the dimensions of which are still hard to calculate.[19]

And fear at the level of panic can be particularly counterproductive. During 2004–5 two experiences in Washington, D.C., with small planes inadvertently violating reserved air space, found federal workers urged from their buildings by supervisors, and told to run for their lives. The response not only heightened further fear; it put employees often at greater risk, had some real attack been involved, than if they had stayed in relatively secure spots within their office complex. The response did, however, exculpate the building administrators, in the best risk-averse fashion. At least they had relocated the danger.

Even aside from panic, the rise of American fear has reduced the capacity for subtlety that many of the issues involved actually require. Distinctions among types of crime yield to fear-derived pressures for mandatory sentencing requirements. Nuances in dealing with foreign governments take a back seat to a with-us-against-us policy that in part results from high emotion.

- Finally, in terms of major drawbacks, fear can distort focus, drawing disproportionate attention to the apparent fear source at the expense of other issues of equal or possibly greater importance. Exaggerated fear of crime has repeatedly drawn resources away from other urban needs. Single-minded concentration on the "war on terror," since September 11, has measurably reduced attention to developments in places like Latin America and China, where changes may have greater implications for American well-being in the long run. It has forced policies, even toward places like southern Africa, into the awkward antiterrorism mold.[20]

This same narrowing tendency, based on high emotion, leads to a pronounced tendency to overemphasize responses to the last problem, rather than trying to anticipate the next one. Thus fearful French leaders, after the horrors of World War I, built their defensive Maginot Line to prevent the German invasion that occurred in 1914, but it proved irrelevant to the invasion possible by the 1930s. Thus Americans agonize over possible repeats of September 11 that, many critics contend, are less likely than some less familiar probe. The expense and inconvenience directed toward air travel have measurably reduced resources and attention devoted to other security risks—such as trains, where except for new warning signs security procedures changed little. Yet arguably, given some modest new precautions, airplanes were unlikely to be used again, as opposed to other venues. Fascination with fighting the last battle, a clear expression of fear, extends even to the now-classic ritual of shoe removal at airports, thanks to a single incident soon after September 11—despite that fact that security measures outside the United States almost uniformly omit the practice with no apparent ill effects. Excessive fear continues to encourage a further commitment to prevent the past from recurring rather than a calmer and more balanced assessment of threats and corresponding deployment of resources.

Excessive fear, in other words, has many of the consequences socially that it can have for individuals, and it has led—is leading—to undesirable results at several levels.

The culture of fear was sufficiently established before September 11, and then exacerbated by the attack itself, to promote doubts about public reliability in the policy community. Measures that might have been taken, for example to establish watch groups, that would have resembled steps after Pearl Harbor (and also British antiterror programs more recently) were sidestepped, presumably because political leaders worried that fears would simply redouble. The result, some have suggested, actually lost an opportunity to reduce free-floating anxiety with a sense of concrete and responsive activity. Many of our political leaders share public fears; they encourage them; but they do distrust also the public that results.[21]

Still more obviously, American fear culture opens many people to excessive manipulability. This was a concern even before September 11, for example in Barry Glassner's warnings about commercial and political exploitation based on fear and exaggerated perception of risk. The concern has to deepen in the wake of the terrorist attack. Given federal monomania on the subject, an amazing array of interests now find profit in promoting fear campaigns. Industries selling presumably protective items, universities promoting research agendas based on biological or chemical threats, politicians simply touting their own indispensability—all can and do play the fear game. Political exploitation may be most explicit, like the absolutely indefensible effort in the 2004 presidential contest to claim that the election of John Kerry would make a terrorist attack a virtual certainty, but there are many hogs at the trough.[22] Some advocates quite sincerely believe that scaring the public into funding new endeavors is a vital protective step, others are simply scam artists. But collective impact is tremendous, and it both utilizes and further extends the kind of crescendo of fear reactions that has been building for two decades in the United States. The "war on terror," like wars on crime and drugs before it, though on an even larger scale, has become a catchall, available to justify almost anything, often with little thought attached. The military-industrial complex that Dwight Eisenhower warned against almost half a century ago has thrived and expanded, and it has gained great skill in using fear to feed its fiscal appetites. And fear is the emotional deterrent to careful consideration of the trends involved.[23]

And this means, of course, that fear is costly. Where we fear dangers that are in fact improbable, we risk spending money needlessly—on prisons, for example, to house the world's largest jail population despite the decline of crime and the dubiousness of many drug arrests. Where we focus on single issues, including battling past foreign threats regardless of their likelihood of literal recurrence, we pour money into activities with disregard for the impact on other areas of need, regardless indeed of longer-term fiscal health. It's not that we shouldn't spend big money to prevent danger—and the conflict with terrorism, though not the only threat around, certainly warrants this kind of commitment. But when fear is evoked, whether the subject is the cold war or terror, it becomes almost impossible to discuss rational limits or larger fiscal consequences—hence the horrendous budget and balance of payments deficits of the 1980s and the 2000s, which will have their own impact on the national future. Americans are not good, socially or personally, at setting spending limits, and our lack of control over fear compounds the problem.

In the process, ironically, excessive fear can trump some of the values of constructive fear. Again in response to terrorism: color coding, which served to maintain high anxiety with no particular focus, while potentially exculpating government authorities should something actually happen, substituted for more careful organization of public watchfulness. A possible if brief opportunity to use emotion to build tighter community was dissipated in favor of a laissez-faire strategy in which individual Americans were essentially urged to keep shopping while worrying a lot.

American policies in response to fear have had their successes. The nation has not collapsed in anxiety. But fear has limited responsible public discussion. It has distorted many government measures and civic responses to these measures. It has joined leaders and wider public in policies that are excessively narrow, costly, and sometimes clearly counterproductive. It has also encouraged pitchmen of various sorts, including many leaders, to take advantage of public emotionality, toward self-interested and sometimes undesirable purposes. The emotion, intended to warn against danger, has become dangerous.

It's always hazardous to predict how subsequent historians will view a present condition, but it's doubtful that they will find American reactions to September 11, over time, one of the nation's finest hours. To be sure, there was no retreat; this was not an American Vichy; indeed, if anything the problem was a fear-induced excess of belligerence. But the extent to which fear caused Americans to accept overgeneralized repression, torture, and military aggression will not sit well with later observers of the early twenty-first century. Nor will the extent to which it encouraged bad and duplicitous budgeting. Sorting out the role of emotion versus leadership incompetence will not be easy, but a safe conclusion will surely involve both factors. By 2006, amid growing prejudice against foreigners, and particularly Muslims, both political parties seemed to be competing for fear votes at the national level. Republicans vied for police powers attention: in their fear vocabulary, arbitrary wiretaps and seizures were vital to prevent terrorist infiltrations. But Democrats risked competing at least as irresponsibly for primacy in measures to restrict foreign involvement in American life. No large leadership group seemed willing to stand up against excessive fear itself. The result was lowest-common-emotional-denominator politics that jeopardized constructive policy debates and choices.

REDUCING FEAR

What is to be done? The most obvious injunctions—to urge people to fear less—offer dubious utility. Most people would fear less if they easily could. There is no panacea. But one of the advantages of exploring the historical origins of contemporary American fear is to suggest also that it can be modified: what cultural forces have helped create, a new set of forces can potentially undo. The fact that American fear levels are not simply inevitable, not part of some set of inexplicable forces, is ultimately encouraging—which is the justification for the historical analysis in the first place. Nor, as we've seen, is unusual sensitivity to fear part of some timeless national character, despite two deeply rooted components; for the most part, the sensitivity is a more recent historical product. To be sure, history does not tell us how to undo, and the combination of trends that have built American fear suggest that modifications will be difficult. Still, simply thinking more objectively about fear, and grasping its historical context, will help in reducing the contagion effect. Seeking to banish most fear and risk, modern American culture has actually opened the door to new, and often, needless anxieties; understanding this historical process is the first step to redress.

Addressing what can fairly be called the fear problem involves responsibilities from leadership and the general public alike. Leadership involvement must include an awareness of the pitfalls of current American fear culture. Most obviously, rousing unnecessary fears, or sending panic signals as a means of deflecting involvement in possible risk, is irresponsible in the extreme, whether the goal is political or commercial. The same applies—and here the focus is diplomatic and military—to dubious foreign adventures that fan fears for a war-weary population. But expecting widespread emotional fragility is equally unnecessary, and encourages free-floating anxieties rather than constructive community action. Public responsibilities are considerable as well, and hopefully they can derive from a better understanding of fear issues and their causes. We need to work toward a public pride in facing (and not necessarily always articulating) fears and risks and toward a greater intolerance for excess and exaggeration. Based on recent national experiences, whatever the proper level of fear over the currently fashionable danger, whether it is crime or health threats or terrorism, it is unlikely to be as great as many will be tempted to assume. Fear must not make us respond to invocations of a menace like terrorism like a Pavlovian dog, ready to sign off on whatever the latest initiative is without serious consideration.

Four targets warrant particular attention. The first involves some reconsideration of our socialization process, toward a greater willingness to allow children to have experiences of courage, to encourage them to learn to deal with certain fears with less adult guidance and intrusion. This is not an invitation to crazy risk taking, for there are plenty of fears without daredevil behaviors. It is an invitation to rethink character building, to do more than cite distant heroes or great generations in the past, but to shape more opportunities to encounter and overcome fears in more personal terms.

Most developmental psychologists and historians of American childhood believe that children's strength and resilience have been seriously underestimated over recent decades. It is neither irresponsible nor farfetched to believe that an approach to children, and through them to adults, that urges a greater willingness to face certain fears and learn from the experience, rather than sidestepping or compensating at every opportunity, could produce real benefits. Changing socialization is, of course, a challenging task, but it can occur and fear is a good place to start. And consciously thinking about the temptation to bypass emotional sturdiness, in favor of some kind of sugarcoating, can set the process in motion, one parent at a time.

Second, and this can be part of socialization as well, though it must continue in adulthood, we desperately need a better approach to assessing magnitudes of risk. Knowing that, aside from September 11, Americans in the past decade have been much more likely die from a lightning strike or even drowning in a bathtub than at the hand of terrorists does not mean we should not fear terrorism, but it certainly provides some degree of perspective that can help hold emotion in check. There's an obvious educational challenge here involving more functional training in statistical assessment. More broadly, we need larger doses of critical skepticism when risks are cited, whether the subject is child abduction or the likelihood of mass casualties from a dirty bomb. Americans must develop a better capacity to calculate probabilities and to make decisions on this basis rather than through misleading invocations of fear or a foolish quest to eliminate even the slightest likelihood of risk. They must insist on greater accuracy from leaders and media, and punish consistent exaggerations with loss of votes or subscriptions. We may, on occasion, decide to spend massively to reduce still further an improbable danger, but this should be a matter of sober deliberation, not emotional neediness.

There is simply no question that, on issues ranging from physical dangers to children, to crime rates, to terrorist probabilities, we have become terrible estimators of the reality of threat. We constantly rush to monitor situations unlikely to occur and to anticipate problems that are unlikely to materialize. The tide of free-floating anxiety rises too high. We need to become better calculators, and to insist on more careful calculations from those who purport to advise us. We need more conscious, rational control over our level of worry and our choice of targets. We need to be able to develop the political and social capacity to discuss excessive fear. One of the consequences of changes in emotional standards, of the sort we have probed for fear, involves shifts in evaluations of one's own and others' emotion. This has certainly occurred in fear: more Americans, whether more fearful or not in fact, have felt increasingly authorized to discuss their fears openly and often. And, more important, few Americans have felt comfortable—as their ancestors surely would have—in suggesting that some groups are too afraid. We may think this privately, but given the new cultural standards it seems uncouth to say so. As a result, we are hampered in our ability to deal with public fears as a political issue, and we should work to improve on this impasse. Fears are legitimate topics for public, if respectful, debate. As with the patterns of socialization we have fallen into, this will require real effort, but it is well worth the exertion.

We need, finally, to work hard to control the media or at least our reactions to media fearmongering—and advertisers and political campaigners fall squarely in this category as well. Again, a critical capacity is crucial here. Certain kinds of fear appeals should simply be laughed off the stage. Political fair practice standards must include some criteria in this area. To revert to a 2004 example: it was obviously appropriate discuss different strategies toward averting terrorist attacks, as part ᴏɪ the presidential campaign; but to permit an emotion-laden assertion that one party made terrorist incursions virtually inevitable (with the attendant implication that the other party could assure the contrary) must not be allowed to happen again. Where media or politicians remain reluctant to self-police—and given several decades of successful appeals to fear, this will be some time in coming—we need an active public monitoring system to call them to account, and a public willingness to withdraw support. A fear calculus must become a central part of assessments of negative campaigning, with a willingness to call manipulators to account. It is not safe, where fear is concerned, to continue to take so many emotional cues from media and partisan sources.

These injunctions are written at the time when the nation has in fact been spared a terrorist attack for over four years. They are not, however, the product of this period of grace, and would apply equally strongly should another attack occur. Terrorism is a genuine problem; it warrants all sorts of sensible precautions; it can cause huge destruction. It is not, however, the scourge our fears have made it out to be. We must hope that it can be deterred, but we must also hope to be able to handle it with some degree of emotional balance, if only because its range of damage depends so greatly on the reactions it produces.

For the manipulative incitements to fear have become far more harmful than the common targets of sexual titillation or casual violence. The danger exists regardless of motivation—sincere, exploitative, or merely participant in the general culture. Consumer organizations and political watch groups need to resist excessive appeals to fear, deliberately offering more sober assessments of risks. The American public must be encouraged to assess and respond to problems without an extra goad of fear. And the public must learn to punish the merchants of fear at the sales counter, in the ratings, and at the polls. It is vital to develop the capacity to debate claims of risk and fear, and to summon up a new severity against those who abuse a national emotional vulnerability.

FEAR AND SELF-CONTROL

Various American observers, over recent decades, have worried loudly about American capacity for self-control. There are certainly legitimate subjects for discussion, from sexual permissiveness to overeating. The capacity is not, however, uniformly defective. For example, Americans brawl less than they did a century ago. Despite misleading campaigns over road rage, most Americans self-regulate their driving better than their counterparts in many countries. We are not, overall, a people running amuck. We have learned to handle several emotions, like anger and jealousy, more responsibly—in terms of operating in a complex managerial society—than was once the case. But, though it's an unfamiliar category, we have seen our capacity for self-control over fear deteriorate, and it is vital to identify a real need here and to work to regain a wider measure of public composure. Excessive fear has become the emotional equivalent of smoking, hurting individuals and society alike, and we must attend to it.[24]

The solutions are not easy, since, unlike smoking, we neither can nor should go cold turkey on fear altogether. The process of remediation begins with a real effort at understanding our current emotional vulnerabilities and the historical processes involved. As many Americans know from individual experience, but as we need now to promote on a wider social level, the capacity to control excessive fear begins with some ability to think about it, to step back from it, in all but the most urgent panic situations. Emotions, even basic ones like fear, are open to rational evaluation and a considerable degree of rational control, but the process starts with rethinking our cultural standards, and the way they have come to inform our emotional cognition, such that a degree of dispassion replaces a knee-jerk reach for venting and reassurance.

The issue is not primarily personal emotional comfort, though it is clear that a better handle on fear, a greater ability to evaluate risk, would really bring some solace to many individual Americans. Given the role fear has come to play in policy making, from crime to key facets of diplomacy, and even in budget decisions, it is not farfetched to argue that a vital part of the nation's future depends on an ability to gain better emotional control in this area, where policymakers and general public alike have faltered so noticeably in recent decades.

The New Deal aphorism, uttered in a different time and a substantially different culture, undeniably oversimple even then, deserves to be recalled. Franklin Roosevelt's memorable phrase highlighted the early part of his first (1933) inaugural address. He directed it against the emotional corollaries of economic depression. His phrase derived from writings of Thoreau ("nothing is as much to be feared as fear") and others in the American and Western intellectual heritage, and it recalled (as we can see today) an earlier popular emotional tradition as well. The full phrasing has even more merit than the familiar quote: "Let me assert my firm belief that the only thing we have to fear is fear itself—nameless, unreasoning, unjustified terror which paralyzes needed efforts to convert retreat into advance. In every dark hour of our national life a leadership of frankness and vigor has met with that understanding and support of the people themselves which is essential to victory."

American society, with many strengths but many problems, has a clear emotional issue. More than in the 1930s, with a wider range of consequences, fear itself has become, in truth, a legitimate target of fear—the kind of constructive fear that can produce positive results.

ENDNOTES

PREFACE

1. Linton Leeks, "Fear Factory," *Washington Post*, Style Section, December 4, 2005.
2. G. T. W. Patrick, "The New Optimism," *Popular Science Monthly*, 82 (May 1913): 492–503. See also Basil King, *The Conquest of Fear* (New York: 1921), cited in James Farrell, *Inventing the American Way of Death* (Philadelphia: 1980), who properly notes the link between this new attack on fear and the belief that death could be relegated to old age—a connection we take up later as well.

CHAPTER 1

1. David Greenstone, "Frightened George: How the Pediatric-Educational Complex Ruined the Curious George Series," *Journal of Social History* 39 (2005): 221–28; Margret Rey and H. A. Rey, *The Complete Adventures of Curious George* (Boston: 2001).
2. Peter N. Stearns, ed., *American Behavioral History* (New York: 2005).
3. Arlie Russell Hochschild, *The Managed Heart: Commercialization of Human Feeling* (Berkeley: 1983) and, with Anne Machung, *Second Shift* (New York: 1989); Carol Tavris, *Anger: The Misunderstood Emotion* (New York: 1982).
4. Peter N. Stearns and Timothy Haggerty, "The Role of Fear: Transitions in American Emotional Standards for Children, 1850–1950," *American Historical Review* 96 (1991): 63–94.
5. Barry Glassner, *The Culture of Fear: Why Americans Are Afraid of the Wrong Things* (New York: 1999); see also Judith Shklar, "The Liberalism of Fear," in *Liberalism and the Moral Life*, ed. Nancy Rosenblum (Cambridge, MA: 1989); Mary Douglas and Aaron Wildavsky, *Risk and Culture: An Essay on the Selection of Technological and Environmental Dangers* (Berkeley: 1982); Cass Sunstein, *The Laws of Fear* (Cambridge: 2005). Joanna Bourke. *Fear: a Cultural History* (Emeryville, CA: 2006), provides an intriguing account of a changing panorama of mostly private fears, arguing that fear has become the dominant emotion of modern—not just American society.
6. Cass Sunstein, *Risk and Reason: Safety, Law and the Environment* (New York: 2002).
7. Corey Robin, *Fear: The History of a Political Idea* (New York: 2004).
8. Theodore Kemper, ed., *Research Agendas in the Sociology of Emotions* (Albany, NY: 1990) and "Social Constructionist and Positive Approaches to the Sociology of Emotions," *American Journal of Sociology* 87 (1981): 336–62; Rom Harré, ed., *The*

Social Construction of Emotions (Oxford: 1986); Catherine Lutz and G. White, "The Anthropology of Emotions," *Annual Review of Anthropology* 15 (1986): 405–36; Owen Lynch, ed., *Divine Passions: The Social Construction of Emotion in India* (Berkeley: 1990).

9. Cas Wouters, "On Status Completion and Emotion Management: The Study of Emotions as a New Field," *Theory, Culture and Society* 9 (1992): 229–52.

10. Peter N. Stearns, *Jealousy: The Evolution of an Emotion in American History* (New York: 1989).

11. Peter N. Stearns, *American Cool: Constructing a Twentieth-Century Emotional Style* (New York: 1994), ch. 5.

12. Susan Matt, *Keeping Up with the Joneses: Envy in American Consumer Society* (Philadelphia: 2003).

13. Herbert Jacob, *Silent Revolution: The Transformation of Divorce Law in the United States* (Chicago: 1988); Stearns, *American Cool*, ch. 8.

14. Shula Sommers, "Adults Evaluating Their Emotions: A Crosscultural Comparison," in Carol Malatesta and Carroll Izard, eds., *Emotion in Adult Development* (Beverly Hills, CA: 1984): 313–36.

15. Mahmut Makal, *A Village in Anatolia* (London: 1954).

16. A. P. Martinich, *Hobbes: A Biography* (New York: 1999), 1–2; cited in Robin, *Fear*.

17. Gregory Smits, "Shaking Up the World: Mid Nineteenth-Century Japanese Urban Society through the Lens of Catfish Prints," *Journal of Social History* 29 (2005): 873–90.

18. Peter N. Stearns, *Global Outrage: The Origins, Evolution and Impact of World Opinion* (London: 2005).

19. Robin, *Fear*.

CHAPTER 2

1. *Washington Post*, A section, January 15, 2005.

2. ABC News, July 7, 2005; *Washington Post*, July 8, 2005. See also CNN Special Report, July 15, 2005, "Your Emails: London Bombings," http://www.cnn.com/2005/WORLD/europe/07/07/feedback.london (accessed October 20, 2005). Here too most entries avoided fear in favor of stiff-upper-lipness.

3. Leonie Huddy, Stanley Feldman, Charles Taber, and Gallya Lahav, "The Politics of Threat: Cognitive and Affective Reactions to 9/11," paper presented at the annual meeting of the American Political Science Association, Boston, August 29–September 1, 2002.

4. Humphrey Taylor, "America Attacked: What the Polls Tell Us," Harris Poll #46, September 19, 2001; Huddy, Feldman, Taber, and Lahav, "Politics of Threat." See also Susan Janssen, "A Kind of September: Impact of Terrorist Attacks on College Students' Lives and Intimate Relationships," D\AA Kind of September-Impact on Student Lives. "National experiment conducted by Carnegie Mellon scientists reviewed impact of fear, anger on American perceptions of terrorism," *APA Online: Psychology in the News*, April 10, 2002.

5. Mark Harris, Franklin Mitchell, and Steven Schechter, *The Homefront: America During World War II* (New York: 1984), 24; see also 17–29.

6. Pauline Parker, ed. *Women of the Homefront: World War II Recollections of 55 Americans* (Jefferson, NC: 2002), 7–12 (on Honolulu), 17–39 (on Japanese Americans), 39–42 (on other early reactions) Eugenia Kaledin, *Daily Life in the United States, 1940–1959* (Westport, CT: 2000), 3–29; Harris, Mitchell, and Schechter, *The Homefront*, 17–29.

7. "Harrell, Charles T." Side B, AFS 6454 (original disc), LWO 3493, Reel 45, Side B.

8. "Mansfield, Matt." Side A, AWS 6445 (original disc), LWO 3493, Reel 45, Side A.

9. "Allen, Matt." Side B, AFS 6453 (original disc), LWO 3493, Reel 45, Side B.

10. Paul Fussell, "The Real War, 1939–45," *Atlantic Monthly* 264 (August, 1989): 33–40 and *Wartime: Understanding and Behavior in the Second World War* (New York: 1989).

11. Tanya Gingerich Warren, Story #9620, The September 11 Digital Archive, September 11, 2003, http://911digitalarchive.org/stories/details/9620.

12. Michelle Moore, Story #10816, The September 11 Digital Archive, September 9, 2004, http://911 digitalarchive.org/stories/details/10816.

13. Nancy, Story #9730, The September 11 Digital Archive, September 11, 2003, http://911digitalarchive.org/stories/details/10880.

14. Blake Buckman, Story #10880, The September 11 Digital Archive, September 30, 2003, http://911digitalarchive.org/stories/details/10880.

15. Brandie Washington, Story #103777, The September 11 Digital Archive, September 3, 2004, http://911digitalarchive.org/stories/details/10777.

16. Stefanie Boaz, Story #10430, The September 11 Digital Archive, February 10, 2004, http://911digitalarchive.org/stories/details/10430.

17. Cynthia Marshall, Story #10279, The September 11 Digital Archive, December 26, 2003, http://911digitalarchive.org/stories/details/10279.

18. Mimi Atkins, Story #9477, The September 11 Digital Archive, September 6, 2003, http://911digitalarchive.org/stories/details/9477.

19. Jessica Story #9396, The September 11 Digital Archive, July 30, 2003, http://911digitalarchive.org/stories/details/9396.

20. Cindy Newkir, Story 9332, The September 11 Digital Archive, June 3, 2003, http://911digitalarchive.org/stories/details/9332.

21. http://911digitalarchive.org (accessed July 9, 2006).

22. Michael Kazin, "12/12 and 9/11: Tales of Power and Tales of Experience in Contemporary History," Georgetown University presentation, February 20, 2005. My thanks to Professor Kazin for a copy of his paper.

23. See note 13 above (Nancy's Story); also Courtney B. Abrams, Karen Albright, and Aaron Panofsky, "Contesting the New York Community: From Liminality to the 'New Normal' in the Wake of September 11," *City & Community* 3, no. 3 (September 2004): 189–220.

24. Parker, *Women of the Homefront*; Kaledin, *Daily Life in the United States*; Harris, Mitchell, and Schechter, *The Homefront*.

25. Bradley Greenberg, *Communication & Terrorism: Public and Media Responses to 9/11* (Cresskill, NJ: 2002). See also Aryah Neier, "America's New Nationalism," *Social Research* 71, no. 4 (Winter 2004), on why terrorism bites so deeply.

26. Peter N. Stearns, *Anxious Parents: The History of Modern Childrearing in America* (New York: 2002); Robert Putnam, *Bowling Alone: The Collapse and Revival of the American Community* (New York: 2000).

27. Gary Becker and Hona Rubinstein, "Fear and the Response to Terrorism: An Economic Analysis" (draft report, August 2004, available from the authors at University of Chicago Department of Economics or Tel Aviv University School of Economics).

28. "Horror Turns to Action in Madrid," *Guardian Unlimited*, March 11, 2004; Tracy Wilkinson, "Millions March against Attacks in Madrid," *Pittsburgh Post-Gazette*, March 13, 2004; Khatya Chhor, "Western Press Review," Radio Free Europe, March 15, 2004.

29. Ian Black, "The European Dilemma," *Guardian Unlimited*, April 2, 2004; J. F. O. McAllister, "Fear Factor," *Time Europe*, November 7, 2005: Al Goodman, "Spain, Poll Triumph for Socialists," *CNN.com International*, March 15, 2004.

30. On Homeland Security, see http://www.ready.gov; on British decisions to allay fears, Kamal Ahmed, Antony Barnett, and Martin Bright, "Security Breach Hits Foreign Office," *The Observer*, December 22, 2002. On color coding and reactions, *Washington Post*, 2002–04; *USA Today*, May 18, 2005, http://www.usatoday.com/news/education/2005-05-18graduates-survey_x.htm; Steve Orr, "Poll: A Fear of Terrorism Persists," Rochester, NY, *Democrat and Chronicle.com*, October 13, 2002; Steven Wax, "Fear in a Time of Terror," *Oregon State Bar Bulletin*, July 2004; Andrew Kohut, "Young People up to Speed on Terrorism News," *Pew Research Center for the People and Press*, January 15, 2002; Evan Vitter, "Students React to Spanish Bombings," *Harvard Crimson*, March 19, 2004; Mason Boothe, "Facing Fear: Curriculum Helps Children Cope with Trauma," *American Red Cross News*, http://www.redcross.org/article/0,1072,0_332_1005,00.html.
31. Carla Marinucci, "Terror Concerns Move More Women into Bush Camp; GOP Sees Security as Key 'Mom' Issue," *San Francisco Chronicle*, September 22, 2004; Rich Lowry, "Momma Gets Tough: Is Tough Counterterrorism the New V-Chip?" *National Review Online*, September 29, 2004, http://www.nationalreview.com/lowry/lowry200409290838.asp (accessed October 20, 2005); Matea Gold, "Women Appear to Lose Faith in Kerry," *Chicago Tribune*, September 22, 2004; Susan Carroll, "Women Voters and the Gender Gap," *American Political Science Association Online*, (2004), http://www.apsa.org/content_5270.cfm (accessed October 20, 2005).

CHAPTER 3

1. See particularly Glassner, *The Culture of Fear* (New York: 1999) and Mark Siegel, *False Alarm: The Truth About Fear* (Hoboken, NJ: 2005). See also Frank Furedi, *The Politics of Fear* (London, 2005).
2. Christophe Lambert, *La société de la peur* (Paris: 2005). See also Joanna Bourke, *Fear: A Cultural History* (Emeryville, CA: 2006), who also seems to invoke a generalized modernity in looking at American fears.

CHAPTER 4

1. John Demos, *Entertaining Satan: Witchcraft and the Culture of Early New England* (New York: 1982).
2. Robert J. Allison, ed., *The Interesting Narrative of the Life of Olaudah Equiano* (Boston: 1995).
3. Gary Nash, *Red, White and Black: The Peoples of Early America* (Englewood Cliffs, NJ: 1974).
4. Scot French, *The Rebellious Slave: Nat Turner in American Memory* (Boston: 2002); Gary Nash and Richard Weeps, eds., *Great Fear: Race in the Minds of Americans* (New York: 1970).
5. Mae Ngai, *Impossible Subjects: Illegal Aliens and the Making of Modern America* (Princeton, NJ: 2004).
6. Barry Glassner, *The Culture of Fear: Why Americans Are Afraid of the Wrong Things* (New York: 1999), ch. 5.
7. Jean Delumeau, *Sin and Fear: The Emergence of a Western Guilt Culture, Thirteenth-Eighteenth Centuries*, tr. Eric Nicholson (New York: 1990).
8. Erik Erikson, *Young Man Luther: A Study in Psychoanalysis and History* (New York: 1958).
9. Timothy Kelly and Joseph Kelly, "American Catholics and the Discourse of Fear," in Peter N. Stearns and Jan Lewis, eds., *An Emotional History of the United States* (New York: 1998), ch. 13. My thanks also to Mary Hildebeidel for suggestions.

10. Philip J. Greven, *The Protestant Temperament: Patterns of Child-Rearing, Religious Experience and The Self in Early America* (Chicago: 1977); Cotton Mather, *Conifactus: An Essay Upon the Good*, David Levin, ed. (Cambridge, MA: 1966), 47; Philip J. Greven, ed., *Child-Rearing Concepts, 1628–1861: Historical Sources* (Itasca, IL: 1973).

11. Mark Shibley, *Resurgent Evangelicalism in the United States* (Columbia, SC: 1996); James Hunter, *American Evangelicalism: Conservative Religion and the Quandary of Modernity* (New Brunswick, NJ: 1983).

12. Philip J. Greven, *Spare the Child: The Religious Roots of Punishment* (New York: 1991); Roy Lessin, *Spanking: Why, When, How?* (New York: 1979); Larry Christenson, *The Christian Family* (New York: 1970).

13. Hillel Schwartz, *Century's End: A Cultural History of the Fin de Siecle From the 990s Through the 1990s* (New York: 1990); Peter N. Stearns, *Millennium III, Century XXI* (Boulder, CO: 1998); Paul Boyer, *When Time Shall Be No More: Prophecy Belief in Modern American Culture* (Cambridge, MA: 1992).

14. Stearns, *Millennium III*, ch. 5

15. Ibid., chaps. 1 and 5.

CHAPTER 5

1. (New York: 1924). See also Douglas Niles, *War of the Worlds: New Millennium* (New York: 2005).

2. Hadley Cantril, *The Invasion from Mars: A Study in the Psychology of Panic* (Princeton, NJ: 1940).

3. Paul Boyer, *By the Bomb's Early Light: American Thought and Culture at the Dawn of the Atomic Age* (New York: 1985).

4. M. Keith Booker, *Monsters, Mushroom Clouds and the Cold War: American Science Fiction and the Roots of Post-modernism, 1946–64* (Westport, CT: 2001).

5. Curtis Peebles, *Watch the Skies! A Chronicle of the Flying Saucer Myths* (Washington, DC: 1994); Benson Salis, Charles Ziegler, and Charles Moore, *UFO Crash at Roswell: The Genesis of a Modern Myth* (Washington, DC: 1997); David Michael Jacobs, *The UFO Controversy in America* (Bloomington, IN: 1975).

6. Susan Sontag, "The Imagination of Disaster," *Against Interpretation and Other Essays* (New York: 1966).

7. It was widely noted that the 2005 film remake of *War of the Worlds* could be seen in terms of an undercurrent of dismay about the failed results of the American invasion of Iraq, and the need to remind the citizenry of the vulnerability that accompanies overassertion.

8. For precontemporary American patterns against which change can be measured, see Robert Wells, *Facing the "King of Terrors": Death and Society in an American Community, 1750–1990* (Cambridge, MA: 1999); David Stannard, *The Puritan Way of Death* (New York: 1991).

9. Elisabeth Küebler-Ross et al., *Death: The Final Stage of Growth* (New York: 1986); David Stannard, *Death in America* (New York: 2003).

10. Paul Rosenblatt, *Bitter, Bitter Tears* (Minneapolis: 1983); Stearns, *American Cool*.

11. Amy Vanderbilt, *The New Complete Book of Etiquette* (New York: 1954).

12. Gary Laderman, *Rest in Peace: Cultural History of Death and the Funeral Home in Twentieth-Century America* (New York: 2003); see also Richard Meyer, ed., *Ethnicity and the American Cemetery* (Bowling Green, OH: 1993).

13. Christie Davis, "Dirt, Death, Decay and Dissolution: American Denial and British Avoidance," in Glennys Howarth and Peter C. Jupp, eds., *Contemporary Issues in the Sociology of Death, Dying and Disposal* (New York: 1996): 198–214.

14. Küebler-Ross, *Death*; Ivan Illich, *Medical Nemesis: The Expropriation of Health* (New York: 1999); Darwin O. Sawyer, "Public Attitudes toward Life and Death," *Public Opinion Quarterly* 46 (1982): 521–33.

15. "Natural Hospice and Palliative Care Upgrading," *NHPCO Facts and Figures* (Alexandria, VA: 2003).

16. Donna Dickenson and Malcolm Johnson, eds., *Death, Dying and Bereavement* (London: 1993); see also an excellent review of post-1960s developments, John W. Riley Jr., "Dying and the Meanings of Death," *Annual Review of Sociology* 9 (1983): 191–216; Margaret Strobe et al., "Broken Hearts in Broken Bonds," *American Psychologist* 47 (1992): 1905–12; Cas Wouters, "Changing Regimes of Power and Emotion at the End of Life," *Netherlands Journal of Sociology* 26 (1990): 151–55. See also Joanna Bourke, *Fear: A Cultural History* (Emeryville, CA: 2006), ch 1.

17. Viviana A. Zelizer, *Pricing the Priceless Child: The Changing Social Value of Children* (New York: 1985).

18. Harold Kushner, *When Bad Things Happen to Good People* (New York: 1981, 2002); Stephen Levine and Andrea Levine, *Who Dies?* (New York: 1982); Katherine Ashenburg, *The Mourner's Dance: What We Do When People Die* (New York: 2002).

19. Shuji Otsuka and Peter N. Stearns, "Perceptions of Death and the Korean War," *War in History* 6, no. 1: 72–87 (1999): 67–83.

CHAPTER 6

1. Dorothy Rowe, *Depression: The Way Out of Your Prison* (London: 1996).

2. David Riesman, *The Lonely Crowd: A Study of the Changing American Character* (New Haven: 1981); Christopher Lasch, *Culture of Narcissism: American Life in an Age of Diminishing Expectations* (New York: 1978); Warren I. Susman, *Culture as History: The Transformation of American Society in the Twentieth Century* (New York: 1985); Matt, *Keeping Up with the Joneses: Envy in American Consumer Society, 1890–1930* (Philadelphia: 2003); Charles W. Sykes, *The Decay of the American Character* (New York: 1992).

3. Peter N. Stearns, *American Cool: Constructing a Twentieth-Century Emotional Style*; Stephanie Shields, *Speaking from the Heart: Gender and the Social Meaning of Emotion* (New York: 2002).

4. Sidonie Gruenberg, ed., *Encyclopedia of Child Care and Guidance* (New York: 1952), 845–52; Stearns, *American Cool*, ch. 4.

5. Lydia Child, *The Mother's Book* (Boston: 1831), 28–32; T. S. Arthur, *Mother's Rule* (Philadelphia: 1856), 289–90; Bernard Wishy, *The Child and the Republic* (Philadelphia: 1968).

6. Horace Bushnell, *Views of Christian Nurture* (Hartford, CT: 1847), 253–55; Arthur, *Mother's Rule*, 288.

7. Oliver Optic (William Taylor Adams), *Now or Never* (Boston: 1856); Harry Castlemon, *George at the Wheel, or, Life in the Pilot-House* (Philadelphia: 1881) and *Frank on the Lower Mississippi* (Boston: 1868), 74–76.

8. E. Anthony Rotundo, "Boy Culture: Middle-Class Boyhood in Nineteenth-Century America," in Mark Carnes and Clyde Griffen, eds., *Meanings for Manhood* (Chicago: 1990), 15–36; Daniel Beard, *Hardly a Man Is Now Alive: The Autobiography of Dan Beard* (New York: 1939); Charles Dudley Warner, *Being a Boy* (Boston: 1897), 50.

9. G. Stanley Hall, "A Study of Fear," *American Journal of Psychology* 8 (1987): 147–298.

10. Peter N. Stearns, *Anxious Parents: A History of Modern American Child Rearing* (New York: 2002).

11. Mrs. Theodore (Alice) Birney, *Childhood* (New York: 1904), 24–29; William Forbush, *The Character-Training of Children* (New York: 1919), 2: 179–87.

12. Shula Sommers, "Adults Evaluating Their Emotions: A Crosscultural Comparison," in Carol Malatesta and Carroll Izard, eds., *Emotion in Adult Development* (Beverly Hills, CA: 1984): 313–36.

13. Alan Fromme, *The Parents' Handbook* (New York: 1956), 101; Ada Hart Arlitt, *The Child from One to Twelve* (New York: 1931), 113; Mary Boucquet, "Baby Fears," *Parents Magazine* (June 1946): 95; Gladys Troves, *Marriage and Family Life* (New York: 1941), 69; "What To Do When Your Child Is Afraid," *Parents Magazine* 2 (March 1927): 25–27.

14. Benjamin Spock, *The Common Sense Book of Baby and Child Care* (New York: 1945), 196–97, 283–97.

15. Fromme, *Parents Handbook*, 102–8; Norma E. Cutts and Nicholas Moseley, *Better Home Discipline* (New York: 1952); B. von Haller Gilmer, *How to Help Your Child Develop Successfully* (New York: 1951); Martin W. Piers, "Who's Afraid?" *Parents Magazine* 24 (June 1949): 6, 95–99.

16. Arthur Jersild et al., *Joys and Problems of Childrearing* (New York: 1949); Arnold Gesell, Francis Ilg, and Laura Ames, *Youth: The Ages from Ten to Sixteen* (New York: 1956), 51, 65, 192.

17. Gary Cross, *The Cute and the Cool: Wondrous Innocence and Modern American Children's Culture* (New York: 2004).

18. Rupert Wilkinson, *American Tough: The Tough-Boy Tradition and American Character* (Westport, CT: 1984); Gillian Avery, *Childhood's Patterns: A Study of the Heroes and Heroines of Childhood Fiction, 1770-1950* (London: 1975); Deirdre Johnson, *Stratemeyer Pseudonyms and Series Books* (Westport, CT: 1982); Franklin W. Dixon, *Secret of the Lost Tunnel* (New York: 1950), 183, 206; Sally McNall, "American Children's Literature, 1880–Present," in Joseph Hawes and H. Ray Hiner, eds., *American Childhood: A Research Guide* (Westport, CT: 1988), 377–411.

19. I am grateful to Deborah Stearns, in the Psychology Department of Montgomery College, for this advance finding from her study.

20. *Washington Post*, February 6, 2005.

21. Stearns and Haggerty, "The Role of Fear: Transitions in American Emotional Standards for Children, 1850–1950," See also Bourke, *Fear: A Cultural History*, ch. 3.

22. Paul Fussell, "The Real War, 1939–45," *Atlantic Monthly* 264 (August 1989): 37–40 and *Wartime: Understanding and Behavior in the Second World War* (New York: 1989); D. L. Kirkpatrick, "How to Select Foremen," *Personnel Journal* 47 (1968): 262–70; Silas Warner, "Spotting the Neurotic—Helping the Maladjusted," *Personnel Journal* 36 (1957): 136–39.

23. Anne Lockard, *American Evangelicals and the United States Military* (Baton Rouge, LA: 1996).

24. Jersild et al., *Joys and Problems of Childrearing*. See also Fussell, *Wartime: Understanding and Behavior in the Second World War*.

25. M. S. Clark and A. M. Isen, "Toward Understanding the Relationship between Feeling States and Social Behavior," in A. H. Hasting and A. M. Isen, eds., *Cognitive Social Psychology* (Amsterdam: 1982), 73–108; S. Schachter and J. Singer, "Cognitive, Social and Physiological Emotion State," *Psychological Review* 69 (1962): 379–99; John Whiting and Irwin Child, *Child Training and Personality* (New Haven, 1953); S. Shott, "Emotions and Social Life: A Symbolic Interactional Analysis," *American Journal of Sociology* 84 (1979): 1317–34.

26. Patricia McDaniel, *Shrinking Violets and Casper Milquetoasts: Shyness, Power, and Intimacy in the United States, 1950–1995* (New York: 2003); Peter Salovey and Judith Roder, "Coping with Envy and Jealousy," *Journal of Social and Clinical Psychology* 7 (1988): 15–33; K. J. Gergen, "Social Psychology as History," *Journal of Personality and Social Psychology* 20 (1973): 309–20; Peter N. Stearns and Deborah Stearns, "Historical Issues in Emotions Research: Causation and Timing," *Sociological Perspectives on*

Emotion 2 (1994); *Parents Magazine*, Childhood Problems (March 1946): 34, (May 1946): 46, (October 1947): 35, (May, 1948): 34; and Children's Welfare Federation of New York City, *Child Care Questions and Answers* (New York: 1948), 103–7.

CHAPTER 7

1. Peter N. Stearns, *Anxious Parents: A History of Modern American Child Rearing* (New York: 2002).
2. Michael L. Ray and William Wilkie, "Fear: The Potential of an Appeal Neglected by Marketing," *Journal of Marketing* 34 (1970): 54–62.
3. "Summer Camps, Then and Now," *Atlantic Monthly*, June 2004, 179–81.
4. See G. Edward White, *Tort Law in America: An Intellectual History* (expanded edition; Oxford: 2003); John Fleming, *The American Tort Process* (Oxford: 1988). On early changes, Alan Alnan, *A Revisionist History of Tort Law: From Holmesian Realism to Neoclassical Rationalism* (Durham, NC: 2005); Robert Rabin, "The Historical Development of the Fault Principle: A Reinterpretation," *Georgia Law Review* 15 (1980–01): 925–61; James Hackney, "The Intellectual Origins of American Strict Products Liability," *American Jounal of Legal History* 39, no. 4 (1995): 443–509; and Edward White, "The Intellectual Origins of Torts in America," *Yale Law Journal* 86 (1976–77): 671–94.
5. Lawrence Friedman, "Civil Wrongs: Personal Injury Law in the Late 19th Century," *American Bar Foundation Research Journal* 12, no. 2–3 (1987): 351.
6. Cited in Friedman, "Civil Wrongs," 357.
7. Sally H. Clarke, "Unmanageable Risks: MacPherson v. Buick and the Emergence of a Mass Consumer Market," *Law and History Review* (Spring 2005), http://www/jostprucppp[eratove/prg/journals/1hr/23.1/clarke.html.
8. Donald Black, "Compensation and the Social Structure of Misfortune," *Law and Society Review* 21, no. 4 (1987): 563, 577, 580–1.
9. Gary Schwartz, "The Beginning and Possible End of the Rise of American Tort Law," *Georgia Law Review* 26, no. 3 (1982): 613.
10. Schwartz, "Beginning," 633.
11. Viviana A. Zelizer, *Morals and Markets: The Development of Life Insurance in the United States* (New Brunswick, NJ: 1983); Tom Baker and Jonathan Simon, *Embracing Risk* (Chicago: 2002).
12. Stuart Bruchey, ed. *Studies in Entrepreneurship and Innovation in the Insurance Industry* (New York: 2001); Tobias Strange and Bill Hartford, *Consumer Reports Auto Insurance Handbook* (Yonkers, NY: 1993), chaps. 2, 6, 7; Auto Insurance FAQ, *Insure.com*, http://www.insure.com (accessd July 9, 2006); http://www.insurance.com/Article.aspx/What_Your_Auto_Insurer_Knows_About_You. (accessed 9/1/2005) and What_Your_Insurer_Knows_About_Your_Driving (accessed 9/1/2005).
13. Joe Frey, "Insurance Adjusters Rewarded for Shrinking Claims Checks," http://info.insure.com/gen/adjusterperformance.html.
14. Theodor H. Moran, ed., *International Political Risk Management* (Washington, D.C., 2002); Baker and Simon, *Embracing Risk*.
15. Peter N. Stearns, *Battleground of Desire, The Struggle for Self-Control in Modern America* (New York: 1999), 141–44.
16. Joel W. Eastman, *Styling versus Safety: The American Automobile Industry and the Development of Automotive Safety 1900-1966* (New York: 1984); U.S. House Committee on Interstate and Foreign Commerce, *Traffic Safety*, Hearings 1956, 225, 863; James Ridgeway, "Car Design and Public Safety," *New Republic*, September 19, 1964, 9; "How Accidents Are Caused," *Newsweek*, April 13, 1953, 81; Harry DeSilva, *Why We Have Automobile Accidents* (New York: 1942), vii, xiv; American Automobile Association, Safety Responsibility Committee, *Safety Responsibility Bill* (n.p.: 1931); American Management Association, *Compulsory Automobile Insurance* (n.p.: 1936);

Automobile Club of Michigan Safety and Traffic Division, "Lecture on Uniform Traffic Law and the Safety Responsibility Bill for Use in Senior and Junior H.S." (n.p.: 1934); American Association of Motor Vehicle Administrators, *Procedure for the Minimum Standard Examination for Drivers* (n.p.: 1939): E. W. Jones, *Improving Driver Responsibility* (New York: 1939) Automobile Club of Southern California, Public Safety Department, *Course of Study in Safety* (Los Angeles: 1928); California Department of Motor Vehicles, *Guide for Instructors of Traffic Schools for Violators* (Los Angeles: 1936); New Hampshire Department of Motor Vehicles, *An Elective Non-Unit Course in Automobile Driving in Secondary Schools, Designed to Prepare for a Driver's License* (n.p.: 1935); National Safety Council, Education Division, *A Program for Organizing a High School Senior Traffic Club* (Washington, D.C.: 1932); California Department of Education, *Manual on Traffic Safety for the California Secondary Schools* (Sacramento: 1936); American Automobile Association, *Sportsmanlike Driving: A Teachers' Outline for a Course in Traffic Safety and Driving for High Schools* (Chicago: 1935).

17. Katherine Fisher, "A Man's Job," *National Safety News* 36 (1937): 40.
18. Joel A. Tarr and Mark Tebeau, "Managing Danger in the Home Environment, 1900–1940," *Journal of Social History* 29 (1966): 797–816; John Burnham, "Why Did Infants and Toddlers Die? Shifts in Americans' Ideas of Responsibility for Accidents—From Blaming Mom to Engineering," *Journal of Social History* 29 (1966): 817–39.
19. Cited in the *New York Times*, November 20, 1996.
20. "Despite Improvements in Knowledge about AIDS, Americans Still Fear Casual Contact with Carriers," *Family Planning Perspectives* 20 (1988): 99–100.
21. Paula Fass, *Kidnapped: Child Abduction in the United States* (New York: 1997).
22. Stearns, *Anxious Parents*, 35.
23. Eric Monkkonen, *Crime Justice, History* (Columbus, OH: 2002).
24. Peter N. Stearns, *Battleground of Desire, The Struggle for Self-Control in Modern America* (New York: 1999), 141–44.
25. Data in this section derive primarily from interviews with two experienced television meteorologists, one in Pittsburgh, and one in Washington, D.C., whose views were quite congruent on the subject of change and on the role of weather reports in local newscasting. They were most generous with their time and insights, but did not wish their names used. See also Mark Svenvold, *Big Weather: Chasing Tornadoes in the Heart of America* (New York: 2005).
26. Svenvold, *Big Weather*. For another take on the contemporary preoccupation with weather, Walter Percy, *Lost in the Cosmos: The Last Self-help Book* (New York: 1983).
27. For a recent comment on how to adapt more sensibly to the dangers of real life, Arthur Kleinman, *What Really Matters: Living A Moral Life amidst Uncertain Danger* (New York: 2006).

CHAPTER 8

1. James Weaver III, and Ron Tamborini, eds., *Horror Films: Current Research on Audience Preferences and Reactions* (Mahwah, NJ: 1996).
2. Patricia Sparks, *Boredom: The Literary History of a State of Mind* (Chicago: 1995).
3. Gary Cross, "Crowds and Leisure: Thinking Comparatively Across the Twentieth Century," *Journal of Social History* 39 (2006): 631–50.
4. Dana Anderson, "Sign, Space and Story: Roller Coasters and the Evolution of a Thrill," *Journal of Popular Culture* 33 (1999): 1–31.
5. Phil Hardy, ed., *The Encyclopedia of Horror Movies* (New York: 2001).
6. Walter Kendrick, *The Thrill of Fear: 250 Years of Scary Entertainment* (New York: 1991).

7. Terry Heller, *The Delights of Terror: An Aesthetics of the Tale of Terror* (Urbana, IL: 1987).

8. Steven Starker, *Evil Influences: Crusades Against the Mass Media* (New Brunswick, NJ: 1989).

9. Heller, *The Delights of Terror*.

10. Weaver and Tamborini, *Horror Films*.

11. Keith F. Durkin and Clifton Bryant, "Tautological Themes in the Tabloids: A Content Analysis," paper presented at Mid-South Sociological Association, Mobile, AL, 1995.

12. M. Dickstein, "The Aesthetics of Fright," in B. K. Grant, ed., *Planks of Reason: Essays on the Horror Film* (Metuchen, NJ: 1991).

13. Weaver and Tamorini, eds., *Horror Films*.

14. Tony Walters, Jane Littlewood and Michael Pickering, "Death in the News," *Sociology* 29 (1995): 579–96.

15. Terence Qualter, *Advertising and Democracy in the Mass Age* (New York: 1991).

16. James Rorty, *Our Master's Voice: Advertising* (New York: 1976).

17. Liz McFall, *Advertising: A Cultural Economy* (London: 2004), 178.

18. Roland Marchand, *Advertising the American Dream: Making Way for Modernity* (Berkeley: 1985), 14, 102, and passim; see also Jackson Lears, *Fables of Abundance: A Cultural History of Advertising in America* (New York: 1994), ch. 6.

19. On fears of insecurity, Stuart Ewen, *Captains of Consciousness: Advertising and the Social Roots of the Consumer Culture* (New York: 1977). See also Ron Beasley and Marcel Danesi, *Persuasive Signs: The Semiotics of Advertising* (Berlin: 2002) and Otis Pease, *The Responsibilities of American Advertising* (New Haven , CT: 1958).

20. On foreign advertising, Eric Clarke, *The Want Makers: The World of Advertising: How They Make You Buy* (New York: 1988), 11–13.

21. McFall, *Advertising: A Cultural Economy*.

22. Marchand, *Advertising the American Dream*.

23. Anthony Pratkanis and Elliot Aronson, *Age of Propaganda: The Everyday Use and Abuse of Persuasion* (New York: 1991); Daniel Pope, *The Making of Modern Advertising* (New York: 1983), 292–93.

24. Brad Edmondson, " The Fear Sell," *American Demographic* 9 (1987): 22.

25. Kate Fitzgerald, "Gizmos Turn Home Protections into a Boom," *Advertising Age* 65 (January, 1994): S1; Jeffery Zbar, "Fear! Weary and Wary of Violent Crime, Americans Seek Help," *Advertising Age* 65 (November 1994): 18–19.

26. Jeffery Zbar, "First Alert Rings Up Sales," *Advertising Age* 65 (November 1994): 12.

27. Bradley Johnson, "IBM Revives Fear to Invigorate PCs," *Advertising Age* 65 (December 10, 1994): 8.

28. Gordon Lewis, "The Goblins Will Gitcha if You Don't Watch Out!," *Direct Marketing* 59 (November 1996): 26.

29. James Rosenfeld, "The World is Ending," *Direct Marketing* 59 (1997): 26.

30. Philip Van Munching, "The Devil's Adman," *Brandweek* 39 (April 1998): 54.

31. Edmund Lawler, "Fear No Evil in Ads," *B to B* 85 (March 2000): 70.

32. Michael Fumento, "Tampon Terrorism," *Forbes* 163 (May 1999): 170.

33. Eleftheria Parpis, "Fear Factor," *Adweek Western Edition* 51 (November 2001): 11.

34. Myra Stark, "Be Fuddled," *Grandweek* 44 (March 2003): 26.

35. Bob Garfield, "Garfield's AdReview," *Advertising Age* 76 (April 2005): 53.

36. Marc Siegel, *False Alarm: The Truth about the Epidemic of Fear* (New York: 2005); but see also Mike Davis, *The Monster at Our Door: The Global Threat of Avian Flu* (New York: 2005).

37 Benedict Anderson, *Imagined Communities: Reflections on the Origin and Spread of Nationalism* (London: 1983).

38. Frank Furedi, "The Market In Fear," Spiked, http://www.spiked-online.com/index. php?/site/article/507/. September 26, 2005, Furedi points to such high culture solicitations as the Museum of Modern Art, with a themed exhibit on the "Perils of Modern Living" or an art biennial in Lyon, France, under the more explicit heading, "The Art of Fear."

CHAPTER 9

1. For U.S. State Department materials, including travel advisories, see http://travel. state.gov/travel, accessed November 22, 2005.
2. French Ministry of Foreign Affairs material can be found at http://www.diplomatie. gouv.fr, accessed November 22, 2005.
3. British Foreign Office guidance is available at http://www.fco.gov.uk/servlet, accessed November 22, 2005.

CHAPTER 10

1. Personal communication from the teacher, Ms. Clio Stearns.
2. M. T. Connelly, *The Response to Prostitution in the Progressive Era* (Chapel Hill, NC: 1980); Michell Jacobson, *Barbarian Virtues: The United States Encounters Foreign Peoples at Home and Abroad 1876–1917* (New York: 2000).
3. Stanley Coben, *A. Mitchell Palmer: Politician* (New York: 1972); *At Home: Readings on American Life, Part II: Peacemaking, 1919–1920: Radicalism and the Red Scare* (New York: 1993); Robert Hill, *The FBI's RACON: Racial Conditions in the United States during World War I* (Boston: 1995).
4. *At Home: Readings on American Life*, Part II.
5. Mikmiso Hane, "Wartime Internment," *Journal of American History* 77 (1990): 569–75.
6. Hazel Erskin, "The Polls: Atomic Weapons and Nuclear Energy," *Public Opinion Quarterly* 27 (1963): 155–90.
7. *New York Times*, August 8, 1945; *Washington Post*, August 26, 1945.
8. *Reader's Digest*, 1946–47.
9. Paul Boyer, *By the Bomb's Early Light: American Thought and Culture at the Dawn of the Atomic Age* (New York: 1985). My debt in this section to Boyer's superb study will be obvious.
10. Jeff Smith, *Unthinking the Unthinkable: Nuclear Weapons and Western culture* (Bloomington, IN: 1969); H. Bruce Franklin, *Star Wars: The Superweapon and the American Imagination* (New York: 1988); Edward Linenthall, *Symbolic Defense: The Cultural Significance of the Strategic Defense Initiative* (Urbana, IL: 1989).
11. Norman Vincent Peale, *Guide to Confident Living* (New York: 1948).
12. Eugene Rabinowitch, "Five Years After," *Bulletin of the Atomic Scientists* 7 (1951): 3; J. Robert Oppenheimer, "Physics in the Comtemporary World," *Bulletin of the Atomic Scientists* 4 (1948): 66.
13. Allan Winkler, "The 'Atom' and American Life," *The History Teacher* 26 (1993): 317–37.
14. David Bradley, *No Place to Hide* (Hanover, NH: 1983).
15. Boyer, *By the Bomb's Early Light*; Winkler, "The 'Atom' and American Life."
16. Boyer, *By the Bomb's Early Light*.
17. Winkler, "The 'Atom' and American Life."
18. L. S. Witmer, *Resisting the Bomb: A History of the World Nuclear Disarmament Movement 1957–1970* (Stamford, CT: 1997).
19. John Hersey, *Hiroshima* (New York: 1966).
20. Spencer R. Weart, *Nuclear Fear: A History of Images* (Cambridge: 1988).

21. W. Warren Wagar, "Truth and Fiction, Equally Strange: Writing about the Bomb," *American Literary History* 1, no. 2 (1989): 448–57.

22. Robert Jay Lifton and Greg Mitchell, *Hiroshima in America: Fifty Years of Denial* (New York: 1995); Robert Jay Lifton and Richard Falk, *Indefensible Weapons: The Political and Psychological Case against Nuclearism* (New York: 1982); John Mack, *Nightmares and Human Conflict* (Boston: 1974).

23. Erskin, "The Polls," 157.

24. David Caute, *The Great Fear* (New York: 1973); Ellen Schrecker, *Many Are the Crimes: McCarthyism in America* (Boston: 1998).

25. Peter Steinberg, *The Great "Red Menace": United States Prosecution of American Communists, 1947–1952* (Westport, CT: 1984); Robert Griffith, *The Politics of Fear: Joseph R. McCarthy and the Senate* (Lexington, KY: 1971).

26. I am grateful to Dr. Ernst Volgenau for this assessment.

27. Arthur Krock, "A Dream Dispelled: Castro serves to remind U.S. that communist threat is not over," *New York Times*, Nov. 4, 1962, p. E 9.

28. Paul Sheatsley and Jacob Feldman, "The Assassination of President Kennedy: A Preliminary Report on Public Reactions and Behavior," *Public Opinion Quarterly* (1984).

29. H. W. Brands, *The Devil We Knew: Americans and the Cold War* (New York: 1993), 159–60.

30. Winkler, "The 'Atom' and American Life"; Jonathan Schell, *The Fate of the Earth* (New York: 1982); Carl Sagan, "Nuclear Winter," *Parade*, October 30, 1983.

31. John Mueller, "Simplicity and Spook: Terrorism and the Dynamics of Threat Exaggeration," *International Studies Perspective* 6 (2005): 208–34; R. H. Johnson, *Improbable Dangers: U.S. Conceptions of Threat in the Cold War and After* (New York: 1994).

32. Andrew Kohut, "Fear of Terrorism Weights Heavily on Public," *Pew Research Center for the People and the Press*, June 29, 2001.

33. Zoe Williams, "Grin and Bear What, Exactly?" *The Guardian*, November 12, 2002; John Wadham, "Terror Suspects Need a New Champion," *Guardian Unlimited*, January 9, 2003.

34. Mueller, "Simplicity and Spook," 208–34; J. C. Kerr, "Terror Threat Level Raised to Orange," *Associated Press*, December 21, 2003.

35. Anonymous, *Imperial Hubris: Why the West Is Losing the War on Terror* (Dulles, VA: 2004), 160, 177, 226, 241–42, 250, 252, 263.

36. David Brooks, "Facing Up to Our Fears," *Newsweek*, October 22, 2001, 62.

37. Tom Raum, "Bush: Radicals Seek to Intimidate World," AP release, October 6, 2005.

38. Mueller, "Simplicity and Spook." See also Robert Higgs, *Resurgence of the Warfare State* (New York: 2005).

39. Cass Sunstein, *The Laws of Fear* (Cambridge: 2005).

40. For stinging commentary on the connections between government reactions to September 11, including indiscriminate imprisonments and torture, and earlier cold war excesses, see *Radical History Review* 85 (Winter 2003), Special Issue: History and Terror.

CHAPTER 11

1. Furedi, "The Market In Fear." Spiked-central, http://www.spiked-online.com/articles/=0000000CAD7B.htm (accessed September 26, 2005). For a more focused assessment of the growing fear literature and its implications for recent history, Peter N. Stearns, "Fear and Contemporary History," *Journal of Social History* 40 (2006, forthcoming).

2. National Science and Technology Council, Subcommittee on Social, Behavioral and Economic Sciences, *Combating Terrorism: Research Priorities in the Social, Behavioral and Economic Science* (Washington, D.C.: n.d.).

3. Christopher Lasch, *Culture of Narcissism: American Life in an Age of Diminishing Expectations* (New York: 1978).

4. In his interesting paper on September 11, Kazin, ("12/12 and 9/11") lamenting the deficiencies in the policy response to terrorism, including the failure to rouse a durable community spirit, adds his dismay about the neglect of political factors in contemporary American historiography, in favor of social and cultural issues that disproportionately omit the state and political actors. Granting that some social historians moved too far away from the political, the argument sketches a false dichotomy: society and politics are typically intertwined, and not simply in the sense of the political shaping the social. The experience of American fear suggests the mutual interconnections, as this book is designed to illustrate.

5. Cas Wouters, "On Status Completion and Emotion Management: The Study of Emotions as a New Field," *Theory, Culture and Society* 9 (1992): 229–52.

6. Carol Z. Stearns and Peter N. Stearns, *Anger: The Struggle for Emotional Control in American History* (New York: 1994).

7. Peter N. Stearns, *American Cool: Constructing a Twentieth-Century Emotional Style* (New York: 1994), ch. 5.

8. Wouters, "On Status Competition"; see also Abram de Swaan, "The Politics of Agoraphobia: On Changes in Emotional and Relational Management," *Theory and Society* 10 (1981).

9. Judith Shkar, *Political Thought and Political Thinkers* (Chicago: 1998), ch. 1.

10. *Washington Post*, September 5, 2005.

11. Barry Glassner, *The Culture of Fear: Why Americans Are Afraid of the Wrong Things* (New York: 1999), xi and passim. For another recent take on the media enhancement of fear, combined with the fearsome impact of government measures and the dehumanizing impact of modern urban design, see Paul Virilio, *City of Panic* (New York: 2005).

12. Bob Garfield, "Maladies by the Millions," *USA Today*, December 16, 1997; William C. Black and others, "Perceptions of Breast Cancer Risk and Screening Effectiveness in Women Younger than 50," *Journal of the National Cancer Institute* 87 (1995): 720–31.

13. On road rage, Glassner, *Culture of Fear*; Peter N. Stearns, *Battleground of Desire: The Struggle for Emotional Control on America's History* (New York: 1999).

14. Martin Gross, *The Psychological Society: A Critical Analysis of Psychiatry, Psychotherapy, Psychoanalysis, and the Psychological Revolution* (New York: 1978).

15. Peter N. Stearns, *Millennium III, Century XXI* (Boulder, CO: 1998).

16. Robert Putnam, *Bowling Alone: The Collapse and Revival of the American Community* (New York: 2000).

17. Stearns, *Anxious Parents: A History of Modern Childrearing in the United States* (New York: 2002).

18. Stearns, *Anxious Parents*; Jackie Orr, *Panic Diaries: A Genealogy of Panic Disorders* (Durham, NC: 2006).

19. On prisoners, see *New York Times*, July 22, 2005.

20. Mueller, "Simplicity and Spook: Terrorism and the Dynamics of Threat Exaggeration; Sean Gorman, "Fear Factor," *National Journal*, May 10, 2003.

21. Kazin, "12/12 and 9/11." For a partisan, but not easily disputable comment on Republican uses of fear, see Al Gore, "The Politics of Fear," *Social Research* 71, no.4 (Winter 2004); see also Barry Glassner, "Narrative Techniques of Fear Mongering," *Social Research* 71, no. 4 (Winter 2004).

22. Mueller, "Simplicity and Spook."
23. Mueller, "Simplicity and Spook."
24. Francis Fukuyama, *America at the Crossroads: Democracy, Power, and the Neoconservative Legacy* (New Haven: 2006).
25. Stearns, *Battleground of Desire.*

INDEX